AN HISTORICAL INTRODU(TO PRIVATE LAW

In this book one of the world's foremost legal historians attempts to explain what produced the private law of the western world as we know it today. Professor van Caenegem pays particular attention to the origin of the Common Law–civil law dichotomy, and how it arose that England and the continent of Europe, although sharing the same civilization and values, live under two different legal systems. The chronological coverage extends from the Germanic invasion in the early Middle Ages to the present day, incorporating analysis of the medieval Roman and canon law, both products of the law schools, and that of the School of Natural Law which inspired the great national codifications of the modern age.

Professor van Caenegem evaluates the role of the lawgivers – emperors, kings and parliaments – and that of the judges, particularly, of course, in the lands of the English Common Law. He deals with the great phases of legal development and the main bodies of doctrine and legislation, rather than offer an analysis of the legal norms themselves; substantive private law – family and status, property, contract, inheritance, trade – and with the organization of the courts and the forms of process.

An Historical Introduction to Private Law is based on both an extensive secondary literature in several languages, and on evidence accumulated by Professor van Caenegem over the past forty years.

AN HISTORICAL INTRODUCTION TO PRIVATE LAW

R. C. van CAENEGEM

Professor of Medieval History in the Faculty of Letters and of Legal History in the Faculty of Law, University of Ghent

TRANSLATED BY D. E. L. JOHNSTON

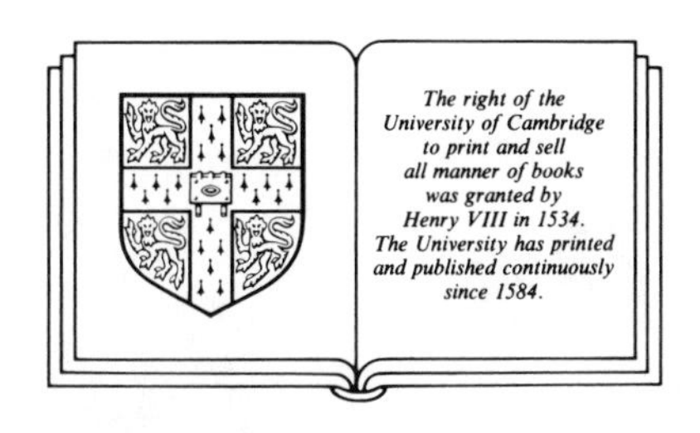

CAMBRIDGE UNIVERSITY PRESS

Cambridge

New York Port Chester

Melbourne Sydney

Published by the Press Syndicate of the University of Cambridge
The Pitt Building, Trumpington Street, Cambridge CB2 1RP
40 West 20th Street, New York, NY 10011–4211, USA
10 Stamford Road, Oakleigh, Victoria 3166, Australia

Originally published in French as *Introduction historique au droit privé*
by Editions Story-Scientia 1988

First published in English by Cambridge University Press 1992 as
An Historical Introduction to Private Law

Printed in Great Britain at the University Press, Cambridge

A catalogue record for this book is available from the British Library

Library of Congress cataloguing in publication data

Caenegem. R. C. van.
[Introduction historique au droit privé. English]
An historical introduction to private law / R. C. van Caenegem:
translated by D. E. L. Johnston.
p. cm.
Translation of: Introduction historique au droit privé.
Includes bibliographical references (p.).
ISBN 0 521 40514 9
1. Civil law – Europe – History. I. Title.
KJC956.C34 1992
346.4 – dc20 91-22841 CIP
[344]

ISBN 0 521 405149 hardback
ISBN 0 521 427452 paperback

UP

Contents

Preface to the English-language edition

Private law is concerned with individual men and women whose relations, one hopes, will be harmonious; otherwise the courts intervene and settle their disputes peacefully and authoritatively. Since this extensive and pervading body of law regulates our daily lives, we may well pose the question as to how and when it was created. If we all happened to live under one and the same civil code, conceived and rapidly penned by Napoleon, the answer would be wonderfully simple. Legal history unfortunately is not that straightforward: one complication is that the law of our present-day western world consists of two quite different systems, English Common Law and continental civil law, also called the law of the Roman-Germanic family. How these legal systems, both of European origin, came into being, went through various stages of development and always remained alien to each other is one of the themes of the present Introduction, where the continental lawyer may learn something about his own heritage but also about events across the Channel, and vice versa. At a time when British judges sit with their continental brethren in European courts of law, this may be especially welcome. National legal histories are readily available, and so are works on Roman and canon law – my Introduction is, of course, largely based on them – but studies that transcend national frontiers and attempt to weave the historic threads of common and civil law into one fabric are still rare. This may go some way towards justifying the present survey, which is the fruit of my teaching in the Law Faculties of the Universities of Ghent and – during the academic year 1984–85 – of Cambridge.

This short book, which covers the period between the sixth and the twentieth centuries, does not attempt to present an analysis of the substance of private law, but merely an external history, explaining who were the great lawgivers, jurists and judges who shaped it, and what texts their endeavours produced. The legal norms themselves are only occasionally discussed, in order to illustrate factors which influenced the course of events.

I hope that the English-reading world will welcome this attempt, and judge that the trees felled to produce the paper on which to print it have not fallen in vain.

It is my pleasant duty to thank the translator, Dr D. E. L. Johnston, who has devoted much of his precious time to this ungrateful task. I would also like to thank the Syndics of the Cambridge University Press who, having welcomed several of my earlier manuscripts, have once again decided to publish my work under their illustrious imprint.

Ghent R. C. VAN CAENEGEM

CHAPTER I

The origins of contemporary private law, 1789–1807

THE *CODE CIVIL* OF 1804: AN END AND A NEW BEGINNING

1 This book does not aim to sketch out a 'universal' history of law[1] but to give a historical introduction to the development of the private law currently in force in Belgium and the Netherlands. That law is made up of very old as well as very modern elements, and during its development it went through periods of stagnation and periods of rapid change. The most important of these periods was that of the great Napoleonic codifications, in particular the *Code civil des Français* promulgated in 1804. The *Code civil* is the culmination of several centuries of French legal evolution: much of it is old law, some of which goes back directly or even literally to the customary and Roman law of the Middle Ages and early modern times. None the less the *Code civil* of 1804 marked a decisive break in the gradual evolution of the law. It replaced the variety of the old law with a single and uniform code for the whole of France; it abolished the law which had previously been in force, in particular custom and Roman law (art. 7 of the law of 31 March 1804); it incorporated several ideological measures inspired by the Revolution of 1789; and it attempted to make the traditional role of legal scholarship superfluous, by forbidding doctrinal commentary on the codes, in the belief that the new legislation was clear and self-sufficient.

The French *Code civil* immediately came into force in Belgium, whose territory had been annexed to France and divided into *départements*. As in France, so in Belgium: the *Code* has never yet been replaced, although numerous measures have been amended, omitted

[1] See the encyclopaedic work of J. Gilissen, *Introduction historique au droit. Esquisse d'une histoire universelle du droit. Les sources du droit depuis le XIIIe siècle. Eléments d'une histoire du droit privé* (Brussels, 1979).

or repealed by legislation or case law. The *Code civil* was also introduced in 1810–11 in the Netherlands, which were annexed to France later than Belgium. But it was replaced by a new code in 1838 which, although a Dutch adaptation, is still very close to the 1804 *Code.*

THE *CODE CIVIL* IN EUROPE

2 Our main concern is with the history of law in France and in the Belgian and Dutch provinces, but the rest of Europe will not be left out of account. That would in any case be impossible. The notion of national law – a single, exclusive code and a single, exclusive system of national courts for each country – is a recent and transient phenomenon. For centuries law had been local or regional (customs and charters) and also cosmopolitan and supra-national (the Roman law taught at the universities, the canon law of the church). And after the Second World War came the rise of European law, which involved the creation of a supra-national legislature and courts, to which national statutes and courts were subordinate.

Historically, the major elements of the law belong to a common European inheritance: ancient and medieval Roman law, canon law, old Germanic law, feudal law, medieval municipal law, the natural law of early modern times. All these elements had their influence in different degrees on all the countries of Europe.

COMMON LAW AND RECEPTION

3 In some regions, such as Italy and the south of France, there was a gradual, spontaneous process of change which led to the replacement of old customary law by the rediscovered Roman law. This occurred very early, from the twelfth century onwards. Elsewhere, in northern France and the southern Netherlands, customary law persisted, and was actually established and promulgated by central authorities ('homologation of customs'). Even there, however, Roman law had an important supplementary role and remained the basis of learned commentaries. In the northern Netherlands, the position was different again. Although there was an order to unify customs, it was hardly implemented at all and the resulting gap in the law led to the creation of Roman–Dutch law (*Rooms–Hollands*

recht) in the seventeenth century. This was a jurisprudential synthesis of Roman and customary law, and the predominant element in it was the Roman one. The influence of Roman law was even more marked in the German empire, where it was decided towards 1500 to abandon medieval customs and 'receive' (*recipere*) Roman law as the national law: this phenomenon is known as the reception. Consequently modern German law has, paradoxically, a markedly more Roman and less Germanic character than French law.

Developments in England were entirely different. There is no doubt that England too was affected by the learned law, which then constituted the common law of Europe, both through canon law in the church courts of the Roman Catholic Church and then the Anglican Church, and also through Roman law in university teaching and in the practice of certain specialist courts. None the less the most important element of English law, the Common Law,[2] was developed from Germanic customary law and feudal law, quite independently of Roman law. As a result the common-law system differs fundamentally from the continental system. A further significant difference is that England developed a national law much earlier than other countries. A Common Law for the whole of the kingdom of England was developed by the royal courts from the twelfth century and was then expounded and commented on in legal works. A final peculiarity of English law is its continuity; there was no break in its development comparable with that caused by the great modern codifications on the continent. Not only was the law never codified, but the old law was never abrogated and replaced by a modern, let alone a revolutionary, legal system. So the system of Common Law is characterized by historical continuity; the statutes in force and the authoritative judgments may be very ancient or they may be quite recent.

[2] There are good reasons for preferring the expression 'le common law' to 'la common law', by analogy with the arguments which Criscuoli has put forward in favour of 'il common law' rather than 'la common law' in Italian. The main argument is that the masculine refers to law (*droit*) and the feminine to *loi* (statute): the common law is a *droit* and not a *loi* (G. Criscuoli, 'Valore semantico e contenuto dommatico dell'espressione "common law" nel linguaggio giuridico italiano', *Rivista trimestriale di diritto e procedura civile* (1967), 1,466–73. Yet the question is not simple, and the confusion surrounding the term 'common law' – common *droit* or common *loi* – is very old, going back in England itself to the Middle Ages. Thus, 'common law' was translated as 'lay commune' in 1297 and as 'comun dreit' in the *Miroir des Justices* of 1290; in 1377 the curious form 'commune Droit' is found; see C. H. McIlwain, *Constitutionalism and the changing world* (Cornell, 1939), 128, 132, 137.

THE COMPILATION AND PROMULGATION OF THE *CODE CIVIL* OF 1804

4 The *coup d'état* of 18 Brumaire (9 November 1799) marked the beginning of the Napoleonic regime, the re-establishment of martial law and the end of the most turbulent decade of French history. 'The Revolution is in thrall to the principles which inspired it: it is over.' One of Napoleon's concerns was to provide the nation with a collection of codes. The prevailing legal uncertainty was to be brought to an end by the use in legal practice of universally valid codes. During the Revolution, the old law had certainly been abrogated to a large extent, but this process had not been complemented by the introduction of a new legal system which was recognised as being generally applicable. Only some areas of law had been subject to new legislation;[3] and all attempts at codifying the civil law had failed. These draft codes had been conceived rather vaguely more as rules of conduct for the benefit of good citizens than as laws, and were never promulgated in the form of statutes. In any case, depending on the political inclinations of successive regimes, the draft codes were regarded at one time as excessively traditional and at another as insufficiently revolutionary. The various drafts were compiled between 1793 and 1799 by different commissions presided over by the lawyer and statesman J. J. de Cambacérès, who was a member of the National Convention in 1792. The Revolution also changed and democratized the administration of justice profoundly, while the universities and their law faculties had been abolished in 1793, and new schools of law did not open until 1804.

In order to bridge the gulf opened up by this revolutionary upheaval, Napoleon decided to introduce effective legislation in France by promulgating 'his' codes. Naturally 'his' codes does not mean that the general and first consul compiled the *Code civil* at his desk with his own hands. The codes are 'Napoleonic', because it was owing to Napoleon's political will and determination that the 1804 *Code civil* in particular was compiled in record time. In August 1800 a commission of four lawyers was instructed to carry out the task.

3 For example, in the field of private law, the great systematic statutes of lasting importance on divorce, marriage and civil status (1792), illegitimacy (1793), inheritance (1794), privileges, hypothecs and the transfer of property (1798). This period of so-called 'intermediate law' (an interval or transitional law between the old law of the *ancien régime* and the new law of the Napoleonic codes) also saw the promulgation of a penal code in 1791 and a code of crimes and penalties in 1795.

Barely four months later it was complete. Its authors were professional lawyers who had been educated under the *ancien régime* and had pursued careers as advocates or magistrates: Fr. Tronchet, J. Portalis, F. Bigot-Préameneu and J. de Maleville.

Tronchet, a distinguished specialist in customary law, came from the north. Portalis, the most brilliant of the four, was a Romanist from the south. He was profoundly learned in philosophy, and conceived law not merely as a skill but as an important element in the social development of his time. His views emerge particularly clearly from his well-known *Discours préliminaire*, which is the introduction to the draft code of 1801: in it he expounds the philosophy of the *Code civil* (a question to which we shall return).

The draft put forward by this commission was submitted to the Tribunal de Cassation and Tribunaux d'Appel; after revision to take account of their comments, it was laid before the Conseil d'Etat presided over by Cambacérès. Cambacérès was hostile to the doctrinal approach to law, and above all to general formulations and definitions. Napoleon himself took part in the debate and sometimes imposed his own views,[4] and it was in the Conseil d'Etat that the *Code* took on its final shape. The Tribunat raised political and ideological objections, but Napoleon was able to overcome the opposition and achieve his own ends. The promulgation of the *Code* by the Corps législatif met with no further obstacles: from 5 March 1803 to 21 March 1804 a series of thirty-six statutes was passed, and on 21 March 1804 consolidated into 2,281 articles constituting the *Code civil des français*. The name was changed by law in 1807 to Code Napoléon, but the new name disappeared with the fall of the emperor. In the field of private law,[5] the *Code civil* was followed by the *Code de procédure civile* of 1806 which came into force on 1 January 1807, and in 1807 by the *Code de commerce* which came into force on 1 January 1808.

[4] The first consul himself presided at thirty-five of the eighty-seven sessions. His personal views strongly influenced, among other things, the provisions on the authority of the paterfamilias for, according to him, 'just as the head of the family is subject in an absolute manner to the government, so the family is subject in absolute manner to its head'. Napoleon's views were also decisive for the subordinate position of (married) women and for the law of divorce (measures on divorce by mutual consent and adoption were introduced at his instance, no doubt for his own political reasons). On the other hand Napoleon had no interest in book II and paid only slight attention to book III.

[5] In criminal law a *Code d'instruction criminelle* and a *Code pénal* were promulgated in 1808 and 1810 respectively. These came into force on 1 January 1811.

THE *CODE CIVIL*: ANCIENT AND MODERN

5 The immediate sources used by the authors of the 1804 *Code civil* were the traditional French common law of the eighteenth century, which was an amalgam of learned and customary law, some of which was very old; and secondly the innovations made during the Revolution. This mixture of old and new suited the political climate of the nation, and after the fall of the *ancien régime* also proved itself well-suited to the middle-class society of the nineteenth century. There had often been hopes of working out a common French law to channel diverse legal currents into a single stream, and during the eighteenth century this project had already made progress through the efforts of the traditional lawyers.

The distant sources of French law (yet to be examined) were (i) the customs, in their codified and annotated form, and in particular the *Coutume de Paris*, which enjoyed great prestige throughout France. The compilers of the *Code civil* made conscious efforts to treat customs and Roman law on an even footing, and they systematically gave preference to formulations conforming to 'natural reason', but customary law was the most important source of the *Code*. (ii) Roman law as systematized by Domat (*d.* 1696),[6] and, to a lesser extent, canon law. Roman law was the basis of jurisprudence, but it was also the law practised in the south, the region of written law (*pays de droit écrit*). The influence of Roman law was particularly marked in the law of obligations. (iii) The law of the three great royal ordinances of 1731 to 1747, which were in fact partial codifications of important areas of law. These ordinances had been the work of Henri François Daguesseau (*d.* 1751), chancellor of Louis XV.[7] (iv) The case law of the *parlements*, especially the Parlement de Paris.

The compilers of the *Code civil* also consulted traditional legal writers, notably François Bourjon (*d.* 1751), author of *Le Droit*

[6] Domat was the author of *Les lois civiles dans leur ordre naturel*, an attempt to arrange the principles of Roman law (which in his view constituted universal guiding principles) in a rational order and according to a system devised by the author himself, as well as to ensure their congruence with the rules of Christian morality. Y. Noda, 'Jean Domat et le Code civil français. Essai sur l'influence de Domat sur le Code civil français', *Comparative Law Review*, 3.2 (1956; Japan Institute of Comparative Law).

[7] The ordinance of gifts of 1731, on wills of 1735 and on fideicommissary substitutions of 1747. The first and third were applicable throughout France, while the second envisaged different regimes for the two law regions, the north (the region of customary law) and the south (region of Roman law).

commun de la France et la Coutume de Paris réduits en Principes;[8] Robert Joseph Pothier (*d.* 1772), a magistrate and professor, author of a commentary on customary law (*Coutumes des duché, bailliage et prévosté d'Orléans*), a work on Roman law (*Pandectae Justinianeae in novam ordinem digestae*) and above all a series of treatises on different topics in civil law. Particularly important was his *Traité des obligations*, whose influence on this subject in the *Code* was decisive. Pothier's authority can be seen even in the texts themselves, since the authors of the *Code* lifted entire passages from his work.

Although the old law was the most important element in the *Code civil*, it was not the intention of its authors to re-establish the legal order of the fallen regime and abandon the advances made in the Revolution. On the contrary, numerous principles which derived from the ideas of the Revolution and the Enlightenment, and which they considered socially beneficial, were enshrined in their legislative work. This applies above all to the actual principle of a codified civil law, unique and uniform throughout France.[9] In fact, the accomplishment of such a code responded to one of the numerous reforms demanded in the registers of grievances in 1788–9, and had already been provided for in the constitution of 1791 ('there shall be a code of civil laws common to the whole kingdom'). Besides, the *Code civil* now assured the recognition of fundamental principles: the equality of citizens before the law; religious tolerance; the disburdening of landed property, which was now freed from the charges imposed by the feudal system and the church law of tithes; freedom of contract, now much greater than under the *ancien régime*. New ideas also appear in certain specific areas, such as civil marriage, divorce, civil status, the transfer of property, and the abolition of the medieval prohibition on interest (usury).

THE SPIRIT OF THE *CODE CIVIL*

6 The general tone of the 1804 *Code* is distinctly conservative: this is indicated by its respect for the family and property rights as the basis of social order. This spirit was best expressed in the work of Portalis,

[8] R. Martinage-Baranger, *Bourjon et le Code civil* (Paris, 1971).

[9] In certain respects, this uniformity was purely formal: e.g. right up to the present, the numerous articles on dowry have hardly ever been applied in the northern regions, since dowry was an institution of Roman law, well diffused in the south but unknown in the north.

in his *Discours préliminaire*, in his *Discours . . . sur le Concordat* (1801), where he emphasizes the indispensable role that religion plays in all civilized societies; and in his posthumous *De l'usage et de l'abus de l'esprit philosophique durant le dix-huitième siècle*. Some quotations sum up his conservative convictions: 'it is useful to conserve everything which it is not necessary to destroy' or 'a bold innovation is often no more than a glaring error'. For Portalis the essential role of the state was to ensure 'preservation and peace'. He also emphasized that the *Code civil* did not represent a collection of entirely new rules, but instead the result of the 'experience of the past, the spirit of centuries'. This foreshadows his celebrated aphorism 'with time codes make themselves; strictly speaking nobody makes them'. Portalis was an admirer of Bonaparte: he saw in him the general who had re-established order and thanks to whom France, after the disorder of the Revolution, once more enjoyed the security of the law, in his words 'the palladium of property'. The absolute right of private property, and the different modes of its acquisition; its administration principally by the paterfamilias, and the means of its transmission: these are the essential concepts of books II and III of the *Code*. The second pillar of the *Code* is the family, whose main characteristic is submission to the power of husband and father (book I).

Another fundamental feature of the *Code* is its positivism, which was to mark the Exegetical School and exercise a predominant influence right through the nineteenth century. The following points allow this aspect of the *Code* to be appreciated. There is no general theoretical introduction to the *Code*, setting out basic principles, a general outline of the contents, and legal definitions. And the first six articles of the *Code* do not make up for this deficiency in any way. Yet it would not have been in the least difficult to provide such an introduction: Portalis' *Discours préliminaire* would have been eminently suitable. The absence is therefore a matter of conscious choice; and this was expressly stated at the Tribunat. Reference was made to the Prussian codification, which was thought to be excessively theoretical. The *Code* was to be conceived first and foremost as a positive legal text, and any doctrinal excess must be avoided; the terms of the statute must not become obscured by theories and lectures. This view accords with the notion of the absolute primacy of statute as a source of law. Doctrinal interpretation, case law (in which the judge is reduced to a passive role as the voice of the statute), and custom are subordinated to the authority of the statute. While custom had been the most important source and expression of the law (a point to which we shall return), it was now relegated to a residual and marginal role. Statute, which at certain stages of legal evolution had been wholly eclipsed, was now the source of law *par excellence*.

The idealism or utopianism of the revolutionary period had disappeared. The *Code civil* bears witness to a sober and realistic reaction. After ten years of the revolutionary regime, the illusion of a new society of honest citizens, in which rules of law were replaced by moral prescriptions enjoining civic conduct, and courts and judgments by friendly conciliation, had been shattered. The aspiration to bring about instant general reforms had been expressed by Cambacérès in 1793, when he declared a desire 'to change everything at once in the schools, in the morals, the customs, the spirits, and in the statutes of a great people'. The Code Napoléon re-established the law and the courts in their full rigour, but the system was now more rational and its functioning more calculable and predictable than under the *ancien régime*.

The elimination of natural law as a source of positive law belongs in this same line of thought. In the eighteenth century the law of reason (*Vernunftsrecht*) had been a powerful instrument in the struggle against the old political regime. During the Revolution, natural law was constantly invoked to justify new rules and new systems. In Portalis' theoretical work natural law plays a very important part. The *Code civil*, on the other hand, rejects all borrowing from natural law: from now on the established order was the *Code*, and all reference to natural law, a perpetual source of inspiration for those opposing the status quo, was out of order. For adherents to the new *Code*, the role of natural law had ended.

So far as liberation and emancipation are concerned, the effect of the *Code* was limited. It is true that many inequalities and burdens (especially feudal ones) were abolished, but the 1804 *Code* introduced new ones. For instance, discrimination against women, especially married women: this can be seen particularly in the restrictions on the right of women to sit on the family council or to appear as witnesses, in a wife's subjection to the authority of her husband and her obligation to adhere to him, as well as in the reservation to the husband of the right to administer his wife's property. There was also discrimination against workers, as the system of workers' files (*livrets d'ouvriers*) shows. The rule in article 1781 of the *Code* was particularly unfavourable: in the case of a dispute between employer and employee on a question of payment or of reciprocal obligation, the employer was believed on his word.[10]

COURTS AND PROCEDURE

7 The triumph of a single, exclusive *Code civil* was achieved by organizing a hierarchy of courts and by promulgating a code of civil procedure in 1806 which was itself common to all civil jurisdictions. Over the centuries of the *ancien régime* there had been a proliferation of jurisdictions, some dependent on the church, others on great landowners. The codification replaced this diversity with a single hierarchy of state courts. It had been customary under the *ancien régime* for worthies who were active in politics and commerce but who had no legal education to sit in the lower courts; but in the nineteenth century the administration of justice in all but the commercial courts was reserved to professional judges educated in faculties of law. The Cour de Cassation was charged with overseeing the uniform application of statutes.

Even more than the *Code civil* of 1804, the *Code de procédure civile* of 1806 owed a debt to the past. Several measures of the *Ordonnance civile sur la réformation de la justice* of 1667 (which we shall deal with later) were repeated word for word. The *Code de procédure civile* also adopted the old idea of civil procedure as a dispute between free and responsible citizens in which no initiative or intervention on the part

[10] Article 1781 of the *Code* under the rubric 'Du Louage des domestiques et ouvriers' provides that 'the master is believed on his affirmation about the amount of wages, the payment of the salary for the past year, and the advances given in the current year'. The compulsory workers' file (*livret d'ouvrier*) was introduced by the statute of 22 Germinal Year XI (12 April 1803) on factories and workshops. When the employer wrote a negative comment or retained the file, the worker was condemned to unemployment and, if he moved without his file, risked being treated as a vagabond. He had the right of recourse to the courts, but there found himself faced with article 1781. In Belgium this discriminatory situation was abolished only in 1883, when the compulsory file and article 1781 were abrogated. See J. Bekers, 'Elaboration des lois, 19e–20e siècle: La loi du 10 juillet concernant les livrets d'ouvrier', *La décision politique et judiciaire dans le passé et dans le présent* (an exhibition from 15 April to 17 May 1975 on the occasion of the colloquium 'Sources de l'histoire des institutions de la Belgique' (Brussels, 1975), 27–64; B. S. Chlepner, *Cent ans d'histoire sociale en Belgique* (Brussels, 1958); J. Neuville, *La condition ouvrière au XIXe siècle*, II: *L'ouvrier suspect*, 2nd edn (Brussels, 1980).

of the administration or the judge was required (a principle described in German as *Verhandlungsmaxime*). The *Préliminaire de conciliation*, one of the most popular procedural innovations of the Revolution, was maintained in principle in the *Code* of 1806 but in practice no longer applied. The aim of this revolutionary institution was to avoid litigation and to attempt reconciliation: parties were brought together beforehand for what was intended to be a constructive and reasonable discussion.

The legislation on civil procedure was passed in the same way as that on civil law. Like other 'feudal laws', the *Ordonnance civile* of 1667 had been criticized and was abrogated by a statute of 3 Brumaire of Year II (24 October 1793). This statute aimed (rather idealistically) to abolish all formal procedure and open the way to a system of administering justice without formal legal proceedings. In Year V a draft code of procedure was compiled but the text was never promulgated. Under the consulate a statute of 27 Ventôse of Year VIII (17 March 1800) established a new judicial system and reintroduced the *Ordonnance* of 1667. The *Code* of 1806, one of whose principal authors was E. Pigeau (*d.* 1818), took up again the broad lines of the 1667 system, although it did retain a number of revolutionary innovations. In some cases (notably the *Préliminaire de conciliation* just mentioned), the preservation of these new institutions was more apparent than real. But other achievements of the Revolution did last, such as the creation of justices of the peace; the obligation to deliver reasoned judgments; the reduction in the number of appellate courts; and the abolition of the secret examination of witnesses.

THE MERITS OF CODIFICATION

8 The revival of legislative activity from the twelfth century and the proliferation of statutes which followed soon brought about a need for systematic collections of the law in force. In the Middle Ages and in early modern times, both church and state promulgated such collections. In compiling them, the authorities attempted to organize, to prune and to adapt bodies of sometimes very disparate rules. The sixth century *Corpus iuris civilis* of Justinian was the ancient model for the new compilations, the first of which was the *Decretales* of Gregory IX of 1234 and the last the *Polnoe Sobranie Zakonov* published in forty-five volumes in Russia by Tsar

Nicholas I in 1830 and followed in 1832 by fifteen volumes of the *Svod Zakonov.*[11]

These compilations of old and new statutes did rearrange the law and bring it up to date, but they differ fundamentally from codes in the strict sense. A true codification is an original work and, in contrast to a compilation, must be intended as a general, exhaustive regulation of a particular area of law (for example, civil law or civil procedure). Furthermore, the drafting of a code involves a coherent programme and a consistent logical structure. The language of a modern code ought to be accessible to all and, as far as possible, free from archaisms and technical professional jargon. Codes of this type appeared only from the eighteenth century onwards.[12]

In theory two types of code can be imagined: a codification with the sole aim of (re)formulation and systematization of the law in force, which avoids all substantial reform and all revolutionary innovation, and which faithfully reflects the past, limiting itself to recording and ordering the existing law.[13] On the other hand, a codification can be conceived as an instrument of social reform aimed at the future. In fact all modern codifications belong, no doubt in differing degrees, to the latter category. In the eighteenth century insistent demands for codification were expressions of a desire for innovation and progress, rather than of a hope that the existing legal order would be compiled and ordered. The promulgation of codes was sometimes the work of enlightened despots, acting on their own initiative and on their own paternalistic convictions, and influenced by the ideas of the Enlightenment. There are examples in the German culture of the period. In other cases, the people or its representatives rebelled and decided to proclaim a code inspired by radical ideas. This was the case with the codifications of the years of intermediate law.

[11] The first contained 30,920 statutes and ordinances arranged in chronological order from 1649–1825; the second was a systematically ordered selection which contained elements of Roman law. In spite of efforts under Tsar Alexander I, inspired by the model of the *Code civil* of 1804, Russia had no civil code in the nineteenth century.

[12] Certain major ordinances of Louis XIV (for example that of 1667 already mentioned) can be considered codifications of particular areas of law. At the same time, however, some scholars envisaged more ambitious projects of codification (e.g. Leibniz' *Praefatio novi codicis* of 1678). Guillaume de Lamoignon (to whom we shall return) hoped to compose a code applicable throughout France and based on the different sources of French law, ordinances, case law and customs, especially the custom of Paris. His attempts did not progress beyond a first sketch under the title *Arrêtés*, completed about 1672. Daguesseau too wished to codify French law; but his work was limited to a few main ordinances in the area of civil law.

[13] One thinks for instance of the formidable 'Restatement of the Law' in the United States.

OPPOSITION TO CODIFICATION

9 The codification movement spread throughout Europe from the eighteenth century. Codes are now a source of law characteristic of the legal system of the various European countries, apart from England, which even now has not got beyond the stage of setting up a law commission to study the problems a codification of the Common Law would present. At first sight this anomaly is the more surprising, as one of the most eloquent exponents of the principle of codification was an Englishman, Jeremy Bentham (*d.* 1832). The difference between the English and the European approach is to be explained largely by the preponderance of case law as a source of law in England, as well as by suspicion among the English ruling classes of all codification, which tended to be associated with ideas of radical or even revolutionary reform. All the same, on the European continent too the codification movement encountered opposition: in Germany it gave rise to a celebrated controversy between A. F. Thibaut (*d.* 1840), who in 1814 published *Uber die Nothwendigkeit eines allgemeinen bürgerlichen Gesetzbuches für Deutschland*, and F. C. von Savigny (*d.* 1861) who in the same year replied with a publication criticizing the idea of codification, *Vom Beruf unsrer Zeit für Gesetzgebung und Rechtswissenschaft*.

All codifications have advantages and disadvantages. Among the advantages are (i) legal security: a code contains the whole of the law. Any rule which is not in the code or which contradicts it is invalid. The text of the code takes precedence over legal doctrine (which is often divided) and case law. This situation is entirely different from that which prevailed before the codifications, when there was a jumble of legal authority: a complex and sometimes incoherent body of customary rules (some of which had not even been set down in writing); diverse and contradictory learned opinions; judicial decisions, from different countries and several centuries. (ii) Clarity: the ability to ascertain the content of the law.[14] A code deals with the whole of a subject systematically, in language accessible to non-lawyers. These qualities are an important advance from an earlier stage, at which law was written in obscure technical language, often in a Latin unintelligible to any non-initiate. (iii) Unity on the scale of a state, kingdom or empire. This is to be

[14] See section 70 below.

contrasted with the inextricable entanglement of ordinances and local customs in the old law.

The main argument against codification is immobility. This criticism was already levelled by Savigny, the founder of the Historical School. A code corresponds to the state of legal development at a given moment and it aims to fix that state so that it will not be changed. The settled text can, at the very most, be the object of interpretation. Now, according to the Historical School, law is the result of the historical evolution of peoples and must adapt itself to that evolution. The fixing of the law by codification causes internal contradictions and intolerable tensions within a society. Every codification therefore poses a dilemma: if the code is not modified, it loses all touch with reality, falls out of date and impedes social development; yet if the components of the code are constantly modified to adapt to new situations, the whole loses its logical unity and increasingly exhibits divergences and even contradictions. These dangers are real, for experience shows that the compilation of a new code is a difficult enterprise which rarely meets with success.

The *Kodifikationsstreit* was also inspired by ideological differences. The adversaries of codification conceived of law as the result of a continually developing history: they, together with their leader Savigny, were the conservatives. On the other hand, the proponents of codification belonged to the progressive camp: the appeal of codification was to break with the past, further the promises of the future, and smash the ascendancy of judges and advocates. In this respect, Portalis' attitude is revealing. As a co-author of the *Code civil*, he was of course in favour of the idea of codification but at the same time conscious of the risks a code entailed. This explains why the *Code* of 1804 drew largely on the old law, and why innovations were introduced only with extreme caution; the revolutionary zeal of the preceding years was now tempered. Portalis also had a sense of the dangers of finalizing the law. To prevent petrification of the law, he formulated these principles: a code must not become too detailed, and must leave a reasonable freedom of judgment to assess the individual cases which arose in practice; to reconcile the contradictions between social development and the law settled by the code, it was proper to turn to natural reason; the task of legal scholarship and case law would be to ensure by means of interpretation that the code remained living law. It is in this sense above all that Portalis' remark 'with time codes make themselves' is to be understood.

BIBLIOGRAPHY

10 Arnaud, A.-J., *Essai d'analyse structurale du Code civil français. La règle du jeu dans la paix bourgeoise*, Paris, 1973; Bibliothèque de Philosophie du Droit

Les origines doctrinales du Code civil français, Paris, 1969

Bloch, C. and Hilaire, J., 'Interpréter la loi. Les limites d'un grand débat révolutionnaire', *Miscellanea forensia historica Prof. de Smidt*, Amsterdam, 1988, 29–48

Garaud, M., *Histoire générale du droit privé français (de 1789 à 1804)*, I: *La révolution et l'égalité civile*, II: *La révolution et la propriété foncière*, Paris, 1953–8

Garaud, M. and Szramkiewicz, R., *La Révolution française et la famille*, Paris, 1978; Publications Fac. Droit et Sciences sociales Poitiers, 7

Halperin, J.-L., *Le tribunal de cassation et les pouvoirs sous la Révolution (1790–1799)*, Paris, 1987; Bibliothèque d'histoire du droit et droit romain, ed. P. Timbal, XXIII

Huussen, A. H., 'Le droit du mariage au cours de la Révolution française', *Revue d'histoire du droit* 47 (1979), 9–52, 99–127

Kan, J. van, *Les efforts de codification en France. Etude historique et psychologique*, Paris, 1929

Lafon, J., 'Le Code civil et la restructuration de la société française', *Mémoires de la société pour l'histoire du droit et des institutions des anciens pays bourguignons, comtois et romands* 42 (1985), 101–8

Maillet, J., 'Codifications napoléoniennes, développement économique et formation de la société française capitaliste', *Quaderni fiorentini per la storia del pensiero giuridico moderno* 2 (1973)

Naissance du Code civil an VII – an XII, 1800–1804, Paris, 1989

Sagnac, P., *La législation civile de la Révolution française (1789–1804). Essai d'histoire sociale*, Paris, 1898

Savatier, L., *L'art de faire des lois: Bonaparte et le Code civil*, Paris, 1927

Schimsewitsch, L., *Portalis et son temps. L'homme, le penseur, le législateur*, Paris, 1936; Thèse Droit

Schioppa, A. P. 'Napoleone e il Code de commerce', *Diritto e potere nella storia europea. Atti in onore di Bruno Paradisi*, I, Florence, 1982, 1,041–68

Vanderlinden, J., *Le concept de code en Europe occidentale du XIIIe au XIXe siècle*, Brussels, 1967

Wilhelm, W., 'Gesetzgebung und Kodifikation in Frankreich im 17. und 18. Jahrhundert', *Ius commune* 1 (1967), 241–70

'Portalis et Savigny. Aspects de la restauration', *Aspekte europäischer Rechtsgeschichte. Festgabe für Helmut Coing*, Frankfurt, 1982, 445–56

CHAPTER 2

Antecedents: the early Middle Ages, c. 500 – c. 1100

THE CHARACTER OF THE PERIOD

11 The Roman empire had been the political form of the ancient Mediterranean civilization of southern and western Europe, North Africa and Asia Minor. When it fell, three new civilizations grew up: the Graeco-Christian Byzantine empire (in which the ancient Roman empire scarcely survived); the Arab-Islamic world; and the Latin-Christian West, made up of the old Roman population and the Germanic peoples who had just settled there. In western Europe, imperial authority had declined in the fifth century, and the old Roman state had been divided among several Germanic tribal kingdoms. In the centuries which followed, the Frankish kings of the Carolingian dynasty, the Germanic kings of the Saxon dynasty and their successors all made attempts to restore the previous supranational authority of Rome. But these were without exception in vain.

The differences between the new Roman-Germanic society of the West and the ancient world were not just political. The upheavals which had brought about the fall of the Roman state had also affected the economy. In the western societies of the early Middle Ages, urbanization and the circulation of money had hardly begun, and agriculture remained more or less at subsistence level. The new culture of the West was different too. It was dominated by the Roman church and the Latin language; it did borrow from the remnants of Antiquity, but it simplified them drastically. The early Middle Ages, which were a primitive period in European history, lasted until about 1100. At that point a new movement radically transformed society and allowed it to attain the level of the two other great cultures, Byzantium and Islam. When the early Middle Ages drew to a close, the western world was in the course of total change:

the economy expanded and diversified; cities reappeared; the advances made in rational thought and in the universities were consolidated. The organization of the church and secular power became more complex; feudalism was in decline.

ROMAN LAW

12 The disappearance of the Roman state and the growing influence of the Germanic peoples were decisive for the evolution of Roman law. The old Roman legal order was not entirely eclipsed but, with the decline of the institutions of Antiquity, it lost its predominant position. The principal changes were these: under the empire the whole population had been subject to Roman law, but now only the *Romani*, the descendants of the old indigenous population, were subject to it. The Germanic tribes retained their own customary law. In this period Roman law became more and more remote from its classical model, owing to the disappearance of the main components of ancient legal culture, namely the tradition of the major schools of law, the learning of the jurists, imperial legislation and case law. Besides, the West no longer remained in intellectual contact with the Greek East, which in its day had greatly contributed to the development of the classical Roman law. To these circumstances may be added the intellectual impoverishment of the western world. Roman law was reduced to being a provincial customary law, the 'Roman vulgar law' which prevailed in Italy and the south of France. Vulgar law was used to some extent in the rudimentary compilations made, on the orders of Germanic kings, for the benefit of their Roman subjects.[1] The compilations of Justinian (*d.* 565) were the most important legacy of Roman law. Yet Justinian's legislative work did not come into force in the West. And it remained unknown for the first centuries of the Middle Ages, owing to the isolation of the West and the failure of Justinian's attempts at reconquest of the territories invaded by the Germans.

The *Corpus iuris civilis* of Justinian (the name goes back to the twelfth century) is one of the most celebrated legislative projects in

[1] The *lex Romana Visigothorum* or *Breviarium Alarici* was a compilation of Roman law promulgated by Alaric, King of the Visigoths, in AD 506. For centuries after the fall of the empire it was one of the main sources of knowledge of Roman law in the West. The important *lex Romana Burgundionum* should also be mentioned; its date is not earlier than the reign of King Gundobad (*d.* AD 516).

history. It represents the ultimate expression of ancient Roman law and the final result of ten centuries of legal evolution. At the same time the *Corpus iuris* was to be a message to future lawyers. Justinian had aimed to compile a substantial selection of the works of the classsical jurists and imperial legislation. The texts chosen were revised, systematically arranged, and then published and promulgated. The *Corpus iuris* is made up of four collections: the most important, on account of its scale as well as its quality, is the *Digest* or *Pandects* (to use the Greek name) completed in AD 533. This contains excerpts from the works of the jurists, the principal craftsmen of Roman law. The second collection, the *Codex*, brings together imperial constitutions and rescripts. A first edition was completed in AD 529, a second in AD 534.[2] The *Codex* is supplemented by the *Novels* (*Novellae Constitutiones*), a collection of laws promulgated by Justinian himself between AD 534 and AD 556.[3] Finally, the *Corpus iuris* also contains the *Institutes* (*Institutiones*), intended as an introduction for the use of students and promulgated in AD 533. This work (not least its title) derives largely from the *Institutes* of Gaius, a work compiled about AD 160. In the eastern empire, Justinian's compilations remained in force: they were commented on in teaching and in scholarship. But in the West their historical role began only towards 1100.[4]

THE GERMANIC NATIONAL LAWS

13 Before the invasions, the Germans were ruled by the primitive law of their tribes, which was based on immemorial customs handed down by a purely oral tradition. In their new kingdoms, these national laws were sometimes set down in writing, under the influence of ancient models: these were the *leges nationum Germanicarum* (or in German, *Volksrechte*).[5] Yet the compilations were no more than clumsy attempts to express in Latin a primitive law which

[2] Only the text of the second edition has come down to us.

[3] As imperial constitutions, the *Novels* clearly had the force of law, and it is natural that they would have been later incorporated into the *Corpus iuris*. But there was no official compilation, and they have come down to us through private collections. The best-known Latin collections are the *Authenticum*, whose date and origin are uncertain, although its name recalls the fact that it was for long thought to be an official or 'authentic' collection, and the *Epitome* of Julian, who was a professor of Byzantine law. Many of Justinian's statutes were issued in Greek or in both Greek and Latin.

[4] See below, section 29.

[5] They are also described with some disdain as *leges barbarorum*.

was devoid of all general principle and consequently any analytical tradition. These compilations contained mainly rules of criminal law, taking the shape of detailed scales fixing fines and compensation in the case of homicide and various injuries, as well as rules of procedure and the (still primitive and irrational) law of evidence. Such rules faithfully reflected the archaic agrarian society from which they derived; the best known is the *lex Salica*, the law of the Salian Franks, the oldest version of which dates back probably to the last years of the reign of Clovis (*c.* AD 507–11). In it are to be found 'malbergic glosses', old Frankish legal terms which appear in the Latin text and are so called because they are the ritual words pronounced on the 'malberg', that is the hill on which the court (*mallus*) sat.

Important compilations of Germanic laws outside the Frankish kingdom should also be mentioned, such as the Edict of King Rothari of AD 643 in the Italian lands conquered by the Lombards. In England the Anglo-Saxon kings from King Aethelberht of Kent (*d.* AD 616) also promulgated an important series of 'statutes' (*dooms*), but in contrast to other compilations these English ones were composed in the vernacular.

The Germanic kingdoms of the continent – Franks, Ostrogoths, Visigoths and Lombards – united peoples of Roman and of Germanic origin. The *Romani* remained subject to Roman vulgar law, the Germans to the law of their own tribe. This is the principle of the 'personality' of law: whatever his place of residence and whoever the sovereign of that place, an individual remains subject to the law of his own people of origin. So in the vast Frankish empire of Charlemagne, in addition to the *Romani*, there were several Germanic nations ruled by their own law. In order to overcome the inconvenience arising from this complexity, Charlemagne attempted to impose a kind of legal unity, but without success. It was not until a later period that the principle of personality of law was abandoned in favour of the principle of territoriality, under which the customary law of the region was applicable to all those living in it regardless of their ethnic origin. This development is to be connected both with the dwindling of old tribal loyalties and with the emergence of a new sense of political unity, which was now based not on ethnic ties but on adherence to the sovereign of the region.

FEUDAL LAW

14 From the eighth century, feudal law developed and spread first through the Frankish kingdom and subsequently through other western lands. It is an original system of law, which was not connected with any nation in particular and was created in the Middle Ages quite independently of Roman law or Germanic national laws. Its general characteristics are none the less Germanic rather than Roman: the importance of personal relations and landed property; the absence of any abstract conception of the state; the lack of writing and formal legislation. Feudal law was a complex body of legal rules which, above all in the area of landed property, was sustained for several centuries. It took shape and developed for four centuries without the intervention of any significant legislation, and without any teaching or legal scholarship. Its development depended on customs, and occasionally on the involvement of a sovereign who was concerned to regulate a question of detail or to innovate on a particular point. The *Leges feudorum*, the first account of feudal (in fact Lombard) law, did not appear until the twelfth century.

LEGISLATION: GENERAL POINTS

15 The Roman emperors were great legislators. In promulgating their constitutions and in addressing their rescripts, they were conscious of taking an active part in the formation of law. By means of their legislation the emperors clarified, made more specific, and interpreted rules of law; they also gave new direction to the legal order. This legislative activity collapsed at the same time as did the Roman state in the West. Naturally the Germanic kings lent their authority to the process of writing down and promulgating traditional laws, and sometimes took the opportunity to innovate, but their primary aim was to set out the old law of the tribe. The decline of legislation at this time is not to be explained solely by the disappearance of the empire; it is also bound up with the conceptions of the Germanic peoples about royalty and law. In their view, law was not a social technique which could be manipulated and adapted just as the central authorities wished, but an eternal[6] reality, a fixed and

[6] Hence the expression *ewa* (cf. the German *ewig*, the Dutch *eeuwig* meaning 'eternal') for the old law.

timeless guiding principle which could be clarified and interpreted but not fundamentally altered. It was recognized that the king had the power to declare the meaning of the law and to develop legal principles, while respecting the existing, unchallengeable foundations, but even he could not in any way alter the ancient law. It is therefore unsurprising that, right through the early Middle Ages, genuine statutes are encountered very rarely indeed, and even subsequently sovereigns were slow and indecisive in resuming legislative activity.

LEGISLATION: THE CAPITULARIES

16 Although the climate was unpropitious, the Frankish kings made important legislative efforts in the eighth and especially the ninth centuries. The restoration of the Roman empire in the West made legislation ('capitularies') possible. The capitularies[7] consist of various types of legal disposition, corresponding in today's terms to statutes, orders, directives and regulations. Contemporaries already regarded the capitularies as an important element in legal practice, as the collections made during this period show. They contain very disparate material: little civil law, but numerous dispositions on criminal law, procedure and feudal law, as well as administrative directives, orders and regulations dealing with military organization. The capitularies therefore reflect the attempts of sovereigns to order society, to improve administration and, under Christian influence, to protect their poorest subjects (*pauperes*) against their most powerful ones (*potentes*).

Kings both protected the church and intervened in ecclesiastical affairs. This led them to promulgate numerous *capitularia ecclesiastica* (as opposed to *capitularia mundana*). Although these capitularies deal with ecclesiastical questions, they emanate from the Frankish kings and not from the ecclesiastical authorities, who held their own councils and promulgated their own decrees. After the coronation of Charlemagne, the entwining of the interests of church and state was a distinctive and a fundamental element in the organization of

[7] A royal constitution (*capitulare*, plural *capitularia*) was made up of several chapters (*capitula*) and this legislation owes its name to these 'chapters' (the title means little, since statutes, ordinances and charters were often made up of articles or 'chapters'). The term *capitulare* appears for the first time in the reign of Charlemagne (cap. de Herstal, in AD 779). Prior to this the terms *decretum*, *edictum*, *praescriptio* and others were used.

medieval society. This went back in fact to the first Christian emperors, who had already intervened in the affairs of the church.

Capitularia legibus addenda are a separate category: these were capitularies complementary to national laws which aimed, in conjunction with them, to establish legal unity within the empire. They are to be contrasted with *capitularia per se scribenda* ('self-justifying capitularies'), independent dispositions which were not ancillary to national laws.

Apart from their brevity (the average length is from ten to twenty articles), the capitularies differ significantly in form. Some are duly dated and begin with a solemn preamble, while others can be dated only approximately and contain neither initial protocol or eschatocol. Sometimes the text is not made up of sentences but simply of rubrics whose exact meaning can only be guessed: for instance 'on fugitives, to whom one persists in giving hospitality'. This is the case with *capitularia missorum*, which are the verbal instructions of sovereigns to *missi dominici*, the royal messengers sent through the country to supervise the application of law or to introduce new rules. The essential point of their mission was explained to them orally, and what has come down to us of these capitularies is no more than an *aide-mémoire*. The ideas of the time regarded the word of the king as the essential constitutive element which gave a document the force of law. This fits with the very ancient idea that the spoken word prevails over the written, not merely in legislation but also in contract and in evidence. The superiority now accorded to the written word is the outcome of an evolution which does not go back beyond the end of the Middle Ages.[8]

Capitularies, although they were promulgated by the king did not derive from his sole authority: the king did not legislate until he had obtained the support of a consensus, that is the agreement of the *populus Francorum* (the leading men of the kingdom), which was supposed to represent the Frankish people. The king always referred expressly to the consensus, but its true importance depended on the political situation and the balance of power. When the sovereign was a powerful leader like Charlemagne, consensus was practically guaranteed in advance, whereas in the time of his grandson, Charles the Bald (whose political position was at times extremely insecure) the wishes of the aristocracy could not be ignored.

[8] This phenomenon is closely associated with cultural development; in the past people listened much more than they read, and even reading was done aloud.

Under the Merovingians, capitularies still played a modest part. The great period of capitularies coincides with the Carolingian dynasty which came to power in AD 751: it is the ninth century, and above all the reigns of Charlemagne (who after his coronation as emperor was deeply conscious of his legislative role), Louis the Pious and Charles the Bald. But already by the end of the ninth century capitularies had disappeared, first in the eastern kingdom, later in the West.[9] The fact that they were proclaimed for the whole kingdom[10] and applicable throughout it meant that they formed a law superior to the various tribal laws and were thus a factor in legal unification. On the European continent legislation on a kingdom-wide scale disappeared after the capitularies; fresh attempts are to be found only in the twelfth century. In England, on the other hand, the national monarchy still promulgated important *dooms* in the tenth and eleventh centuries. The political unity of England explains why the situation there was quite the reverse of that in Europe, where at the same time the political division of kingdoms was taking place.

The importance of capitularies was recognized very early on, and collections intended for court practice and other legal purposes were compiled. These unofficial collections, which almost all date from the ninth to eleventh centuries, merely repeat the capitularies in their original form, and provisions are left in historical rather than systematic order, even though a systematic arrangement would have had certain advantages. Two collections became well known: that of Ansegisus, abbot of St Wandrille (AD 827), in which an article from one capitulary is sometimes transposed to a different context when the author thinks this more logical; and that of 'Benedict the Levite' (AD 847–52), a pseudonym under which the author brought together various legal sources (mainly ecclesiastical texts) in a collection which was intended to complement and continue the work of Ansegisus. Several of the documents in the collection of the Levite are either false capitularies or authentic sources which have been falsified; the falsifications largely relate to questions of the ecclesiasti-

[9] In the Frankish kingdom of the West (prefiguring France), the last capitularies date from AD 883 and 884; in the eastern kingdom (later, Germany) no capitulary was promulgated after the division of the empire (Verdun, AD 843); in Italy capitularies are rare after AD 875, and the last dates from AD 898.

[10] Some capitularies were promulgated both for the Frankish and for the Lombard kingdoms; others were applicable only in one or the other of the two kingdoms (which were united in AD 774 by a personal union).

cal hierarchy, which was probably one of the main preoccupations of the author.

JURISPRUDENCE

17 During the first centuries of the Middle Ages legislation had only a secondary importance. Jurisprudence as such did not exist: there is no trace of legal treatises or professional legal teaching. The collections of capitularies, which are sometimes found in the same manuscripts as the texts of national laws, were written for the use of practitioners and were not subject to doctrinal exposition in commentaries or manuals. Some rudiments of Roman thought were known through such texts as the *lex Romana Visigothorum*[11] or the *Etymologiae* of Isidore of Seville, a small encylopaedia which distilled the knowledge of Antiquity. But these isolated traces of ancient legal culture were not studied or analysed. In any case the law schools and lawyers who would have been capable of such work had disappeared. The sources of the period reveal ignorance of Roman law, and sometimes of the law of the capitularies, even among those whose professional activities in principle required them to be acquainted with them. Thus it is, not surprisingly, extremely rare to find a qualified and independent author expressing any critical opinion; but precisely this should be the role of any jurisprudence. An exceptional figure of this kind was Agobard of Lyon (*d.* AD 840) who dared to attack the ordeals and the personality principle of the application of law. Even canon law, which enjoyed considerable prestige,[12] inspired no study or theoretical commentary: the authors of collections contented themselves with bringing together the existing rules, and the promulgation of new rules by the pope or by the councils (especially the Frankish councils) was most infrequent.

The law therefore remained essentially an oral law, whose principal source was custom. The law of the kingdom was not unified but varied from tribe to tribe (initially) and from region to region (in later centuries). Apart from the capitularies, the only supra-national law was the law of the Latin church, which was authoritative

[11] See above section 12, note 1.

[12] Dionysius Exiguus in AD 489–501 compiled a collection which was recognized in the Frankish kingdom under Charlemagne. It was known as the *Dionysio-Hadriana*: Hadrian I presented it in AD 772 to Charlemagne in Rome, and in AD 802 at Aix-la-Chapelle he proclaimed it the canonical and authoritative collection for the empire.

throughout the West but important only in church affairs, largely of an administrative nature. None of these sources of law was the object of study or scholarly commentary.

THE COURTS AND PROCEDURE

18 The courts of the early Middle Ages bear no resemblance to those of the late Roman empire, as the following points show. The hierarchy of courts, with the possibility of appeal to Rome, had disappeared and was replaced by a system of local jurisdictions, the *mallus* of the county (*pagus*) in the Frankish kingdom. There was no centralization nor any procedure for appeal. The professional official judges of the late empire gave way to casual judges without legal education or particular qualifications, such as the Merovingian *rachimburgii*. From the reign of Charlemagne, however, resort could be had to permanent judges (*scabini*, aldermen) who, although they were not professional magistrates, at least provided greater stability in the administration of justice. The Frankish monarchy succeeded at least partly in realizing its policy of centralization and uniformity by entrusting important cases, submitted to the king as supreme judge, to a court official, the count of the palace (*comes palatii*); and by having the *missi dominici* supervise the workings of local jurisdictions in the name of the king.

The development of feudal law produced a parallel system of feudal courts, juxtaposed to the old court organization of different areas (*pagi* – counties – and smaller districts). The vassals of a lord sat in the feudal courts under his presidency and resolved disputes about their fiefs (e.g. succession) or among themselves (e.g. disputes between vassals or between a lord and his vassal). With the manorial system[13] there also came 'seigneurial' courts with jurisdiction over the subjects of the manors. To complete the picture, the church courts and (at a later period) the municipal courts should also be mentioned. This variety and fragmentation of the organization of justice (if it may be called organization) lasted to the end of the *ancien régime*.

The procedure adopted by the courts and tribunals of the early Middle Ages was of course very different from the procedure *extra*

[13] This is a type of agricultural concern based on the great estate. It has an economic and a public order aspect, since it is exploited economically, but also ruled and administered by the lord and great landowner.

ordinem of the late empire. Cases were now heard in public in the open air near a sacred place, perhaps a mountain, tree or spring. The people took an active part in the administration of justice, and expressed agreement or disagreement with the proposed verdict; the procedure was oral, with very limited use of written documents; no minutes or pleadings were in writing, and no records were kept; the case was essentially a dispute between the parties, in which the role played by the legal authorities was limited to formal control and simple ratification of the victorious party. The most striking expression of this conception of procedure is without doubt the judicial duel, which is nothing but an institutionalized combat designed to resolve the dispute.

Modes of proof were for the most part irrational. Justice made use of divine and supernatural powers, as in the case of judicial duels and other ordeals, and also in the oaths taken by one party and his supporters. Rational proof by means of documents and witnesses was not excluded, but proof by confronting the witnesses for either party with each other was undeveloped and highly formalistic. When the witnesses of the two parties refused to retract their testimony and the judges consequently found themselves in an impasse, a duel was the only possible outcome. In any event, the judges did not undertake any critical examination of the parties or witnesses which might have exposed a contradiction. By contrast with this purely mechanical confrontation of witnesses for and against, the royal *inquisitio* came much closer to an inquiry into the actual facts. The *inquisitio* was a Carolingian innovation, which consisted in having the inhabitants of an area interrogated under oath by royal agents. It mainly related to questions of landed property in which the king or the church had an interest. This *inquisitio* (which is no relation of the Inquisition instituted in the thirteenth century to repress heretics) is the historical origin of the jury system in both criminal and civil procedure.

EVALUATION

19 Each age has the law it deserves. It is therefore natural that the West in the early Middle Ages had a law adapted to the new political, economic and intellectual situation; and so a system of administering justice which was fragmented, but adequate for the needs of an agrarian and military society. The law of the period was

inevitably lacking in complexity, devoid of theory and general principles, imbued with irrational and sacred elements, and knew nothing of learned jurists or professional practitioners. It goes without saying that one of the great changes which took place in western society from about 1100 was the development of a new type of legal order. None the less the imprint of the great events of the early Middle Ages was not completely erased in the following centuries and can still sometimes be detected. The legal dualism characteristic of continental Europe – that is, the coexistence of Roman and Germanic laws – corresponds to the cultural dualism of the Roman-Germanic world of the early Middle Ages.[14] In some countries such as England (where the legacy of Roman civilization was entirely lost) as well as in the regions east of the Rhine which escaped Romanization, canon law was the only Roman element in legal practice. On the other hand, in the Mediterranean countries, notably Italy, Roman law remained the foundation of the legal order (even though the contribution of the great Lombard nation should not be underestimated; in northern Italy the *Lombarda* for a long time exercised a considerable influence on legal practice). France is a special case: in the south, which corresponds roughly to what is now the Languedoc, Germanization was superficial (*Herrensiedlung*) and the main principles of Roman law were maintained; in the north, on the other hand, the territories which were later to become French-speaking, the invasions were followed by a massive occupation by Germanic tribes (*Bauernsiedlung*) and Roman law was lost. Consequently, until the end of the *ancien régime* France was divided. In the north, the region of customary law, the law was based on Germanic and feudal oral custom; while Roman law remained in the south, the region of written law ('written' because it was set down in the *Corpus iuris* and in the works of the learned jurists). The persistence of different matrimonial regimes illustrates this legal division: in the region of customary law, the Germanic regime of community of property was followed; in the south, the dotal system of Roman law was maintained.

Some features of the archaic law of this period disappeared as a more advanced society developed, but have been appreciated again

[14] This is the basis of the expression 'Roman-Germanic family' proposed by the comparatist R. David, *Grands systèmes de droit contemporain* (Paris, 1969), to describe western European law (which is itself one of the major systems of law alongside the Common Law, the law of socialist states, and religious law).

in more recent times. The oral and public character of the administration of justice, for example, was suppressed to a large degree in early modern times. Yet nowadays importance is once again attached to the democratic and non-bureaucratic character of such principles.

BIBLIOGRAPHY

20 Amira, K. von, *Germanisches Recht I: Rechtsdenkmäler*, 4th edition by K. A. Eckhardt: Berlin, 1960; Grundriss der Germanischen Philologie 5/1

Astuti, G., *Lezioni di storia del diritto italiano. Le fonti. Età romano-barbarica*, Padua, 1953

Bognetti, G. P., *L'età Longobarda*, 4 vols., Milan, 1966–8

Buhler, A., 'Capitularia relecta. Studien zur Entstehung und Uberlieferung der Kapitularien Karls des Grossen und Ludwigs des Frommen', *Archiv für Diplomatik* 32 (1986), 305–501

Clercq, C. de, *La législation religieuse franque*, I: *De Clovis à Charlemagne*, II: *De Louis le Pieux à la fin du IXe siècle*, Louvain, Paris, Antwerp, 1936–58

Conrat, M., *Geschichte der Quellen und Literatur des römischen Rechts im früheren Mittelalter*, I, Leipzig, 1891

Davies, W. and Fouracre, P. (eds.), *The settlement of disputes in early medieval Europe*, Cambridge, 1986

Dilcher, G. and Diestelkamp, B. (eds.), *Recht Gericht Genossenschaft und Policey. Studien zu Grundbegriffen der germanistischen Rechtstheorie. Symposion für A. Erler*, Berlin, 1986

Diurni, G., *L'expositio ad Librum Papiensem e la scienza giuridica preirneriana*, Rome, 1976; Biblioteca della Rivista di storia del diritto italiano, 23

Le situazioni possessorie nel medioevo. Età longobardo-franca, Milan, 1988; Quaderni di studi senesi, 64

Foviaux, J., *De l'Empire romain à la féodalité*, Paris, 1986; Droit et institutions, I

Ganshof, F. L., *Qu'est-ce que la féodalité?*, 5th edn, Paris, 1982

Recherches sur les capitulaires, Paris, 1958; Société d'Histoire du Droit

Gaudemet, J., 'Survivances romaines dans le droit de la monarchie franque du Ve au Xe siècle', *Revue d'histoire du droit* 23 (1955), 149–206

Guterman, S. L., *From personal to territorial law. Aspects of the history and structure of the Western legal–constitutional tradition*, Metuchen, NJ, 1972

Hägermann, D., 'Zur Entstehung der Kapitularien', *Festschrift für Peter Acht*, Kallmünz, 1976; Münchener historische Studien, Abt. geschichtliche Hilfswissenschaften, 15, 12–27

Hannig, J., *Consensus fidelium. Frühfeudale Interpretationen des Verhältnisses von Königtum und Adel am Beispiel des Frankenreichs*, Stuttgart, 1982; Monographien zur Geschichte des Mittelalters, 27

Kaufmann, E., *Aequitatis iudicium. Königsgericht und Billigkeit in der Rechtsordnung des frühen Mittelalters*, Frankfurt, 1959

Kern, F., 'Recht und Verfassung im Mittelalter', *Historische Zeitschrift* 120 (1929), 1–79
King, P. D., *Law and society in the Visigothic kingdom*, Cambridge, 1972; Cambridge studies in medieval life and thought
Köbler, G., *Das Recht im frühen Mittelalter*, Cologne, Vienna, 1971; Forschungen zur deutschen Rechtsgeschichte 7
'Vorstufen der Rechtswissenschaft im mittelalterlichen Deutschland', *Zeitschrift der Savigny-Stiftung für Rechtsgeschichte* (G.A.) 100 (1983), 75–118
Kop, P. C., *Beschouwingen over het zgn. 'vulgaire' Romeinse recht*, Leyden, The Hague, 1980
Krause, H., 'Königtum und Rechtsordnung in der Zeit der Sächsishen und Salischen Herrscher', *Zeitschrift der Savigny-Stiftung für Rechtsgeschichte* (G.A.) 82 (1965), 1–98
Levy, E., *West Roman vulgar law: the law of property*, Philadelphia, 1961; Memoirs of the American Philosophical Society 29
Mayer-Homberg, E., *Die fränkischen Volksrechte im Mittelalter*, I*: Die fränkischen Volksrechte und das Reichsrecht*, Weimar, 1912
Mitteis, H., *Lehnrecht und Staatsgewalt*, Weimar, 1935
Nehlsen, H., 'Aktualität und Effektivität der ältesten germanischen Rechtsaufzeichnungen', *Recht und Schrift im Mittelalter*, ed. by P. Classen, Sigmaringen, 1977; Vorträge und Forschungen hg. vom Konstanzer Arbeitskreis für mittelalterliche Geschichte, 23
Roels, W., *Onderzoek naar het gebruik van de aangehaalde bronnen van Romeins recht in de Lex Romana Burgundionum*, Antwerp, 1958; Vlaamse Rechtskundige Bibliotheek 41
Scovazzi, M., *Le origini del diritto germanico. Fonti, preistoria, diritto pubblico*, Milan, 1957
Sprandel, R., 'Uber das Problem neuen Rechts im früheren Mittelalter', *Zeitschrift der Savigny-Stiftung für Rechtsgeschichte* (G.A.) 79 (1962), 138–63
Weitzel, J., *Dinggenossenschaft und Recht. Untersuchungen zum Rechtsverständnis im fränkisch-deutschen Mittelalter*, Cologne, 1985; 2 volumes; Quellen und Forschungen zur höchsten Gerichtsbarkeit im alten Reich, 15, I, II
Wenskus, R., *Stammesbildung und Verfassung. Das Werden der frühmittelalterlichen Gentes*, Cologne, Graz, 1961

CHAPTER 3

Europe and Roman-Germanic law, c. 1100 – c. 1750

CHARACTER OF THE PERIOD

21 At the end of the eleventh century, western European society finally left behind the archaic feudal and agrarian structures which had characterized the early Middle Ages. Important advances were made in the course of this transformation of the West. The sovereign nation state became the dominant form of political organization, and its symbol was the absolute monarch of early modern times. The society of the late Middle Ages, in which the various social orders had managed to obtain a share of power by means of a system of representative 'estates', was no more than a passing phase in the evolution of the state, as was the political independence of the great cities at that time. The emergence of national authorities was at the expense of the empire, and it obstructed German attempts to restore the universal power of the Roman empire. The same development also meant that the power of feudal lords diminished to the same degree that central governments asserted and reinforced themselves.

The organization of the church had a similar centralist tendency. Here power was concentrated at a supra-national level, and allowed a bureaucratic and hierarchical church to take shape under the direction of the papacy.

The closed and essentially agricultural manorial economy was replaced by a market economy. This was sustained by the development of international commerce and industry, an intense circulation of capital, and the development of a banking system: in other words, a renewal and transformation of economic activity in general, assisted by the rise of numerous cities. In spite of the dampening effects associated with corporatism and mercantilism, free enterprise was the driving force of the new economy. The scale of capitalist enterprise in the late Middle Ages was still modest, as it was restricted by the economic power of cities or independent city republics. From early modern times, however, capitalism could mobilize the resources of an entire nation and work on a world scale. This economic expansion is reflected in urbanization: the population of the large cities of the Middle Ages was still of the order of 100,000, yet in early modern times it reached a million. The social consequences were clear. The commercial success of urban businesses now set the pace for economic development in the country; social emancipation also extended beyond the cities into the country. The cities and their liberated citizens, by exerting this two-pronged pressure, therefore made a decisive contribution to the abolition of serfdom. And as agriculture became commercialized, the social and economic structure of the old manor disappeared.

There was also a profound intellectual development. The general cultural level rose markedly, and this is reflected particularly in increased literacy and increased written use of the vernacular languages; rational thought also continued to gain ground. It was at this time too that universities came into being and spread throughout Europe. They carried with them an intellectual discipline based on the great philosophical and legal works of Graeco-Roman Antiquity. Ancient thought was the object of intense study, which culminated during the Renaissance; it was subsequently supplanted by modern scientific method, which was experimental and had freed itself of dogma and arguments based on authority.

BEFORE AND AFTER 1500: CONTINUITY

22 This chapter deals with the period until about the middle of the eighteenth century. It therefore ignores traditional periodization and the conventional break – about 1500 – between the Middle Ages and modern times.[1] It is true that traditional periodization corresponds to important changes: the fracturing of the unity of the medieval church, the rise of absolutism, great discoveries. The effect

[1] Many historians, dissatisfied with traditional periodization, argue that a break just as important as that around 1500 should be made around 1100, and consequently propose to distinguish between the early and late Middle Ages. Others go further and divide the history of Europe after Antiquity into three phases: archaic (until 1100), Old Europe (until the eighteenth century), and the industrial period. This periodization is followed especially in the *Zeitschrift für historische Forschung. Halbjahrschrift zur Erforschung des Spätmittelalters und der frühen Neuzeit*, launched in 1975, in which the second period is described as the 'old-European period'.

of these changes must not be misunderstood, yet it is all the more important to underline the continuity which existed between the Middle Ages and modern times. The rise of the national sovereign state clearly began during the last centuries of the Middle Ages and reached its apogee in modern times. Criticism of, and attacks against, absolute power became an important political consideration only in the eighteenth century (except in England where they began in the seventeenth century). Dogmatic Christianity also survived the Middle Ages: although the meaning of Christian dogmas was sometimes in dispute, it was not possible to place the dogmas themselves in doubt. Yet this prohibition lost all significance with the diffusion of the ideas of the Enlightenment in the eighteenth century. Economic development was retarded by the limitations imposed by the inadequacy of available sources of energy right up until the machine age and the industrial use of steam. Throughout the *ancien régime*, industrial production and transport had to make use of primitive resources: the physical power of man, animal, water or wind. And the succession of famines and epidemics, a constant characteristic of the Middle Ages, persisted long after 1500.

The fundamental transformations which occurred in these various areas profoundly changed the society of the *ancien régime* in the course of the eighteenth century. The Industrial Revolution brought about a vast increase in potential energy, and laid the foundations for mass production. It was this, together with scientific advances, which shaped the modern technical and industrial age, in comparison with which all earlier history may be called pre-industrial.

The Enlightenment (*Aufklärung*) signified a new mode of thought and a new conception of man and the universe: from now on the foundation was human reason and no longer revealed religion. This movement towards rational ideas and discoveries broke with a thousand years of European history and prepared the way for a new philosophy – and at the same time for a new society, since the old social structures were intimately bound up with religious conceptions of the universe. Monarchy by divine right is an example. The exponents of new ideas attacked absolutist regimes precisely because they were steeped in dogmas which had now been declared to be obsolete and contrary to the freedom of the individual. None the less in Europe the old political system managed to survive until the end of the eighteenth century; the only exception is England, where absolutism received a decisive setback at the end of the seventeenth century. In some states the durability of the old political structures can be explained because sovereigns favourable to the ideas of the Enlightenment pursued policies of modernization. In other countries, France above all, it was largely political inertia which kept the monarchy in power. Modernization struck late in France, with all the more force, and led to the destruction of the political system of the *ancien régime*, first in France and soon in other European countries too.

THE DEVELOPMENT OF THE LAW: OUTLINE

23 In the development of private law there is no dramatic divide between the fifteenth and the sixteenth centuries. Admittedly, it was towards 1500 that the reception of Roman law in Germany took place; some decades later the homologation of customs began in the Netherlands; and the sixteenth century saw jurisprudence dominated by the Humanist School. All these events, however (which will be examined in detail), are simply one stage in a long evolution which goes back to the Middle Ages. The reception was a consequence of the revival of Roman law in the twelfth century, and merely one of the many forms of interaction between Germanic customary law and the 'learned' Roman law which took place over several centuries throughout Europe. Similarly, legal humanism was no more than a new episode in the long history of assimilation of ancient law by European man. As for the reduction of customs to writing, which was first decreed in the fifteenth century in France, it cannot be understood except in the context of a fundamental question which preoccupied the authorities and the lawyers from the Middle Ages onwards: 'was it or was it not necessary to preserve customary law?' To appreciate the significance of this crucial problem in Europe under the *ancien régime*, the following points should be noted.

As soon as customary law no longer met the requirements of society, the need for modernization appeared more and more pressing. It could be achieved either by internal transformation of the 'native' law or by receiving into that law an existing system, which was more sophisticated and better able to meet new demands: in the event, Roman law. In their attempts to modernize traditional customary law and assimilate learned doctrine, European countries tried both methods, and consequently the old European law can be called a Roman-Germanic system. The coexistence of the two elements, however, and their influence on one another varied greatly from one country to another, as is typical in Europe. Germany is the extreme case of a massive reception of learned law; by contrast, English Common Law is the most radical example of a rejection of Roman law.[2]

After several centuries of diffusion, the learned law had finally established itself in the sixteenth century in the various countries and regions of continental Europe. The development was to be expected in the Mediterranean regions, where learned law had already acquired a predominant position in the Middle Ages, as well as in Germany, where it had been introduced by way of authority. Yet a similar development is to be observed in the areas where homologated customs were in force. Several factors may explain this diffusion of Roman law in the regions of customary law: legal scholarship there was wholly under the influence of learned law; the courts of justice were peopled by lawyers whose university education was based on Roman law; and the customs themselves (once homologated) often recognised Roman law as having a binding supplementary role. The sixteenth and seventeenth centuries, the classical age of political absolutism, also coincided with the classical age of modern Roman law. But the Roman law of that time was essentially an academic legal system, a 'professors' law' barely accessible and intelligible to an uninitiated public. It was employed in practice in secret bureaucratic procedures, which aimed as far as possible to avoid any direct contact with the people to whom the law applied.

The meaning of the law was frequently unclear, and certainty in the law elusive. It was an improvement when customs were set down in writing, first on individual initiative and later by official order, but the written versions were often highly imperfect and had to be supplemented by learned law. But the learned law itself (and this was not the least of the practitioners' difficulties) was at that time made up of a mass of works which were sometimes inordinately long, and which were written by innumerable jurists who were inclined to contradict one another. Although there was also progress in legisla-

[2] But it should be emphasized that even after the reception in Germany, the old Germanic law (Saxon law among others) did not lose its importance in legal practice. In England too the Common Law, while an essential component of English law, was not the only system in force; in parallel courts such as the Court of Chancery and the High Court of Admiralty (and obviously in the church courts) the learned law was applied (see below, section 38).

tion, until the mid-eighteenth century no general codification was achieved. The most successful attempts still restricted themselves to ordinances in specific areas of the law (some important, of course) or simply to collecting statutes promulgated over the various centuries of the Middle Ages and *ancien régime.* The variety of jurisdictions inherited from the Middle Ages had been curtailed by a progressive limitation of the role of the municipal, ecclesiastical and corporate courts in favour of the court system of the modern state, but this limitation fell short of actual elimination. Yet plans for a rational court system under the control of central authority were far from being accomplished in practice, and sometimes met with tenacious opposition: the enlightened reform which Joseph II tried to introduce into the Austrian Netherlands triggered off revolution there.

The eighteenth century marked the end of the old European legal order. Various factors contributed to its disappearance: a refusal to submit to the authorities of Antiquity, notably Roman law; the search for a new legal order based on reason, or on the nature of man and society as conceived and defined by reason; the triumph of the idea of codification; and the will to make the closed and esoteric world of law and justice accessible and democratic.

CUSTOMARY LAW

General development

24 Custom was originally the most important of the sources of old European law, and in the following centuries too it played a significant part, particularly in northern France and the southern Netherlands, the regions of customary law. During the *ancien régime* customary law changed profoundly, notably in the following respects. It tended towards a greater unity: in the post-Carolingian age, there were many local and regional customs, owing to feudal fragmentation and the independence of cities. This diversity was progressively reduced by a process of concentration and unification. In England in the reign of Henry II (1154–89) the central royal courts had already created a single national customary law, the Common Law, which was 'common' to the kingdom, and as such contrasted with local customs of lesser importance.[3] In other

[3] The term 'Common Law' nowadays also has other connotations, particularly that of judge-made law, that is, case law based on binding precedent, in contrast to statute law passed by Parliament.

countries the concentration was less radical, and the diversity of customs was reduced but not eliminated. In the south of France, the revived Roman law became the common basis of legal practice at a very early date. In the north, on the other hand, customs were more tenacious, although the prestige and influence of the *Coutume de Paris* led to a relative standardization of customary law, at least in the northern regions. In the southern Netherlands, the homologation of customs brought about the disappearance of many customs and a relative (essentially regional) unification of customary law.

There was also an increasing tendency to set customs down in writing. At first sight this is a contradiction in terms, because the qualities *par excellence* of custom are the adaptability, flexibility and fluidity with which it arises[4] and disappears. Once a customary rule has been reduced to writing, however, the written version takes on a life of its own and a certain permanence; the writing fixes the text and restricts all further modification. These effects had already been felt in private compilations made on the initiative of practitioners, and the official compilation of customs followed by their promulgation with the force of law completed the development. The end product of this operation, known as the recording or 'homologation' of customs, is a hybrid source of law. On the one hand, the written customs are customary law. That is how they are presented, and the fact that they were compiled on the basis of statements by witnesses who had experience of local usages confirms their customary origin. On the other hand, the collected texts were promulgated after revision by the central authorities, and the courts were then bound to apply them to the exclusion of all other contrary custom. Since it is rare (as history shows) for a promulgated version to be adapted or modified later, the established text resembles a statute even more. The homologated customs therefore represent a transitional phase between the true customs spontaneously formed and developed in the early Middle Ages, and the true legislation of the following period.

In the Netherlands, where the authorities were plainly influenced by the French example of the fifteenth century,[5] Charles V decreed

4 The appearance of a custom was sometimes confirmed by judicial investigation: according to some medieval teaching, two judgments sufficed to prove the existence of a custom.

5 *Ordonnance* of Montil-lez-Tours, promulgated by Charles VII in 1454; the text of the custom of Burgundy had already been promulgated in 1459 by Duke Philip the Good. After a change of method, the official compilation of customs was carried out largely after 1497; and between 1500 and 1540 almost 600 customs, mostly from central and northern France,

homologation in 1531. His order was evidently addressed to the whole of the seventeen provinces, as at this point there was no reason to predict the secession which took place in the reign of Philip II. The accomplishment of the programme of homologation was very slow, and the order had to be reiterated several times, first by Charles V himself, then by Philip II, still later by the Archdukes Albert and Isabelle. There were various stages involved in the procedure of homologation: first, a draft had to be produced by the local authorities; this was examined by the provincial and regional councils or by the courts of justice; it was then revised by the Conseil Privé at Brussels; finally the sovereign confirmed and promulgated the definitive text by decree. With a few exceptions, this process did not envisage any participation by representative institutions such as the state assemblies.

In total 832 customs were reduced to writing and 96 were homologated. Since homologation was conducted effectively only from the second half of the sixteenth century, and since political circumstances made it difficult to carry out royal instructions in the northern provinces at that time, the vast majority of the homologated customs are from the southern provinces.[6] The programme of homologation aimed to improve legal certainty, and this aim was largely attained. Some of the compilations of customs were virtual codes, such as the (non-homologated) version of the Custom of Antwerp of 1608, which contains no fewer than 3,832 articles. But most were much more modest. To fill the gaps in customary law, the learned law (i.e. Roman and canon law) was declared compulsorily applicable, and this is what is meant by the supplementary role of the 'written common law'. Even at the stage of compilation and revision, the learned law had invariably managed to influence the terminology of the texts, and sometimes the actual substance too. A further aim of homologation was unification of the law, but this objective was only very partially attained. In some provinces, mostly rural regions such as Namur, Luxembourg and Frisia, a single provincial *Coutume* was decreed, and all local customs were accordingly abrogated. In Hainaut and in Artois, a provincial custom was

were set down in writing. The vogue for compilation was followed in the years 1555 to 1581 by a reform of customs. The reformed customs remained in force until the end of the *ancien régime*. In the course of the seventeenth and eighteenth centuries very little new compilation was attempted.

[6] Thus in Holland customs were not homologated and, in the seventeenth century, scholarship filled the gap by creating Roman-Dutch law.

superimposed on local customs, while in Flanders and the Brabant a large number of different and independent customs persisted in the absence of a 'common' customary law at the provincial level.[7] In spite of the abrogation of nearly 600 customs, the Netherlands preserved about 100 homologated customs, and more than 800 written ones; homologation therefore did limit the fragmentation of law, but it also contributed to maintaining the diversity of customs up to the end of the *ancien régime*.

Custom became the subject of learned legal studies, which certainly affected its original spontaneity. It was above all the homologated customs which were subject to such studies; although the works of the legists were inspired primarily by the principles of Roman law in which they had been schooled, it was not beneath them to comment on this new 'written law' which had acquired the force of statute. On the continent compilations and accounts of local and regional customary law appeared in the thirteenth century. In the earliest works no trace of learned law is to be detected, but very soon university teaching was reflected – in degrees varying from one author to another – in the use of the learned law. The supple and the somewhat naive character of custom was inevitably lost when it was subjected to a scholarship based to a greater or lesser extent on Roman law. The following sections note the major customary works of France and the Netherlands.

The French 'coutumiers' of the Middle Ages

25 The most celebrated of the French customary works (*coutumiers*) of the thirteenth century is that of Philippe de Beaumanoir, the *Coutumes de Beauvaisis*, written about 1279–83.[8] The author, an official of the royal courts, was a practitioner first and foremost, but had probably been educated at university. His clear and well-informed account deals with the customary law of Beauvaisis as well as the customs of Vermandois and Paris. He also draws on case law,

[7] In Flanders 227 customs were reduced to writing and 37 homologated; in Brabant and Limburg the figures were 124 and 8.

[8] Modern edition by A. Salmon in 2 volumes, 1899–1900 (reprinted 1970), completed by a third volume: G. Hubrecht, *Commentaire historique et juridique* (Paris, 1974). P. Bonnet-Laborderie (ed.), *Actes du colloque international Philippe de Beaumanoir et les Coutumes de Beauvaisis (1283–1983)* (Beauvais, 1983). The work so well characterizes old medieval law that it was even translated into Japanese by Hiroshi Hawawa in 1971; there is great interest in western feudalism in Japan.

in particular that of the Parlement de Paris, and on the learned law, both Roman and canon. Beaumanoir was the initiator of the genre and his attempt at formulating and at the same time systematizing the customary rules was fairly successful. His work was written in French and could be used in everyday legal practice. It helped to impart the terminology, principles, and legal doctrine of the learned law to a wide audience.

Two other important works on custom appeared at the end of the fourteenth century. The first dealt essentially with the *Coutume de Paris*, and the second with the customary law of the north. Jacques d'Ableiges, who was the king's bailiff in various regions, was the author of a work completed about 1388 known as the *Grand Coutumier de France*. The title (a more recent coinage) is misleading: d'Ableiges did not deal with French customary law in general (the variety of the customs anyway made that impossible) but with the *Coutume de Paris* and surrounding areas, which was later to play a major part in the formation of French common law. His sources were the case law of the Châtelet (the court of first instance in Paris) and the Parlement de Paris, but he also drew on his own judicial experience. His work was extremely influential.[9]

Jean Boutillier was also a royal agent with duties in (among other places) Tournai, which was then a French royal burgh, and in which he was legal counsellor and magistrate. His *Somme Rural*, which probably dates from 1393–6, was conceived as an account of the customary law of the north of France and at the same time as an introduction to the learned law for the general reader without university education. The author's intention to write a popularizing work emerges even from the title *Somme rural*, which suggests a general work accessible to those from rural backgrounds. The fact that the book was written in French at once sets it apart from contemporary learned treatises, in which the use of Latin was *de rigueur*. Boutillier used the sources of Roman and canon law, and case law familiar to him both from his own experience and from consulting the records of the superior courts of justice, especially the Parlement de Paris. This introduction to learned law in the vernacular proved useful and popular. Since the customary law examined in Boutillier's work was close to that of the Netherlands, it is not

[9] Modern edition by E. Laboulaye and R. Dareste (Paris, 1868).

surprising that it was equally successful there, and was soon printed there and translated into Dutch.[10]

French commentators of modern times

26 In the sixteenth century the tradition of *coutumiers* continued. It culminated in the work of Charles Du Moulin (*d.* 1566), the most eminent learned commentator on French customary law. Du Moulin was expert in Roman law, to which he devoted several original works which attest his qualities as a Romanist.[11] But he dedicated his main studies to customary law: his grand design was to set out from the principles of the *Coutume de Paris* and to arrive at the unification of French customary law. The significance of Du Moulin's fundamental choice can be appreciated only by considering the relations between customary law and the *ius commune* in other countries in the same period. Germany and Scotland had opted for the introduction of learned law. In principle, this solution would have had the same advantages in France, for the legal techniques of learned law were without doubt superior to those of customary law, and in the southern territories of the kingdom the written law was generally used. Du Moulin none the less opposed the adoption of Roman law as the common law of France, yet he was convinced of the need for a unified French law and intended to base such a unification on the statutes and customs of the kingdom. The common French law was to be formed not on the basis of learned law (the European *ius commune*) but from the common store of French customs: *consuetudines nostrae sunt ius commune* (a phrase from his *De feudis* of 1539).[12]

[10] *Editio princeps*: Bruges, 1479 (numerous reprints); first Dutch edition: Delft, 1483 (also numerous reprints). In the absence of a modern critical edition, the preferred edition is that published at the hand of L. Charondas le Caron (Paris, 1603). On Boutillier, see G. van Dievoet, *Jehan Boutillier en de Somme rural* (Louvain, 1951); R. Feenstra, 'La source du titre des droits royaux de la "Somme rural" de Boutillier', *Revue de Nord* 40 (1958), 235–44; R. Feenstra and M. Duynstee, 'Les "cas brief selon le droit civil". Annexe de la Somme rural de Jean Boutillier empruntée aux "Casus legum" des Decretales', *Revue d'histoire du droit* 51 (1983), 365–400.

[11] See especially works on the law of obligations, which are the basis of some doctrines of the *Code civil* (see articles 1217–25 and its theory of divisible and indivisible obligations). J.-L. Thireau, 'Aux origines des articles 1217 à 1225 du Code civil: l'extricatio labyrinthi dividui et individui de Charles du Moulin', *Revue d'histoire du droit* 15 (1938), 51–109. J.-L. Thireau, *Charles du Moulin (1500–66). Etude sur les sources, la méthode, les idées politiques et économiques d'un juriste de la Renaissance* (Geneva, 1980).

[12] In the same vein see *Oratio de concordia et unione consuetudinum Francie* (posthumous edition, 1576).

Du Moulin's reservations about Roman law were of course essentially political: Roman law was the 'imperial' law, and in Du Moulin's day the Holy Roman Empire under the Habsburgs was the most redoubtable enemy of France. To this objection of principle were added legal objections: customs were admittedly imperfect, but Roman law itself could lay no claim to perfection. The work of the Humanist School had made it possible to see that the *Corpus iuris* was a product of human history, and lawyers were now all the more conscious of its defects. The erudite humanists had also shown how much had been misunderstood by the medieval commentators, who were still highly authoritative in the sixteenth century. Budé made a list of these misunderstandings in his *Annotationes in XXIV libros Pandectarum* (1508). Donellus (*d.* 1591), in his *Commentarii de iure civili* of 1589–90, even expressed serious reservations about the quality of Justinian's compilations. And if Roman law was not the perfect, intrinsically superior expression of universal reason, why should the heritage of French law be sacrificed to it? Another French jurist, François Hotman (*d.* 1590), a Huguenot and opponent of absolutism, spoke out to the same effect. His *Anti Tribonianum sive dissertatio de studio legum* of 1567 is both a virulent attack on Roman law, and a plea in favour of a unification of French law based on national customs, studied with the exactness of the learned lawyer, and enriched by medieval legal doctrine.

Du Moulin's main work was his commentary on the *Coutume de Paris*. The text of the *Coutume* had been published in 1510, and the significance of Du Moulin's work is illustrated by the fact that the main modifications and corrections made at the time of the 'reform' of the *Coutume* in 1580 derived from his critical commentary. Du Moulin also made *Notae solemnes* (1557) on the custom of Paris and elsewhere. He still hoped for the unification of French customary law, but his hope was never fulfilled.

Among other renowned learned commentators on French customs should be mentioned Bernard d'Argentré (*d.* 1590), the commentator on the custom of Brittany; Guy Coquille (*d.* 1603), who commented on the custom of the Nivernais[13] and wrote an *Institution au droict des François* (1607), in which he expounded the general principles of French law; and Antoine Loisel (*d.* 1617), author of the

[13] *Coutumes du pays et duché de Nivernais, avec les annotations et commentaires de M. Gui Coquille* (Paris, 1605).

very influential *Institutes coutumières* of 1607.[14] Loisel attempted to separate and order systematically the subject-matter and elements common to the various customs, and to this end he referred principally to the *Coutume de Paris*.

If the work of these authors on custom illustrates how much progress had been made since the first sketches and drafts of the thirteenth century, it also shows how great a contribution to customary literature had been made, over the centuries, by learning based on the *Corpus iuris*.

Commentators in the Netherlands

27 In the old Netherlands, particularly the old county of Flanders, local customary law was also set down in *coutumiers* (in Dutch, *rechtsboeken* or 'books of law'). The anonymous *coutumier* known as *Facet* deals with the custom of St Amand-en-Pévèle (in the chatelainry of Douai) and dates from 1265–71. The original version showed no Roman law influence, in contrast to the additions of the fourteenth and fifteenth centuries.[15] The author of the *coutumier* of Lille, however, is known: it was the secretary of the city, Roisin. Lille was already important in the Middle Ages, and this work, which is known as the *livre Roisin*, was composed around 1280 (the oldest parts date from 1267). It was based entirely on customary law, and learned law appeared only in additions made in the following century.[16] Similarly, two anonymous *coutumiers* from the small Flemish town of Aardenburg are devoid of learned elements: *Wettelijchede* and *Tale en Wedertale*.[17] These works closely follow court practice and procedure: the summons and the defences of the parties or their advocates (*taelmannen*) are often repeated verbatim, giving a very vivid picture of the practice of the time. The best-known of the Dutch *coutumiers*, the *Rechtsboek van Den Briel*, by Jan Matthijssen (*d.* 1423), a town clerk, also belongs to the tradition of *coutumiers* without Roman law elements. Matthijssen's work is remarkable above all for

[14] Cf. M. Reulos, *Etude sur l'esprit, les sources et la methode des Institutes coutumières d'Antoine Loisel* (Paris, 1935).

[15] Modern edition by E. M. Meijers and J. J. Salverda de Grave, *Les lois et coutumes de Saint-Amand* (Harlem, 1934).

[16] Modern edition: R. Monier (Lille, 1932).

[17] Edited by G. A. Vorsterman van Oyen (The Hague, 1892).

its complete and exact description of both substantive and procedural aspects of civil and criminal law.[18]

From the fifteenth century, the learned law is to be found in the Dutch *coutumiers*, among them those of W. Van der Tanerijen and Ph. Wielant. Willem Van der Tanerijen (*d.* 1499) from Antwerp was educated at university, and followed a career as an official and magistrate, especially as counsellor at the Council of Brabant and the Great Council of Mary of Burgundy. Owing to his duties at the Council of Brabant, he had at his disposal the means for describing Brabant customary law in his *Boec van der loopender Practijken der Raidtcameren van Brabant* (1474–6, the last edition dating from 1496). In it Van der Tanerijen pleaded for the diffusion of Roman law, and drew on numerous Roman elements in his account of Brabant law. Some chapters, on obligations for instance, look more like a treatise on Roman law. In the absence of detailed historical studies, it is difficult to tell whether the practice of the Council of Brabant was in fact so strongly impregnated with the *Corpus iuris* as Van der Tanerijen suggests. It is in any case astonishing that this vast and very well-structured work does not seem to have been widely available; until a modern scholarly edition of it was produced, it remained virtually unknown.[19]

The work of Philippe Wielant (*d.* 1520) of Ghent met with greater success. Like Van der Tanerijen, Wielant was university-educated and had a career (among other things) as a magistrate in the Parlement of Malines (1473), Great Council (1477), Council of Flanders (1482) and finally the Great Council of Malines (1504). His work, however, is closer to provincial customary law, and he managed to identify and formulate its common features better than his contemporaries. Wielant's great ambition was to produce an account of contemporary Flemish criminal and civil law, but to do so without turning his back on his university education in Roman law. This aim emerges above all from the structure of his work, from the terminology employed, and from his approach to procedure. His two principal works were *Practijke criminele*, probably written about 1508–10 and devoted to criminal law and procedure,[20] and *Practijke civile* (1508–19), devoted to civil law and particularly to civil

[18] Edited by J. A. Fruin and M. S. Pols (The Hague, 1880).

[19] Edited by E. I. Strubbe (Brussels, 1952). On Van der Tanerijen, see *Nationaal Biografisch Woordenboek* v (1972), col. 877–81.

[20] Edited by A. Orts (Ghent, 1872).

procedure.[21] Wielant shows himself to be neither in favour of abolishing customary law nor blind to the European diffusion of the learned law. His work aims at a synthesis which preserves the fundamental position of customary law, while assimilating the doctrinal advances of academic law, especially of the Bartolist School. These qualities assured Wielant's works, which were written in Dutch, a wide audience in legal circles, in which few practitioners were sufficiently educated to embark on large Latin commentaries, but in which the learned law could no longer be ignored. Wielant's work was typical of the general direction of the law of the Netherlands during the sixteenth century: customary law was maintained, but at the same time the legal order was open to the contributions of the European *ius commune*. Through translations into French, German and (in particular) Latin, Wielant's work obtained a great circulation beyond the Netherlands. Joos de Damhouder (*d.* 1581), a lawyer from Bruges, published Latin translations of Wielant's two principal works (*Praxis rerum criminalium* and *Praxis rerum civilium*) under his own name, without mentioning that of Wielant.[22] He also wrote a treatise (all his own work, this time) on tutelage and curators.[23]

In the seventeenth and eighteenth centuries, several lawyers in the southern Netherlands wrote treatises or commentaries on the law in force in their provinces. These works were largely based on customs, ordinances and case law, although they were still strongly infused with Roman law. Works deserving mention in this period are those of François van der Zype (*d.* 1650), author of the *Notitia juris belgici* and works on canon law which had an international circulation; Antoon Anselmo (*d.* 1668) author (*inter alia*) of the *Codex Belgicus*; Georges de Ghewiet (*d.* 1745), author of a *Précis des Institutions du droit belgique* and *Institutions du droit belgique*; Jean-Baptiste Verlooy (*d.*

[21] *Editio princeps*, Antwerp, 1558. The first edition that does justice to Wielant's work is that of the advocate to the Great Council, A. van Tsestich (reprinted, with an introduction, by E. I. Strubbe, Amsterdam, 1968). Wielant also produced the *Recueil des antiquités de Flandre*, an essay of institutional history, and a study on Flemish feudal law. In 1503 he devoted a work to the law of the city of Haarlem. D. van den Auweele, G. Tournoy and J. Monballyu, 'De bibliotheek van Mr Filips Wielant (1483)' in *Lias. sources and documents relating to the early modern history of ideas*, 8 (Amsterdam, 1981), 145–87.

[22] For the *Praxis rerum criminalium* Damhouder made substantial additions of his own, which was not the case in his edition of the *Praxis rerum civilium*.

[23] See *Nationaal Biografisch Woordenboek* v (1972), col. 1009–19. On Damhouder, *ibid.*, col. 273–84, and E. I. Strubbe, 'Joos de Damhouder als criminalist', *Revue d'histoire du droit* 38 (1970), 1–65.

1797), author of the *Codex Brabanticus*, an attempt to rationalize and codify the legislation in force in the Brabant, under alphabetically ordered rubrics. He made use of scholarship and also of customary law in his systematization; and his work was the more useful (as well as the more difficult to complete) as the sources studied and ordered in it extended over seven centuries.[24]

Northern Netherlands: customary law and Roman-Dutch law

28 There was no shortage of works on regional customs in the United Provinces. But in Holland, by far the most important province, the development was unique and remarkable. Customs had not been homologated there, and so Roman law had greater influence, but traditional customary law was not superseded altogether. The result was a synthesis of Roman law (primarily) and Dutch customary law (secondarily). Until the end of the *ancien régime*, this synthesis had a major influence on the law of the Republic; and nowadays it still subsists in South Africa. The creator of this synthesis, which he outlined in his *Inleidinge tot de Hollandsche Rechtsgeleertheyd* (1620, first published 1631), was Hugo de Groot (Grotius), the most eminent jurist the Netherlands have produced in modern times, best known as the leading figure in the Natural Law School.[25]

THE EUROPEAN *IUS COMMUNE*

The rediscovery of the 'Corpus iuris'

29 Towards 1100 the West rediscovered the *Corpus iuris civilis* of Justinian. This was not simply a matter of finding the whole text of the compilation again; it meant that from now on the text was studied, analysed and taught at universities. Legal scholars glossed and commented on the authoritative ancient compilations, and gradually built up a neo-Roman or medieval Roman law[26] which

[24] Cf. J. van den Broeck, 'J. B. C. Verlooy, Codex Brabanticus (1781)', *Revue d'histoire du droit* 46 (1978), 297–325; J. van den Broeck, *J. B. C. Verlooy, vooruitstrevend jurist en politicus uit de 18e eeuw, 1746–97* (Antwerp and Amsterdam, 1980).

[25] The expression 'Roman-Dutch' was not used by Grotius, and appeared only in 1652 in Simon de Leeuwen's *Paratitula juris novissimi, dat is een Kort Begrip van het Rooms Hollands Regt* (in the 1664 edition the subtitle has become the main title).

[26] In French it has been suggested that by analogy with *Médio-latin*, one might speak of *médio-romain* for medieval Roman law.

became the common basis for university teaching and legal science throughout Europe.[27] Medieval Roman or 'civil' law together with canon law (which was itself strongly influenced by Roman law) made up the learned law common to the whole of the West: hence the name *ius commune*. The Roman component of this written common law was the essential one, for it was the principles, terminology and doctrine of Justinian's law which were the basis for the study of canon law, rather than the reverse.[28]

Ius commune is to be contrasted with *ius proprium*, the 'particular' law which was in force in its countless variations in the various countries, regions and cities of Europe, in the form of customs, ordinances and charters.[29] The study of Roman law in the Middle Ages might perhaps have limited itself to purely academic research, like our own approach (for instance) to ancient Egyptian law. But it did not. Over the centuries, Roman legal doctrine permeated legal practice by various paths (which will be examined), and the medieval learned law thereby influenced the development of law to a greater or lesser extent in all parts of western Europe. This reception of a foreign law may be called legal acculturation or a 'legal transplant'.[30] For the West in the late Middle Ages, Roman law was a new and foreign law: decisively so in the northern regions; but even in the Mediterranean regions where, under Germanic and feudal influence, the law had travelled some distance from ancient law.

There is nothing exceptional about the reception of a foreign legal system which is regarded as technically superior. Sometimes this is a sudden, deliberate process; sometimes a slow infiltration, a gradual, imperceptible osmosis. A well-known example of assimilation of the first kind (apart from the reception in Germany at the beginning of modern times) is the decision of the Japanese authorities in the nineteenth century to introduce western (mainly German, although also French) civil law, in a conscious policy of westernization aiming

[27] Except for Russia and the territories occupied by the Turks.

[28] This is the meaning of the maxim '*legista sine canonibus parum valet, canonista sine legibus nihil*' (*Decretum* c.7 D. 10). Cf. F. Merzbacher, 'Die Parömie legista sine canonibus parum valet, canonista sine legibus nihil' *Studia Gratiana* 13 (1967), 273–82.

[29] The term is no doubt borrowed from *Institutes* 1.2.1.: 'quod quisque populus ipse sibi ius constituit, id ipsius proprium civitatis est vocaturque ius civile, quasi ius proprium ipsius civitatis'.

[30] Cf. A. Watson, *Legal transplants* (Edinburgh, 1974).

to free the country from its feudal shackles.[31] In this instance Japan opted for a foreign law, but for a live contemporary one. By contrast, the assimilation of *ius commune* in the Middle Ages depended on the law of an empire and civilization which had vanished centuries ago, and of which the *Corpus iuris* was (so to speak) merely an embalmed relic. Thus the thread of a thousand-year evolution, which had provisionally broken off in sixth-century Byzantium, was taken up again in twelfth-century Italy.

The enthusiasm which characterized the study of the *Corpus iuris* as it spread from Italy into the various societies of the West was simply part of a more general cultural renaissance, one aspect of which was the founding of universities. Besides ancient law, Greek philosophy (Aristotle) and Graeco-Arabian science (medicine, physics, mathematics) were discovered, translated and commented upon. The authority of ancient learning was absolute: what Holy Scripture was to theology, Aristotle was to philosophy, Galen to anatomy, and the *Corpus iuris* to the law. But additional motives and demands sustained the interest in ancient Roman law: expanding cities and principalities needed a legal framework adapted to new administrative structures; and during the investiture contest, each side sought arguments to support its cause in the texts of the *Corpus iuris*.

Three great schools of study of Roman law may be distinguished according to approach and method: the glossators from the twelfth century to the first half of the thirteenth; the commentators in the fourteenth and fifteenth centuries; and the humanists of the sixteenth century.

The glossators of Roman law

30 The *Corpus iuris* studied by the glossators (to whom it owes its name) was the entire Justinianic compilation which had been

[31] Cf. the general observations of W. Wilhelm, 'Bemerkungen zur Rezeption ausländischen Rechts', *Ius commune* 5 (1975), 122–37; A. B. Schwarz, 'Rezeption und Assimilation ausländischer Rechte' in H. Thieme and F. Wieacker (eds.), *Gesammelte Schriften von A. B. Schwarz* (Karlsruhe, 1960); W. Fikentscher (ed.), *Entstehung und Wandel rechtlicher Traditionen* (Freiburg, 1980; Veröffentlichungen Inst. hist. Anthropologie, 2). On Japan, W. G. Beasley, *The Meiji Restoration* (Stanford, 1973); Z. Kitagawa, *Rezeption und Fortbildung des europäischen Zivilrechts in Japan* (Frankfurt, 1970); R. W. Bowen, *Rebellion and democracy in Meiji Japan* (Berkeley, 1981); T. M. Huber, *The revolutionary origins of modern Japan* (Stanford, 1981); Y. Okubo, 'Gustave Boissonade, père français du droit japonais moderne', *Revue historique de droit français et étranger* 59 (1981), 29–54.

rediscovered in the eleventh century.[32] The text which the glossators studied and taught is known as the *Littera vulgata* ('vulgate', in the sense of standard edition) or *Littera Bononiensis* (that is, the version taught at Bologna, the university where the School of Glossators flourished). This medieval edition was fairly close to, but not identical with, the authentic text promulgated by Justinian;[33] but it was certainly adequate for the needs of the time.

Naturally the *Digest* was the most important part. It seems to have been unknown in the West from the seventh century until a sixth-century manuscript reappeared in south Italy in the eleventh century: the *Littera Pisana*.[34] This manuscript was evidently the basis for a copy made about 1070 which, with other manuscripts, was the basis for the standard edition followed by the glossators. The *Codex* of Justinian had not entirely disappeared in Italy in the early Middle Ages but it was known only in a ruthlessly abridged version; as with the *Digest*, the complete texts reappeared only in the eleventh century.[35] By contrast, the whole text of the *Institutes* was not lost in the early Middle Ages, at least not in Italy. In addition the glossators were able to study the *Novels* in the compilation known as the *Authenticum*,[36] the extant manuscripts of which go back no earlier than the eleventh century.[37]

The glossators had to devise methods and principles for assimilating and comprehending the *Corpus iuris*. Their main aim was like that of the scholastic theologians: just as the theologians aimed by the light of human reason to elucidate a Scripture whose authority was absolute, so the jurists attempted to understand the *Corpus iuris*

[32] Cf. section 12 above.

[33] Attempts to restore and reconstitute the original Justinianic text go back no further than the Humanist School; the first editions of the *Corpus* still follow the *littera Vulgata*. It was only in the nineteenth century that modern historical method was in a position to produce a complete critical edition of the supposed original. The critical edition still in use is by Th. Mommsen, P. Krüger, R. Schöll and G. Kroll (Berlin, 1868–95).

[34] So called because the manuscript was in Pisa until 1411 when, following the conquest of that city in 1406, it was taken to Florence where it is still preserved in the Biblioteca Lorenziana. Since then the manuscript has been known as the *Codex Florentinus*, and the text is referred to as the *littera Florentina*. E. Spagnesi, *Le Pandette di Giustiniano. Storia e fortuna della littera Florentina. Mostra di codici e documenti* (Florence, 1983). See S. Kuttner, 'The revival of jurisprudence' in R. Benson and G. Constable (eds.), *Renaissance and renewal in the twelfth century* (Cambridge, Mass., 1982), 299–323.

[35] At least the first nine books; the last three books reappeared later. Hence in the Middle Ages *Codex* meant books I to IX; books X to XII formed a separate group known as *Tres libri*.

[36] Cf. above, section 12.

[37] The *Epitome Juliani*, which was widely known in the early Middle Ages, was little used by the glossators.

with the aid of formal logic. The first task was to grasp the exact meaning of the Justinianic text by explaining it word for word or by paraphrasing the difficult or obscure terms and passages of the *Corpus*: the name of the School of Glossators denotes precisely that the principal activity of these jurists was to 'gloss'[38] the Roman texts.

'Glosses' in the sense of explanations or clarifications sometimes went beyond purely literal exegesis, for example where the meaning of a rule was elucidated by reference to other passages of the *Corpus* ('parallel texts') containing other principles or qualifications which contributed to a better understanding of the text. It follows from the structure of the *Corpus iuris* that the same subject-matter can be dealt with in different places, both in the *Codex* (when it is a matter of an imperial constitution) and also in the *Digest* (when for instance it is the opinion of a jurist). Reference to parallel texts certainly permitted a better overall view on a given question.

These cross-references at the same time brought to light disparities, and sometimes even contradictions, which Tribonian and his colleagues had not succeeded in avoiding in the compilation. Nowadays it seems only natural that a compilation of materials from various sources and different periods should not always display a perfectly coherent whole. For the jurists of the Middle Ages, however, the *Corpus* represented perfection itself, and so contradictions in it could not be genuine but must be merely apparent.[39] The glossators therefore attempted to eliminate these antinomies, particularly by resorting to the technique of *distinctio* (a minute distinction between the different meanings of a particular word).[40] In applying this technique, they were sometimes tempted into excessive subtleties or logical artificialities. Such excesses may explain the unfortunate reputation of the learned jurists, who were accused of

[38] *Glossa* means 'word' (as in 'malbergic glosses') as well as 'exegesis of a word'.

[39] Hence the medieval expression *in hortulo juris nil spinosum* ('there are no thorns in the garden of the law'). Even in the eighteenth century Jean Bouhier (*d.* 1746) subscribed to the declaration by Claude de Ferrière (*d.* 1715) that 'Roman law is founded on natural reason and the principles of equity; it is a ray of divinity which God has communicated to man.'

[40] For example, the constitution C. 4.35.21 *in re mandata* affirms that each man is '*suae rei arbiter*' while D. 4.8.51 *si de re sua* claims that none can be *de re sua arbiter*. The apparent contradiction is avoided by distinguishing the meaning of the two expressions: in the first case each is the master of his own property and can take the responsibility of disposing of it; in the second it is a question of an arbiter called on to judge his own case. Cf. R. Feenstra, 'Historische aspecten van de private eigendom als rechtsinstituut', *Rechtsgeleerd Magazijn Themis* (1976), 248–75.

distorting the law by misrepresenting the true meaning of the texts. On the other hand the same methods had more than merely academic uses, and these lawyers proved themselves formidable advocates even in other areas of law.

One teaching technique which was widely employed was the *casus*. Originally this was a presentation of a fictitious case, in which whatever rule of law was being studied had to be applied. Later the same expression was used to describe an account of a complex question. *Notabilia* and *brocardica*, that is brief, striking aphorisms summing up a rule of law, were also very popular.[41]

The premisses from which the glossators set out imposed certain restrictions. In their view there was no question of casting doubt on the doctrine of the *Corpus iuris*, as it expressed *ratio scripta*, written reason. An assault on the texts was therefore (literally) unreasonable and senseless. Nor did they see the *Corpus iuris* as the product of a given civilization; far from considering it a historical document, they elevated it to the status of a universal and eternal model, a revelation. A further consequence of this attitude was that the glossators did not go beyond the *Corpus iuris*. In their scholarship and teaching they did not deal, for instance, with feudal institutions or with irrational modes of proof, although ordeals were still current in their own age. The *Corpus* did not raise these questions, and the glossators therefore felt entitled to ignore them. Thus Accursius could declare that according to Roman law the emperor was not subject to any jurisdiction, and it is typical that he paid not the least attention to the political reality of the time, which he knew perfectly well: that the authority of the pope undeniably extended to emperors and kings, and that pontiffs had even exercised their authority in practice by pronouncing interdicts, excommunications, and sometimes even orders for deposition.[42] The converse, however, was not true: if the learned lawyers ignored customary law in their studies, they did not hesitate to employ their own arguments on the *Corpus iuris* when consulted by litigants, or when they appeared as advocates.[43]

[41] E.g. *actor sequitur forum rei*; *locus regit actum*; *in dubio pro reo*.

[42] Cf. B. Tierney, 'The prince is not bound by the laws. Accursius and the origins of the modern state', *Comparative Studies in Society and History* 5 (1962), 378–400; D. Wyduckel, *Princeps legibus solutus. Eine Untersuchung zur frühmodernen Rechts- und Staatslehre* (Berlin, 1979).

[43] A. P. Schioppa, 'Le rôle du droit savant dans quelques actes judiciaires italiens des XIe et XIIe siècles', *Confluence des droits savants et des pratiques juridiques. Actes du colloque de Montpellier 1977* (Milan, 1979), 341–71.

Legal science acquired a very pronounced abstract character, since it concentrated on the legal system of a bygone age, and did not develop, as is more usual, from the encounters of daily practice and the experience of generations. Yet the researches of the glossators revealed ancient law to the world of the late Middle Ages, and their works of exegesis gave access to the *Corpus iuris*. The School of Glossators thus prepared the way for the jurists who subsequently tried to produce a synthesis of medieval customs, legislation and Roman law.

The scholarly work of the glossators took various shapes. First, of course, glosses. These were originally brief isolated notes inserted between the lines or in the margin of the text of the *Corpus*. Little by little these glosses built up and took on the form of a continuous commentary (*apparatus*). In manuscripts, as well as in old editions of the *Corpus*, the page is laid out with the *textus* in the centre, completely surrounded by the glosses (which often exceed it in length). The great merit of Accursius (*d.* 1263) was to make a selection from the thousands of scattered glosses which his numerous scholarly predecessors had written. His version rapidly became the standard gloss and was therefore known as the *glossa ordinaria* (*c.* 1240); the *apparatus* fixed by Accursius represented the culmination of the School of Glossators.

Some glossators wrote original treatises, in which they discussed the law of the *Corpus* as a whole. The *Summa Codicis* of Azo, written about 1208–10, is the best known of these: while he follows the rubrics of books I to IX of the *Codex*, Azo in fact gives a systematic account of the subject-matter of the *Corpus*. This 'summary' was for long the classic Roman law manual which the jurists consulted in conjunction with the glossed *Corpus*.

Little evidence about the first glossators has come down to us. The first name to appear is that of Pepo, who is said in a legal action towards the end of the eleventh century to have referred to the *Codex* and *Institutes*, and to have begun in Bologna *auctoritate sua legere in legibus*. After him, Irnerius undertook the teaching of the whole *Corpus iuris*, again in Bologna. He had been educated in the *artes*, and applied his literary knowledge and skill to the legal texts. Among his pupils, most is known of the 'Four Doctors' (*quattuor doctores*), Bulgarus, Martinus Gosia, Hugo, and Jacobus. Their teaching made Bologna the indisputable capital of legal studies; their influence extended far beyond the circle of their students, and even great figures of the time such as Frederick I Barbarossa sought their opinions.[44]

The commentators of Roman law

31 Nowadays the jurists of this school are referred to as 'commentators'; previously they were known as 'post-glossators', owing to the fact that they taught after the glossators and in a sense continued their work. Yet that name wrongly implies that the new school amounted to no more than an unoriginal continuation of the work of its precursor. The name 'commentators' emphasizes that these jurists wrote important commentaries on the *Corpus iuris* as a whole. In addition they wrote numerous *consilia* or legal opinions, delivered on actual questions on which they had been consulted: hence the name *consiliatores* has also been proposed to describe this school. The zenith of the School of Commentators was in the fourteenth and fifteenth centuries; its authors too were mostly Italian. Their aims and methods were these.

The *Corpus iuris* and the Gloss formed the basis of their works. The importance accorded by them to the Gloss was such that it sometimes eclipsed the original texts.[45] The commentators' method was strongly influenced by scholasticism, which had reached its high point in the thirteenth century, and which had imbued subsequent scholarly thought with Aristotelian logic. In particular the commentators adopted the system of argumentation, disputation and polemic typical of scholasticism. They also took up its excesses, and this is the origin of their interminable discussions on trivialities, their excessively subtle analyses of authorities, and their exaggerated reliance on the technique of successive distinctions. The work of the commentators is essentially academic, and this is to be associated largely with university teaching, which was then undergoing a major expansion. Universities had first been founded in Italy and in France, but rapidly spread in Spain, England and then in the other

[44] Of Irnerius' work, only glosses are preserved; of the four doctors', some other rather brief works have also survived. Some short anonymous treatises of the twelfth century are also known; cf. e.g. G. Dolezalek, 'Tractatus de diligentia et dolo et culpa et fortuito casu. Eine Abhandlung über die Haftung für die Beschädigung oder den Untergang von Sachen aus dem zwölften Jahrhundert', *Aspekte europäischer Rechtsgeschichte. Festgabe für Helmut Coing* (Frankfurt, 1982; Ius commune Sonderheft, 17), 87–122.

[45] Hence Cynus' aphorism *sicut antiqui adorabant idola pro deis, ita advocati adorant glossatores pro evangelistis* ('just as the ancients adored idols as gods, so advocates adore the glossators as evangelists').

countries of continental Europe (e.g. Louvain 1425). The law conceived in the law faculties was inevitably a learned and academic law, a professors' law.

None the less the School of Commentators differs from the glossators in that its authors took a greater interest in the law outside the *Corpus iuris civilis*, and in their scholarly work even paid attention to the social realities of the time. Thus the commentators had firm views on the sources of non-learned law too, such as customs and ordinances. In spite of their positions in universities, they were realistic enough to appreciate that it was inconceivable in their time (no doubt in the future too) for learned law to become the common law for all Europe. Regional customs, feudal principles, municipal regulations and statutes, and royal ordinances were much too firmly anchored in practice and much too intimately bound up with vested interests to be swept aside and replaced with an academic system from Bologna. On the other hand, the commentators also appreciated that the learned law would play only a trifling part if it remained confined to the narrow artificial context of the *Corpus iuris* and the ancient world. The commentators adapted the learned law to the needs of their time; they worked out doctrines of practical value; they allowed the learned law to complement and enrich the other sources of law without eliminating them; and so they enabled it to play an effective and vital role in legal practice.

Learned law could also provide a method and principles suitable for the scholarly study of non-Roman laws. Here the distinction made by the commentators between *ius commune* (the 'common', cosmopolitan and learned law of the whole of the West) and *ius proprium* (the law 'proper' or particular to a country, region, town or corporation) took on a major importance. Although the commentators recognized and respected the significance of *ius proprium*, they urged that it should be studied and that gaps in it should be filled by the learned law and its method. Their interest in *ius proprium* also led them to deal with real problems, often taken from everyday life. An example is their theory of statutes (which is still applicable in private international law), which was developed from the conflict of laws between statutes and the other municipal laws of Italian cities. It should not be forgotten that these professors were often directly involved in legal practice as judges or advocates.

The typical works of the School of Commentators are in line with this approach to law: the commentators were first and foremost professors, and their teaching remained based on Justinian's compilations. Their courses (*lecturae*) still scrupulously followed the order of the *Corpus*. Most authors gave *lecturae* only on certain parts of the *Corpus*, but sometimes the teaching of a professor extended to the whole of the compilation. *Lecturae*, once filled out with academic debate and discourses on specific problems, sometimes grew into the encyclopaedic commentaries which gave their name to the school. Another genre, treatises, allowed the authors to leave the confines of the *Corpus*: the point of departure was no longer a particular text drawn from the compilation, but a real instance or problem of legal practice to which the jurist attempted to give a satisfactory solution by making use of the learned law. Examples are the treatise of Bartolus on arbiters or that of Cynus on intestate succession. Closer still to legal practice were the numerous *consilia* written by the authors of this period: the *consilium* was a legal opinion, often very detailed, given by one or more professional lawyers on an actual case, at the request of an individual or an institution. Even the courts requested such opinions (and even in the nineteenth century, German law provided a procedure under which the courts could in certain circumstances request an opinion from the faculties of law). It is largely in the mass of extant *consilia* that the experience and learning of the commentators are to be found.

The School of Commentators produced many authors and an impressive volume of their work survives. Mostly Italians, they maintained the traditional pre-eminence of their nation in the area of legal science. French jurists, however, the best known of whom are Jacques de Révigny (*d.* 1296) and Pierre de Belleperche (*d.* 1308), had been the precursors of the Italian commentators in the second half of the thirteenth century. Their doctrines were diffused in Italy by Cynus of Pistoia (*d.* 1336), the first great author of the School of Commentators. After him the school reached its scholarly summit with Bartolus of Saxoferrato (*d.* 1357) and Baldus de Ubaldis (*d.* 1400). The tradition was continued in the fifteenth century by many other Italian jurists, such as Paulus de Castro (*d.* 1441) and Jason de Mayno (*d.* 1519). Italian pre-eminence was such that this school was known as the *mos italicus iuris docendi* ('Italian method of teaching law'), as opposed to the French school or *mos gallicus*, by which is meant the approach of the sixteenth-century humanists, who were essentially connected with France.[46]

The Humanist School of Roman law

32 Sixteenth-century jurisprudence was dominated by the achievements of the Humanist School of Roman law. The last school to profess the primacy of the *Corpus iuris*, it none the less adopted an approach very different from that of the glossators and commentators. Its rise was but one manifestation of the renaissance of Antiquity which, from the end of the Middle Ages, profoundly influenced European science, arts and letters. The impulse once again – but for the last time – came from Italy. The positive stimulus for the Renaissance was a new enthusiasm for the culture of Antiquity. This was a rediscovery of ancient culture more profound, precise and complete than the somewhat naive and blind admiration characteristic of the Middle Ages. The negative side was the often harsh disdain the humanists directed towards the 'Middle Ages', an expression they coined to describe the obscure centuries between the cultural peaks of Antiquity and their own time. They accused the people of the Middle Ages of having bastardized classical Latin through neologisms and stylistic imperfections which were incompatible with the ancient language of culture; and they reproached them for their ignorance of Greek.

The humanist approach to law brought about a revival of studies of Roman law and the civilization which had created it. The original element in the humanist approach was to apply both historical methods, in order to understand the social context of legal rules, and philological methods, in order to determine the exact meaning of Latin and Greek texts. These principles enabled the humanists to expose the erroneous and anachronistic interpretations given by their predecessors. Sometimes they launched violent attacks on the jurists of the Middle Ages, describing them as fools and accusing them of having submerged Roman law under a mass of Gothic and barbaric accretions.[47]

46 'Gallicus' here means 'French' rather than 'Gaulish'; this school flourished in France in the sixteenth century. The expression derives from the fondness of the humanists for ancient Latin geographical names (Belgicus for Dutch, Gallicus for French, and so forth).

47 In some caustic remarks, Rabelais described the medieval lawyers as being 'ignorant of everything necessary for the understanding of law', accused them of 'knowing neither Greek nor Latin but only Gothic and Barbarian', and charged them with being totally unacquainted with the letters and history of Antiquity. In humanist circles, vituperation of the lawyers was *de rigueur*, and Petrarch, Filelfo, Valla and Politian were all true to the tradition. On Rabelais, see E. Nardi, *Rabelais e il diritto romano* (Milan, 1912).

The positive results of humanism were considerable. Numerous errors committed by the glossators and commentators owing to their lack of historical and philological expertise were corrected, and knowledge of the ancient world therefore became much more precise and profound; the *Annotationes* of Guillaume Budé, for instance, exposed a whole series of misconceptions by the jurists of the Middle Ages. Their approach enabled the humanists to see the *Corpus iuris* as a historical phenomenon of its own time and place, as a human achievement, and not a 'gift fallen from heaven' as Budé said ironically of the naive medieval approach.[48] Yet humanist criticism had its unfortunate consequences. The Bartolists had adapted the Roman law of the *Corpus iuris* to the needs of medieval society. The humanists rejected these adaptations on the ground that they corrupted the original purity of Roman law; and so they reduced that law to the state of an academic relic, a historical monument, a dead law for scholarly study only. It will be recalled that the Latin language had undergone a parallel evolution: in the Middle Ages Latin had remained a living language, owing to constant adaptation and the introduction of new terms and expressions, but the purism of the humanists turned it into a mere academic tool, a dead language.

By demonstrating the historicity and thus the relativity of the *Corpus iuris*, the humanists destroyed the absolute authority which it had until then enjoyed. If Roman law was no more than the product of a given society of a given period, what reason was there to submit to it in another period, or to accord it an authority superior to the laws of modern peoples?

The founder of the Humanist School was Andrea Alciato (*d.* 1550), an Italian jurist who studied in Pavia and Bologna, where he became the pupil of Jason de Mayno; he then taught at Avignon and Bourges, and later at Italian universities.[49] The university of Bourges became the main centre of the *mos gallicus*, owing principally to Jacques Cujas (*d.* 1590). He was the most outstanding exponent of

[48] Sometimes even the humanists fell into gross errors: U. Zasius, for example, thought the word *carocerus* (the symbolic coach of the city of Milan) was a proper name. On Budé, D. R. Kelley, 'Guillaume Budé and the first historical school of law', *American Historical Review* 72 (1967), 807–34.

[49] Among his many works the *Annotationes in tres posteriores codicis libros* (1513), dealing with the political and administrative institutions of ancient Rome, expresses the novel approach of humanist study.

humanism, and he taught in Bourges (with a few interruptions) from 1555 to 1590. Cujas approached his subject with an exceptional mastery of Roman law and philology, which until the work of Th. Mommsen (*d.* 1903) was to remain unequalled. There were also distinguished German and Dutch proponents of humanism. In Germany, Ulrich Zasius (*d.* 1535), a friend of Erasmus, was one of the first legal humanists. In the Netherlands, the University of Louvain rapidly became a centre of humanism, and jurisprudence was also affected by this cultural revival. At the Faculty of Law, Gabriel Mudaeus (Van der Muyden, *d.* 1560) acquired a great reputation. Among his pupils were Jacob Reyvaert (Raevardus, *d.* 1568) and Mattheus van Wesembeke (Wesenbecius, *d.* 1586). Viglius (*d.* 1577) edited the Greek version of Roman law texts and wrote a commentary on some titles of the *Institutes* according to Alciato's method.

Several jurists of the Humanist School were implicated in the religious conflicts of the Reformation and were compelled to go into exile because of their beliefs. This applies notably to the Frenchman Hugues Doneau (Donellus, *d.* 1591) who took refuge and taught in Germany and in the northern Netherlands. He became one of the leading lights of the University of Leiden (founded in 1575), where he became renowned for his immense learning and total lack of any practical sense. (It is related that the eminent jurist did not know how to make out a receipt for the salary paid to him by the Dutch state.) His *Commentarii iuris civilis* in twenty-eight books had great success in Germany and the Netherlands.

The Humanist School made an unprecedented contribution to broadening and deepening knowledge of ancient law and the ancient world. Even in the nineteenth century, Mommsen was able to start from humanist works published three centuries earlier. Practitioners throughout Europe, however, continued to apply Roman law in the Bartolist tradition, since Bartolist commentaries, treatises and *consilia* supplied solutions to real and present problems. Yet the opposition between *mos gallicus* and *mos italicus* should not be exaggerated. Many lawyers – judges, advocates, and scholars – were inspired by both schools. They still based themselves on the practical work of the medieval Italian school, but from the humanists they acquired a broader conception of law, a more philosophical approach, and the taste for elegant development of their ideas and arguments. These lawyers were above all practical, but they took a lively interest in ancient history and literature.[50] It is quite right, therefore, to speak of the 'Elegant School' to denote the lawyers of the United Provinces who integrated the style and quality of the humanists into their practical work.[51] With other legal historians, we may therefore recognize a third school besides *mos gallicus* and *mos italicus*, made up of lawyers who hoped to preserve the advances of medieval learning but were also disposed to follow the broader lines of the Humanist School, and to assimilate the human and stylistic qualities of classical literature.[52]

This revived academic Roman law was finally supplanted by national codes inspired by the School of Natural Law. The influence of the old schools, however, did not altogether disappear. Traces of the *mos italicus* are still to be found in legal doctrines and in some parts of the modern codes such as the law of obligations; while the *mos gallicus* survives in the more academic study of ancient law, and in the general culture of legal education.

The influence of Roman law on canon law

General considerations

33 The intensive study of Roman law at European universities was not just academic recreation, nor purely historical research. Quite the reverse: it strongly influenced and guided both the practical and the doctrinal development of law. The word 'guided' is used advisedly since, without the renaissance of Roman law, the development of law in Europe would have been fundamentally different. Even without the *Corpus iuris*, the society of the late Middle Ages would have had to free itself from the archaic law of the feudal period and develop a law adapted to its new needs. Such a law would have been the result of original innovation and intellectual effort, its solutions to comparable problems would no doubt some-

[50] E.g. P. Wielant's library (whose catalogue has recently been discovered) contained many humanist literary works.

[51] Among the members of the Dutch Elegant School are Joachim Hoppers (Hopperus, *d.* 1576), Arnold Vinnius (*d.* 1657), Ulrik Huber (*d.* 1694), Johannes Voet (*d.* 1713) and Cornelis van Bijnkershoek (*d.* 1743), as well, of course, as Grotius, a very widely read lawyer who, although best known for his work on natural law and Roman-Dutch law, was also a learned humanist and author of a commentary on the *lex Romana Burgundionum*.

[52] Cf. F. Carpintero, 'Mos italicus, mos gallicus y el Humanismo racionalista. Una contribución a la historia de la metodología jurídica', *Ius commune* 6 (1977), 108–71. Carpintero sees this 'third' school as a transitional movement between the medieval lawyers and the authors of natural law, such as Grotius and Pufendorf.

times have been analogous to those of ancient Roman law, but the whole system of the Justinianic compilations would never have been adopted or reinvented. The Common Law shows exactly how a European post-feudal law might have developed in isolation from the Roman model.

The impact of the *Corpus iuris* and Bolognese teaching in Europe was not directly due to the legislative measures of sovereigns. There are of course measures which have about them something of a 'reception' imposed by the sovereign: in his kingdom of southern Italy Emperor Frederick II promulgated in 1231 the *Liber Augustalis*, which was profoundly influenced by Roman law; the *Siete Partidas* (1256–8) introduced in Castile by Alfonso X the Wise resembles a Roman law treatise; Charles the Bold, having defeated the people of Liège, abolished their customs and imposed Roman law on them. But in spite of these isolated and short-lived measures, the *Corpus iuris* was never imposed by authority. Even in the Holy Roman Empire, where the emperors considered themselves the successors of the Christian emperors of ancient Rome, the reception was not achieved by an imperial act: the decision in favour of reception was taken by the 'Estates' (*Reichsstände*) of the empire, and was based not on a specific statute but on the strongly Romanized case law of the *Reichskammergericht* founded in 1495.[53]

The triumph of the *Corpus iuris* is to be explained first and foremost by its prestige and its intrinsic doctrinal quality: Roman law was authoritative *non ratione imperii, sed imperio rationis*.[54] There are no modern parallels of such a phenomenon, but the role of American Common Law in relation to the diverse laws of the different states of the United States might be mentioned: it supplies guiding principles which are refined by scholarship, but it has no legislative force. Another instance is English Common Law, which in international commercial contracts is frequently declared to be applicable, even when the contracting parties have no connexion with England.

The task now is to study in detail how and by what means the *Corpus iuris* guided the development of medieval law, dealing first with canon law, and then with secular laws.

53 Cf. section 53 below. The *Reichskammergericht* (imperial chamber of justice) was an institution of the *Reichsstände* (Estates of the empire) and not of the emperor; on the contrary, it even encroached on the emperor's own jurisdiction. Towards 1500 many German cities reformed their municipal law under the influence of Roman law (*Reformationen*).

54 'Not by reason of power, but by the power of reason.'

Gratian

34 It is no accident that the study of canon law began in the twelfth century in Bologna, where the teaching of Roman law first flourished. The founder of the scholarly study of canon law was Gratian (who died probably before 1160), a Camaldolese[55] monk who taught theology at the convent of Saints Felix and Nabor in Bologna and who became particularly attracted to the study of the law of the church. His work, composed towards 1140, is entitled *Concordia discordantium canonum* ('reconciliation of conflicting canons') but is more generally known as the *Decretum Gratiani*.[56]

The *Decretum* is a systematic collection of ecclesiastical sources of different origins, and is made up principally of decisions of councils (*canones*: hence canon law to signify the law of the church) and decretals (pontifical letters interpreting or establishing rules of law).[57] Gratian also included various extracts especially from Scripture and the church fathers. His collection was certainly not the first of its kind,[58] but it was by far the most encyclopaedic, and took in practically all the sources of canon law known at the time.[59] Gratian was not content with compiling and ordering his sources. His original contribution was to summarize the texts and define the legal problem with which they were concerned. Furthermore, Gratian attempted, as the title of his work makes clear, to resolve disparities and occasional contradictions between different texts. To do so he established a hierarchy of sources (for instance, an ecumenical council took precedence over a provincial council, a pontifical letter over an episcopal letter). Above all, he employed the tried and tested technique of *distinctio*, which allowed the different meanings

55 The order takes its name from Camaldoli, north of Arezzo, where it was founded as a reclusive order around 1000 by St Romuald. J. T. Noonan, 'Gratian slept here. The changing identity of the father of the systematic study of canon law', *Traditio* 35 (1979), 145–72.

56 From the title of an earlier work, the *Decretum* of Ivo of Chartres (*d.* 1116). The name 'Decretum' also causes confusion, since it suggests a legislative work, although Gratian composed it as a scholar not an official.

57 Decretals (or in full, *litterae decretales*) are so called because they are letters in the form of a 'decree', in the sense that they establish and impose a rule of law. Most are addressed to individuals (usually bishops) who had consulted the pope on a particular question.

58 On many other collections, see A. van Hove, *Prolegomena*, 2nd edn (Malines and Rome, 1945; Commentarium Lovaniense in Codicem Iuris Canonici I, 1), 120–336.

59 Gratian deals with very diverse subject-matter, and in particular with questions more relevant to theology than to law, such as sacraments and liturgy; in his day, canonistic jurisprudence was still taking shape from other disciplines (like the learning of the glossators).

and significations of a word to be distinguished.[60] For example, some canonical texts forbade the participation of the clergy in war, while others seemed to approve it. The solution was to distinguish between a defensive or just war and an offensive or unjust war.[61] The *Decretum* also contains texts which allow lay people to take part in the election of bishops, while others seem to exclude all participation by the people (*populus*) and reserve competence to the clergy (*clerus*) alone. Gratian tried to resolve this contradiction by accepting that lay people could not be ignored at such elections, but limiting their participation to expressing agreement with the choice of the clergy.[62] This example shows that contradictions were sometimes resolved only by means of subtleties and hair-splitting dictated by the need to reconcile the irreconcilable.

Gratian was not only a scholar but a teacher who appreciated the educational value of the concrete case in the study of rules. The second and greater part of his work is made up of fictitious cases (*causae*) which introduce a legal discussion, in which reference is made to the relevant texts and observations are also made by Gratian himself (*dicta Gratiani*). His method may be illustrated by an example from the law of marriage (it also has implications for the law of ordination). The case was the following: a married non-believer (which at this period no doubt means a Muslim) converted to Christianity, and was deserted by his wife, who was opposed to the new religion. He then married a Christian woman and on her death entered the clergy. Later he was elected bishop. Gratian formulates three legal problems (*quaestiones*) in relation to this case: (i) is a marriage between non-believers valid? (ii) May the convert remarry while his first wife is still alive? (iii) Should a man who marries another woman after having been baptized be considered a *bigamista*?[63] The answers proposed by Gratian are (i) between non-believers there can be an honest marriage, but it is not binding; (ii)

[60] An important part of his work is a series of *Distinctiones*.

[61] On the canonistic doctrine of different types of war, see C. Erdmann, *Entstehung des Kreuzzugsgedankens* (Stuttgart, 1933); F. Prinz, *Klerus und Krieg im früheren Mittelalter* (Stuttgart, 1971); F. H. Russell, *The just war in the middle ages* (Cambridge, 1975); E. D. Hehl, *Kirche und Krieg im 12. Jahrhundert. Studien zu kanonischem Recht und politischer Wirklichkeit* (Stuttgart, 1980).

[62] Dist. 62–4. Cf. F. Lot and R. Fawtier, *Histoire des institutions françaises au moyen âge, III: Institutions ecclésiastiques* (Paris, 1962), 165–6; H. Müller, *Der Anteil der Laien an der Bischofswahl* (Amsterdam, 1977); J. Gaudemet, *Les élections dans l'église latine des origines au XVIe siècle* (Paris, 1979).

[63] I.e. a person married twice in succession not (in the modern sense) to two people at once.

in a marriage between non-believers, if the wife leaves her husband, he may remarry even if he has converted in the meantime; (iii) by his second marriage, he none the less becomes *bigamista* and cannot as a result attain to higher orders. The man elected bishop cannot therefore be ordained or installed. (In this example too there are contradictory authorities: St Jerome saw no impediment in the state of 'bigamy', but St Augustine followed by Pope Innocent I asserted the opposite, and Gratian opted for their view.[64])

Gratian therefore combined the qualities of compiler and teacher, and his work was not merely a collection of earlier sources but also a manual for study. For centuries the *Decretum* served as the basis for university teaching, even though it was never officially sanctioned. Gratian's work inaugurated the important studies of the School of Decretists, which was later followed by the decretalists.

The decretals

35 Gratian marks the end of the first millennium of the history of canon law and also the beginning of its new and unprecedented ascendance. Gratian's work and teaching had started and had facilitated the rise of canon law from the twelfth century, but that had been caused above all by a veritable explosion of ecclesiastical legislation beginning even in his time. This legislation included the canons of councils,[65] but was made up principally of pontifical decretals. While no decretal had been promulgated between AD 891 and the mid-eleventh century (the beginning of the Gregorian Reform), there are almost 2,000 for the period from the pontificate of Alexander III (1159–81) to that of Gregory IX (1227–41).

An illustration is the decretal *Veniens ad nos* of Alexander III (x.4, 1, 15) which was decisive for the canonistic theory on the formation of marriage. The decretal was the response to an inquiry from the bishop of Pavia about a specific case: in his diocese a certain G. had been surprised by his host while in bed with the host's daughter. Thereupon the daughter and G. exchanged consents for marriage *de presenti* which, according to contemporary theory, sufficed to form a valid marriage. It then transpired that the man was already living

[64] Cf. C. Brooke, *The twelfth century renaissance* (London, 1970), 79.

[65] For example the Fourth Lateran Council of 1215 was one of the most important in the history of the church.

together with another woman and actually had children, but he had not married her and had merely promised to marry her *de futuro*. Which of these 'marriages' was valid? The decision was referred to the pope, who held that a promise of marriage (*sponsalia de futuro*) followed by sexual relations (*copula carnalis*) formed a valid marriage, and that G. was therefore actually married when he made his declaration of marriage *de presenti* to the daughter of his host. The second marriage was therefore void.[66]

Systematic collections of new decretals were begun very early in order to meet the needs of teaching and practice.[67] A period of legislation and intensive compilation culminated in 1230 when the Spanish canonist Ramón de Peñaforte, chaplain to Gregory IX, was entrusted by him with the task of editing a definitive collection of the constitutions and decretals promulgated since the composition of the *Decretum* of Gratian. In carrying out this task, for ease of consultation Ramón de Peñaforte added to the texts summaries in his own words, and rubrics indicating the subject-matter. The various subjects were ordered and corrected, some were eliminated, and they were regrouped in five books according to an older model: *iudex* (the judge) on the organization of the courts; *iudicium* (process, judgment) on procedure; *clerus* (the clergy) on their rights and privileges; *connubium* (marriage) on the law of the family and persons; *crimen* (crime) on criminal law and procedure. In 1234 the collection was promulgated by Gregory IX: any texts later than the *Decretum* of Gratian which were not included in the new collection were abrogated, and the text of the collection alone was declared authoritative. It is entitled *Liber decretalium extra Decretum vagantium* ('book of decretals current outside the *Decretum*') and is now known as the *Liber extra*. The collection was also intended for teaching: copies were sent to the universities of Bologna and Paris. Just as the School of Decretists had devoted their study and teaching to the *Decretum*, so the decretals now became the object of study by the decretalists.

66 C. Donahue, 'The policy of Alexander the Third's consent theory of marriage', *Proceedings of the fourth international congress of medieval canon law* (Vatican, 1976), 251; *idem.*, 'The dating of Alexander the Third's marriage decretals', *Zeitschrift der Savigny-Stiftung für Rechtsgeschichte* (K.A.), 65 (1982), 70–124.

67 P. Landau, 'Die Entstehung der systematischen Dekretalensammlungen und die europäische Kanonistik des 12. Jts.', *Zeitschrift der Savigny-Stiftung für Rechtsgeschichte* (K.A.) 65 (1979), 120–48.

The canonists also glossed the texts of the *Decretum* and the decretals (just as the Roman texts had been glossed) and composed an *apparatus* on the entire collection. The *apparatus* of Johannes Teutonicus (*d.* 1245 or 1246), revised by Bartholomew of Brescia (*d.* 1258) became the ordinary gloss on the *Decretum*; that of Bernard of Parma (*d.* 1263), based among others on the gloss of Vincentius Hispanus (*d.* 1248), became the ordinary gloss on the *Liber extra*. The *Decretum* and *Liber extra* were also the subject of important *summae* and *lecturae*,[68] as well as repertories, collections of *casus* and other works largely intended for practitioners. New decretals were promulgated after the *Liber extra*, and some popes published partial collections of them, notably the *Liber Sextus* of Boniface VIII (1298)[69] and the *Constitutiones Clementinae* of Clement V (1314, promulgated in 1317 by his successor John XXII).

The *Decretum* of Gratian and the official collections of decretals together make up the *Corpus iuris canonici*, a title used from the fifteenth century (by analogy with *Corpus iuris civilis*). In the sixteenth century the collections were submitted by pontifical order to a commission called the *Correctores Romani* for textual revision. The results of their work were published in Rome in 1582 under the title *Corpus Iuris Canonici* and this was not replaced until 1917 by the *Codex Iuris Canonici* of Benedict XV, which was conceived as a modern code. A revision of canon law was undertaken in connexion with the Second Vatican Council and led to the promulgation of a new code in 1983.

The canonists

36 There are several aspects to the influence of Roman law on canonistic legislation and doctrine. The example of Roman law enabled canon law to establish itself as an independent discipline, distinct although not separate from theology and ethics. This point deserves emphasis, since other religions make no distinction between rules of conduct and religious taboos on the one hand, and rules of

[68] Among the earliest works of the Decretists are the *Summae* of Paucapalea (1140–8), of Roland Bandinelli (the future Pope Alexander III) composed before 1148, and of Stephen of Tournai (not earlier than 1160); the *Summa* of Huguccio (not earlier than 1188) is very important. Among the best-known works of the Decretalists are the *Summa aurea* or *Hostiensis* of Henry of Susa (1250–3) and the commentary of Sinibaldus Fliscus (the future Pope Innocent IV) composed about 1251.

[69] '*Sextus*' because it was intended to complement and continue the five books of the *Liber Extra*.

law on the other; or, in other words, between the confessional and the court. Roman law scholarship at Bologna contributed to the rise of an independent canonistic scholarship which was soon distinguished by its own faculties, schools, classic works and authoritative commentaries. The study of Roman law was (as we have seen) necessary for the education of canonists, for it was in the schools of the civilians that canonists learned the 'grammar' of learned law, and there that they assimilated methods, fundamental concepts and legal terminology.

The *Corpus iuris civilis* gave strong support to the centralist policy of the popes. The Roman emperor as universal legislator and supreme judge served as a model for pontifical aspirations to legislate and to administer justice for the whole of Christendom. The rise of canon law coincided with a marked resurgence of legalism within the church, and a focusing of attention more on questions of competence, justice and fiscality than on teaching, spirituality or asceticism. Although the popes had taken an interest in questions of law even before this time, it is significant that the tradition of pontiff-jurists begins only in the twelfth century. Officials of the church came to be chosen more and more for their legal education and experience, rather than for their aptitude to govern or their personal sanctity or charisma.[70]

Canon law expressly recognized the authority of Roman law, inasmuch as it was the legislation of the Christian Emperor Justinian, at least so far as its dispositions were not contrary to the canons. This doctrine is found in Gratian: the statutes of emperors are to be applicable in ecclesiastical matters unless they are contrary to the holy canons of the church (D. X c.7; *dicta post* D. X c.6 and *post* c.4, C. XV q. 3). The *Decretum* also contains some texts taken directly from Justinian's compilations.[71] The influence of Roman law is also to be found in the application by analogy of some Roman rules to subjects which were peculiarly ecclesiastical. Thus the doctrine of the canonists on *error in persona* as the key to the nullity of marriage is inspired by Roman principles of error in the contract of sale. The

[70] This excessive legalism was attacked by the reformers, who thought the church of the late Middle Ages paid too much importance to institutional and administrative questions and too little to its holiness.

[71] The source of the (much more numerous) additions of canonical texts known as *paleae* (a term whose exact significance is unclear) has not yet been established; they are attributed to pupils of Gratian.

appeal of this theory was such that, in the absence of canonistic scholarship or legislation, the canonists used it to develop rules on error as to person, which vitiated consent and so entailed the nullity of marriage.[72] Canon law criminal procedure is another striking example of the use of the Roman law analogy. For the rigorous repression of heretics, the canonists resorted to the very severe rules provided in Roman criminal law for the crime of treason. In the medieval period heresy as an offence 'against divine majesty' was assimilated to affront to the imperial majesty in ancient Rome. The civilians also contributed so much to creating a modern procedure for the church courts that it is known as Roman-canonical procedure; here Roman and canonical elements became fused.[73]

The influence of canon law on secular law was considerable; in fact the history of law in Europe is inconceivable without the contribution of canon law. The institutional structure of the post-Gregorian church, with its hierarchy, centralization, administration and its bureaucracy, served as a model for the institutions of kingdoms and principalities from the late Middle Ages onwards.

In some important areas of private law even lay people were subject to the jurisdiction of the church courts. The obvious example is the law of marriage and the family. This had inevitable repercussions for the law of succession, in which the question of legitimacy or illegitimacy was often decisive. People encountered the learned law, at least in its canonical form, in innumerable actions on questions of engagement, marriage, separation and paternity.[74] At the same time they encountered Roman-canonical procedure, with its own rules of evidence, judgment and appeal. This was the first experience which many people had of Roman law in practice, since the secular courts actually began to apply Roman law only after church courts

[72] J. Gaudemet, 'Droit canonique et droit romain. A propos de l'erreur sur la personne en matière de mariage', *Studia Gratiana* 9 (1966), 47–64. Obviously error as to person was very rare; but error as to the social status of the spouse was more frequent and, according to some authors, could be assimilated to *error in persona*; thus a free person who married a serf by mistake could invoke error to argue for nullity.

[73] Cf. below section 38.

[74] C. Vleeschouwers and M. van Melkebeek, *Liber sentenciarum van de officialiteit van Brussel 1448–59* (2 vols., Brussels, 1982–3; Commission royale des anciennes lois et ordonnances, Recueil de l'ancienne jurisprudence de la Belgique, 7e série).

had become widespread, even in the Mediterranean regions (and *a fortiori* in more northerly regions).[75]

Some modern legal theory was developed by the medieval canonists. One example is the doctrine of *nuda pacta*, which was inspired by moral considerations (*solus consensus obligat*; *pacta sunt servanda*: every agreement, even if concluded without formalities, must be respected); another is the theory of *causa* in the law of obligations.[76] In criminal law, the canonical theory of culpability[77] prepared the way for modern criminal law, which attaches prime importance to determining culpability (voluntary or involuntary, premeditation, recidivism, mitigating circumstances, and so on), whereas primitive criminal law was interested above all in the harm done and in compensation.

The influence of the 'ius commune' on legal practice in general

37 The glossators (as we have seen) exercised an early and profound influence on canon law. But the spread of learning in Roman law was not limited to canon law, whose field of application was restricted both *ratione materiae* and *ratione personae*. Roman law increasingly affected legal life and practice in Europe in general. The degree of Romanization varied greatly from one country to another, but none completely escaped. The Roman law of the medieval universities therefore shaped and steered the development of law throughout Europe.

Extent and speed of Romanization

38 In some areas of the Mediterranean world, learned law was adopted as early as the thirteenth century as the basis of the legal system. In these areas, the customs and ordinances peculiar to each country or city were regarded as local variants, which were of course

75 In the county of Flanders, for instance, learned law was already to be found around 1200 in the practice of the *officialité* of Tournai, but in secular practice the first traces of the influence of the legists are not to be found until the fourteenth century, particularly in the Audience of the counts of Flanders.

76 Even today there are the two schools of 'causalists' and 'anti-causalists' among the civilians; cf. J. Limpens, *De wording van het contract* (Brussels, 1970; Med. Kon. ve Akad. Wetenschappen, XXII, 3) and H. Capitant, *De la cause des obligations* (Paris, 1927). On medieval theories, see E. M. Meijers, 'Les théories médiévales concernant la cause de la stipulation et la cause de la donation', *Revue d'histoire du droit* 14 (1932), 376; G. Chevrier, *Dictionnaire de droit canonique* III (1942), col. 1–10.

77 S. Kuttner, *Kanonistische Schuldlehre* (Vatican, 1935; Studi e testi, 64).

valid but were of limited application and were anyway subject to the general rules of the learned law. Italy and the south of France, the regions of written law,[78] are the classic instances of this type of Romanization. In Spain, there was a more tenacious tradition of local *fueros* (compilations of local law, sometimes archaic and of Visigothic origin), and the *ius commune* did not succeed in taking over entirely.

In Italy and the south of France the learned Roman law penetrated more easily owing to the tradition of Roman vulgar law. In Italy the university centres of learned law were clearly an important factor in Romanization. Twelfth-century Italy was also the European country in the most advanced state of development, not only politically but also socially and economically. There were strong cultural links between the Occitan region in southern France and Lombardy and Tuscany: the Italian glossators had already lectured in the south of France in the twelfth century, and universities and law teaching emerged there during the first half of the thirteenth century. The conversion of Roman vulgar or customary law into learned law could therefore take place in Italy and in the Midi spontaneously and without official intervention. Practitioners there recognized without difficulty the superiority of the *ius scriptum* taught at Bologna, and naturally preferred it to the local primitive and underdeveloped laws which had grown up over the centuries on the basis of Roman vulgar law.

In France, the voluntary adoption of the *ius scriptum* in the south and the preservation of ancient Germanic customary law in the north brought about and institutionalized a division between the region of written law and the region of customary law which was to last until the end of the *ancien régime*.[79] The Crown tolerated this division, but it always refused to recognize that Roman law was applied in the south because of imperial authority; instead, in its

[78] The boundary between the regions of written law to the south and customary law to the north became established in the thirteenth century. It ran from the Atlantic in the west above the island of Oléron to the north of Saintonge, Périgord and Limousin, then south of the Auvergne, north of the Mâconnais, Bresse and the Pays du Gex to Lake Geneva. It roughly corresponded to the linguistic boundary between French and Occitan, which was just to the south. See the map in H. Klimrath, 'Etudes sur les coutumes', *Revue de législation et de jurisprudence* 6 (1837), 107–35, 161–214, 321–93; the map has frequently been reprinted *inter alia* in J. Brissaud, *Cours d'histoire générale du droit français*, 1 (Paris, 1904); J. A. Brutails, *La géographie monumentale de la France* (Paris, 1923); J. Gilissen, *Introduction historique au droit* (Brussels, 1979), 241.

[79] Its distant origin was examined in the chapter on the early Middle Ages. The dichotomy remained to the end of the *ancien régime*, at least in theory; in practice differences exist even nowadays.

view it was founded solely on the ancient practices of the region, which had to be respected by the king.[80] The decretal *Super specula* promulgated by Pope Honorius III in 1219 at the instance of the king of France[81] made reference to 'Francia[82] and the other provinces' of the kingdom 'where lay people do not live under the rule of Roman law'. In this official document the legal dichotomy in France was openly acknowledged.

At a later period the learned law was introduced and adopted as national law in some northern regions, and replaced disparate and inconvenient customs. This was the case in Germany, where the Reception began towards 1500, and in Scotland, where continental learned law established itself during the sixteenth century. A German version of the *ius commune* was developed in early modern times and is known as the *Usus Modernus Pandectarum* ('new use of the *Pandects* or *Digest*'). The last flourish of the *Usus Modernus* was in the nineteenth century, particularly in the work of B. Windscheid (*d.* 1892), the most important of the pandectists. The legal authority of the *Digest* in particular, and Roman law in general, disappeared when the *Bürgerliches Gesetzbuch* (*BGB*) came into force in 1900. Still, the influence of the Pandectist School continued to be felt; and, besides, Windscheid played a large part in the compilation of the *BGB*. Scotland in the twelfth and thirteenth centuries had been strongly influenced by England, and Scots law had come close to Common Law. This development was interrupted when Scotland and England were at war, and to fill the gaps in its own underdeveloped customary law, Scotland decided to introduce continental *ius commune*, which had all the right credentials. It could give Scotland a sophisticated legal system, which was uniform throughout the regions, and it was also distinct from English law.[83] In these countries the learned law, Roman and canon law, was in principle the national common law; regional laws had a secondary role.

In other regions, northern France and the southern Netherlands,

[80] This conception is found in a royal ordinance of July 1254 about the seneschalsy of Beaucaire. An ordinance of July 1312 provided that the kingdom was not ruled by written law; and although the population of one part of it lived by written law with royal consent, that was not because written law was established, but because their traditional customary law was in conformity with written law. Such political speciousness did not affect the views of the regional counsellors, who sat in the *parlements* of Aix, Grenoble and Toulouse: for them it was enough to apply the *Corpus iuris civilis*, and that was that.

[81] Cf. section 43 below.

[82] I.e. the Ile-de-France, the old *domaine direct* of the Capetians.

[83] For this reason many Scottish students studied Roman law on the continent, initially at Orléans and Louvain, and after the Reformation mainly at Leiden.

official compilations of traditional customary law were made and promulgated. Although this preserved the customary character of these regions for the following centuries, the *ius commune* was not ignored and it played an official supplementary and interpretative role. Even in the customary regions, an education in written law was in any event indispensable for all those laying claim to be lawyers. In the northern Netherlands, Roman-Dutch law was a unique development: in Holland the customs had not been homologated, and the *ius scriptum* had not been formally introduced by way of authority. Jurisprudence therefore evolved a new synthesis of Dutch law and Roman law, adapted to the society of its time. Roman-Dutch law rapidly acquired an uncontested prestige and its influence was considerable right to the end of the *ancien régime*.

The development in England was without doubt the most unusual in Europe. In the twelfth century the royal courts had created an English common law inspired by feudal and customary law and devoid of Roman elements. This Common Law remained the basis of English law and was not affected by the diffusion of Roman law. Other courts, however, were created besides the Common Law jurisdiction. These developed their own case law and their own principles, which were in several respects remote from classical Common Law and closer to continental learned law, especially Roman-canonical procedure. This applies above all to Equity, the case law of the chancellor, who in the Middle Ages was almost always a bishop. He employed a procedure close to the Roman-canonical, which suited him (as a bishop) better than that of the Common Law courts. But the Court of Chancery and the Court of Requests (which was modelled on it) were less marked by Roman law than the Court of Admiralty, where the judges applied pure *ius commune*. There were also canonical elements in the procedure of the Star Chamber. The Church courts also, in England and throughout the medieval West, already applied canonical law and procedure, and that tradition was maintained even after the break with Rome.[84] The learned law in England was not confined to the legal practice of some jurisdictions, but was also taught at Oxford and Cambridge, and the principal Common Law author of the Middle

[84] As the Reformation had abolished the teaching of canon law, the learned jurists of the church courts were usually doctors in Roman law. 'Civilians' are also to be found in the English courts influenced by Roman law, the Court of Admiralty and Court of Chivalry. From the fifteenth century, these lawyers formed a body known as 'Doctors' Commons'.

Ages, Bracton (*d.* 1268) in his celebrated treatise *On the laws and customs of England* betrays a profound knowledge of learned law.[85] Since Vacarius,[86] the *Corpus iuris civilis* had never been completely absent from English legal theory and practice.

The *ius commune* was a true European law which transcended geographical boundaries. Yet it still met with social obstacles, for it was accessible only to a restricted elite of those educated at university, and to the people at large its Latin was a Sibylline tongue.

The dynamic of the 'ius commune': ideas

39 Any historian who is not content merely to recite facts must ask himself what caused the remarkable but incomplete success of Roman law in the Middle Ages and early modern times. In part it must be attributed to the intrinsic qualities of the *Corpus iuris*, which is the product of a highly developed civilization and the long experience of one of the greatest legal nations in history. Although Roman law was several centuries older, it still corresponded to a stage of social evolution incomparably more advanced than that of Europe around 1100. Rome had been a cosmopolitan and sophisticated empire, with a developed urbanized economy. Europe in the eleventh century, on the other hand, was a feudal and agrarian society of provincial scale and style; and in the twelfth century its degree of cultural and intellectual development was still primitive.

Romanization therefore meant modernization. Roman law appeared to be a modern system, progressive, orientated to the future, while customary law was traditional, antiquated and bound up with an increasingly obsolete stage of development. Roman law also had the advantage of being taught and studied in the universities, which in the late Middle Ages represented the centres *par excellence* of learned thought. To appreciate this, it is sufficient to compare the technique and mastery of style, the presentation, and the rigour of reasoning of the civilian treatises and commentaries with the clumsy attempts of their contemporaries who tried to formulate customary law relatively clearly. Jurisprudence was a skill

85 *Bracton on the laws and customs of England*, ed. G. E. Woodbine, trans. with revisions and notes by S. E. Thorne, 4 vols. (Cambridge, Mass. and London, 1968–77; Latin text and English translation).

86 Vacarius was an Italian glossator who taught Roman law at Oxford in the time of King Stephen (1135–54) and produced a cheap abridged version of the *Corpus iuris* for his students, which is known as the *Liber pauperum* ('book of the poor'). See the edition by F. de Zulueta (Oxford, 1927).

which had necessarily to be acquired in the school of Roman law. And when the professors in their teaching paid attention to the practical demands of the time, as did the Bartolists, the appeal of their message was irresistible. It is symptomatic that when Bracton set out to describe and comment on English law (which had escaped the influence of Roman law) he felt obliged to borrow the principles of a 'general theory' of law from Azo and other glossators.

Yet the intrinsic qualities of the *ius commune* do not alone explain the Romanization of the West. The teaching of the Bolognese masters, excellent though it was, would hardly have been sufficient in the absence of other powerful social factors. The rise and fall of legal systems and great legislative projects are in practice determined by the will of the dominant groups and institutions in a given society. The history of law cannot be understood out of the context of political history, and the effect of law on society is itself a political phenomenon in the broad sense. It is proper therefore now to consider what political and social circumstances allowed the learned law to spread through Europe.

The church was the first of the great powers of the medieval world to lend resolute support to Roman law. The education of Church lawyers was based on the *Corpus iuris civilis*, from which the methods and sometimes even the principles of canon law were derived, and the procedure of the church courts was impregnated to such a degree with Roman law that it is called 'Roman-canonical'. Centralization, hierarchy, bureaucracy, rationalization from above, the importance of law and administration: these were all elements contained in Roman law which the church authorities could use. From the Gregorian Reform, they were the broad lines of papal policy, and they were also precisely the characteristics displayed by Roman law, especially the law of the late Roman empire as enshrined in the *Corpus iuris*. The church adopted Roman law without hesitation despite the fact that the principal authors had lived in pagan times, for the law of the *Corpus* was associated with the prestige of the great Christian emperor Justinian.

Kings and emperors also realized the advantages they could derive from Roman law. In the Holy Roman Empire the authority of Roman law was self-evident, as the emperors considered themselves the successors of the Christian *principes* of ancient Rome. Kings too thought of themselves as the successors of the *caesar* or *princeps* of the *Corpus iuris*; the expression *rex imperator in regno suo* ('the king in his own kingdom is [as sovereign as] the emperor') was a commonplace from the twelfth century. For the sovereigns of the late Middle Ages, the *Corpus* was above all an inexhaustible reserve of arguments to reinforce their positions. The *Corpus* says nothing about the rights of the people or limits on the power of the state; it knows nothing of democracy. Principles which support the omnipotence of the emperor and the majesty of the state therefore stand out all the more clearly. Maxims of the type *princeps legibus solutus* and *quod principi placuit legis habet vigorem*[87] suited to perfection sovereigns who were eager to break away from the feudal mould and establish modern political structures. This was why Emperor Frederick Barbarossa approached the four doctors of Bologna at the time of the diet of Roncaglia (1158) seeking a definition (which was to be used against the cities) of *regalia*, the sovereign and inalienable rights of the Crown. In France the legal advisers of Philip IV the Fair employed Roman law to justify the condemnation of the count of Flanders, as vassal of the king of France. Traditional feudal conceptions now came up against modern ideas on the indivisible sovereignty of the state.[88]

For sovereigns pursuing policies of rationalization and unification of the laws of their kingdoms it was tempting to take up the available model of Roman law.[89] No doubt it would be inaccurate to maintain that the rise of the modern sovereign state was a consequence of the teaching of the glossators; and it can in any case be shown that it had already taken shape in England and in Flanders before Roman law appeared there. None the less it is undeniable that the *Corpus iuris* provided authorities and solid compelling arguments for reinforcing state power against feudal fragmentation, and that many commentators on Roman law took the side of absolutism in the great debate of the age on the power of the state.[90] The legists[91] stood at the centre

[87] 'The emperor is not bound by the laws' and 'What pleases the emperor has the force of law.'

[88] The Dutch cleric and scholar Philip of Leiden (*d.*, 1382), who was in the service of count William V of Holland, wrote a *Tracatatus de cura rei publicae et sorte principantis* in which he argued for the extension of royal power and the civil state and against the nobility; for these purposes he made use of the Roman law he had studied at Orléans (he was also a doctor of canon law of the University of Paris). See P. Leupen, *Philip of Leyden. A fourteenth century jurist* (The Hague and Zwolle, 1981; Rechtshistorische Studies, 7).

[89] E.g. Louis IX of France in the ordinances of 1254 and 1258 which attempted to introduce a French version of Roman-canonical procedure. This met with resistance in feudal circles, which preferred such things as duels to inquests.

[90] Baldus, for example, wrote in his commentary on C. 1.14.4 that '*suprema et absoluta potestas principis non est sub lege*'; cf. R. W. and A. J. Carlyle, *History of medieval political theory*, VI (London, 1950), 20. On political exploitation of the *auctoritas* of Roman law, W. Ullmann, *Law and politics in the Middle Ages. An introduction to the sources of medieval political ideas* (London, 1975).

[91] So called as at university they had studied the *leges* of the Roman emperors (i.e. the *Corpus iuris civilis*).

of power, and there they developed doctrines to support the policies of centralization, rationalization and standardization pursued by sovereigns.

The dynamic of the 'ius commune': the jurists

40 The authorities of the emerging nation states not only made use of the principles of Roman law, but also secured the services of graduates of law faculties. In addition to ideas and rules, the universities could supply officials trained in the reasoning and argumentation of the learned law. From the thirteenth century, legists are to be found occupying influential positions in central institutions and courts of justice even beyond the Mediterranean world. In France they sat in the Parlement de Paris[92] from the mid-thirteenth century, and at court proved themselves loyal servants of the imperialist policy of Philip IV the Fair. In the county of Flanders, they appeared from 1279 at the court of Guy de Dampierre. The first councillors were still Italian and French, but in the fourteenth century most were Flemings who had studied at Bologna or Orléans.[93]

Large and powerful cities were also conscious of the advantages to be derived from having officials in their service whose legal education had equipped them to carry out the specialized tasks of municipal administration. The cities preferred to have university graduates to prepare and defend their legal actions. While city magistrates had been unimpressed by the theories in favour of sovereign power, they could see that the professional education offered in the law faculties could be turned to their advantage, and that in the huge arsenal of the *Corpus* it was not too difficult to discover quotations which could support their own interests.

Here it should be noted that medieval thought did not object to citation of ancient sources completely out of context or their application to situations for which the Romans had never intended them. The *Corpus iuris* could therefore satisfy the most diverse demands. The maxim *quod omnes tangit ab omnibus approbetur*[94] was

[92] Cf. section 53 below.

[93] See J. Gilissen, 'Les légistes en Flandre aux XIIIe et XIVe siècles', *Bull. Comm. Roy. Anc. Lois* 15 (1939), 117–231.

[94] C. 5.59.5.3. The rule was wrenched from its context and applied, in favour of the conciliarist thesis, to the organization of both church and state. Cf. J. Maravall, 'La fórmula "quod omnes tangit" y la corriente democrática medieval en España', *Album E. Lousse*, IV (Louvain, 1964), 1–13; A. Marongiu, 'Le "quod omnes tangit" et une légende dure à mourir', *Revue historique de droit français et étranger* 48 (1970), 10–11; W. Ullmann, *Law and politics*, 281–2.

invoked as a fundamental principle in favour of representative institutions and participation by the people in decisions which concerned them. A literal reading could give the maxim a democratic meaning. To find such a rule in Justinian's *Code*, which is after all the work of an authoritarian regime, would be surprising – except that there it has no connexion with state power, and applies instead to a private-law institution, tutorship. Acts of administration which affected the property of a ward had to be approved by all the tutors. For such reasons it was inevitable that from the thirteenth century Italian cities should entice law professors, create universities and appoint lawyers to public office. In the twelfth century Roman law was still regarded as an instrument of imperial power; but its application in the thirteenth century in the cities of northern Italy (where Bologna had become a staunch focus of opposition to the emperor) was such that in 1224 Frederick II created a university in Naples favourable to his own interests, where the *Corpus* would be interpreted and elucidated more 'correctly'. In northern regions there was a comparable development: legists were appointed to the service of cities, and universities were founded on municipal initiatives, for example Louvain in 1425. But all this happened considerably later than in Italy.[95]

Finally, legal circles made their own contribution to the diffusion of the learned law. Advocates, always on the lookout for arguments to suit their own cases, did not hesitate to cite the *Corpus iuris* to impress their audiences.[96] In his defence a litigant had no option but to call another advocate who could either cite other texts of the *Corpus* refuting the arguments of his adversary or show that the texts cited by him were not relevant. From now on mastery of the learned law became an important trump card.[97] Besides, it was useful not just for the parties but for judges too, when confronted with new

95 From 1304 to 1332 Ghent had in its service Hendrik Braem, *legum professor*, at a salary of 100 pounds. Liège obtained the services of John of Hocsem (*d.* 1348), also *legum professor*.

96 For the oldest testimony on this point, see A. P. Schioppa, 'Il ruolo della cultura giuridica in alcuni atti giudiziari italiani dei secoli XI e XII', *Nuova rivista storica* 64 (1980), 265–89; L. Schmugge, '"Codicis Justiniani et Institutionum baiulus". Eine neue Quelle zu Magister Pepo von Bologna', *Ius commune* 6 (1977), 1–9.

97 From the time of the glossators, a letter is extant written by a monk of the Abbey of St Victor in Marseilles who was travelling Italy and sought permission from his abbot to study Roman law; he pointed out that in the future the abbey would thereby be better placed to defend itself against its detractors. The date of the letter is uncertain, but recent research places it between 1124 and 1127. Cf. J. Dufour, G. Giordanengo and A. Gouron, 'L'attrait des "leges". Note sur la lettre d'un moine victorin (vers 1124/1127)', *Studia et documenta historiae et iuris* 45 (1979), 504–29.

problems: the *ius commune* was so extensive and the *consilia* so abundant and detailed that, in the absence of a customary rule, judges could be sure of discovering a principle in the learned law.[98] In great political debates a need was also felt to make reference to Roman law or contradict opponents by quoting the *Corpus*: when Philip IV the Fair attacked the count of Flanders with the aid of the *Corpus iuris*, the count felt obliged in his turn to ask legists for help in defending his position, for the traditional rules of feudal law no longer made any impression.

Learning and the university

41 The university[99] was the common basis of the powerful supranational body of lawyers. Its origins go back to the twelfth century in Bologna, Salerno and Paris. In the centuries which followed, universities spread throughout the West. Although there were important local differences, the medieval universities had various features in common. In the teaching of law the following are notable. In the Middle Ages above all, the university world was cosmopolitan: national frontiers (which at the time counted for little) constituted no more of a barrier than vernacular languages. At all the universities from Poland to Portugal, from Scotland to Sicily, teaching was in Latin, the basic works were the same, and the qualifications were recognized in all countries. Students flocked from all areas of Europe especially to the large universities and organized themselves into 'nations'; at Orléans, for example, the students who came from the German empire formed the 'Natio Germanica' within which students from Brabant, Liège and Holland were strongly represented. The recruitment of professors was also wholly international, and so were the regulations and the syllabuses which the new foundations often borrowed from old and sometimes distant universities.

Like all teaching institutions, the medieval universities had an ecclesiastical character. Most had been created by a pontifical bull and placed under the authority of a cleric as chancellor. Originally

[98] For the circumstances in which the first arguments of learned law were made before the Flemish courts, see E. I. Strubbe, 'De receptie in de Vlaamse rechtbanken van midden veertiende tot einde vijftiende eeuw', *Revue d'histoire du droit* 29 (1961), 445–62 (also in *idem.*, *De luister van ons oude recht. Verzamelde rechtshistorische studies* (Brussels, 1973), 601–15).

[99] Originally *universitas* meant 'group', 'society', or 'corporation'; it came to be used for the associations of professors or students of a town. Little by little, it became the standard term for the body of professors and students of the *studium generale* in a town.

all the students belonged to the clergy, although the great majority had merely entered minor orders, and only a few ended up being ordained priests. Towards the end of the Middle Ages, the clerical character abated, and from then on the majority of the student population was made up of lay people.

The universities of the Middle Ages were fiercely independent in their administrative and financial management. This was natural for the first groups of students which grew up around certain well-known professors; but even after the universities had become institutionalized with charters of foundation, regulations, and financial support from public authorities, they retained extensive independence. State interference in prescribing courses and appointing professors is a late phenomenon more characteristic of early modern times. At that time a certain 'nationalization' of the universities also occurred. From the end of the Middle Ages, some rulers had founded universities specially intended for their subjects and to provide for the needs of their administration and government. In exceptional cases, such as the 'political' university founded in Naples in 1224, study abroad was actually forbidden. In early modern times this type of monopoly tended to multiply: for instance, in the sixteenth century in the southern Netherlands in favour of Louvain and Douai, for motives which were as much political as religious.

The first universities were not deliberate foundations: they were spontaneous associations or corporations (so popular in the Middle Ages) either of *magistri* and *scholares* together or 'masters' and 'students' separately.[100] Some universities originated when professors and students seceded from an existing university, owing to internal differences, longstanding disputes, or conflicts with the municipal authorities, and set up a new university in another town. The University of Cambridge, for instance, was founded after a secession from Oxford. At a later stage the deliberate official foundation of a university went hand in hand with the setting up of an official organization and the granting of state or local endowments. In several Italian cities professors were paid out of the municipal budget; at Vercelli in 1228 the community undertook payment of the salaries of seven professors of law. This meant progressively

[100] Sometimes professors were appointed and paid by the student body: in the thirteenth century the University of Bologna was a student corporation with an independent administration, and many students were men with legal and administrative experience. In the fourteenth century, administration fell into the hands of the town itself.

greater interference by the authorities in the internal affairs of the universities.

The universities were elitist, first in the intellectual sense. The courses of study were long (seven years or more was normal) and demands were high. Familiarity with Latin was essential in order to take part in 'disputations', as well as to learn the *Corpus iuris* (often by heart) and the Gloss. Secondly, the small circle of students[101] was elitist by social origin. Studies were often pursued abroad and were expensive; bursaries were rare.[102] Some students did manage to pay for their studies by working in the service of wealthy students,[103] but most belonged to the nobility or the *haute bourgeoisie*, which in early modern times supplied the administrative classes and the *noblesse de robe*. The *petite bourgeoisie*, artisans and countrymen were hardly represented. Finally, the students made up an elite by virtue of their rights: members of the university enjoyed numerous privileges, notably that they were not subject to the jurisdiction of the ordinary courts. The constitution *Habita* of 1158 of Frederick Barbarossa had already given important privileges and exemptions to university scholars. In early modern times in particular the circle of university-educated lawyers tended to form an exclusive elite. Alliances within the homogeneous social class of senior officials and magistrates were frequent; an introduction or a promotion often depended on family connexions. Yet the lawyers, in spite of this influence, did not succeed in extending their grip beyond administration and legal practice. Political decisions remained in the hands of the sovereign, and the attempts of some courts of justice such as the Parlement de Paris to play a political role provoked several grave conflicts with the Crown.

In early modern times university syllabuses and the elitism of the lawyers hardly changed. Roman law and canon law still had almost

[101] Around 1200 the University of Bologna, the main institution for legal education, is thought to have had around 1,000 students. Orléans and Avignon towards the end of the fourteenth century had significantly fewer (256 bachelors and 368 students at the former, 339 bachelors and 467 scholars at the latter). At Cologne, probably the most important faculty in fifteenth-century Germany, the estimate of law students is 100 or 200. In general the larger universities had from 500 to 1,000 students, and the smaller about 100.

[102] The complete set of the five manuscript volumes of the glossed *Corpus* cost as much as a town-house. Bursaries were sometimes awarded by municipalities in the hope of attracting to themselves a devoted lawyer; most bursaries were awarded for the same reason by ecclesiastical bodies (chapters or abbeys) to their most promising members.

[103] They were inscribed as *pauperes* in the registers and exempt from matriculation fees.

a monopoly on the subjects taught.[104] On the one hand the state increasingly interfered in university affairs, while on the other the intellectual level and originality of legal teaching declined.

The university and the theoretical approach

42 The fact that for centuries leading lawyers were educated in law faculties had great importance for the development of law in Europe. It gave continental European law not only its Romano-Germanic basis but also its typically theoretical and conceptual character. In a general historical perspective, it is rather surprising that these lawyers received their professional education far away from daily legal practice; their education instead took place in universities and consisted in an initiation lasting several years into the 'sacred books' of their discipline. The education of common lawyers is much more typical: young people who wanted to devote themselves to a legal career were taken on as apprentices with an established practitioner and worked as clerks or assistants in practice in London, where the royal courts sat. They lived in institutions for students, the Inns of Court, where they received lodging and a training which was basic and not to be compared with a university syllabus. There was no requirement for university study of law until the twentieth century in England, and the most eminent lawyers (the judges of the higher courts) were not graduates in law but practitioners who had learned their skills on the job. Only recently did it become the norm for intending lawyers to study law at university and to obtain a degree in law.[105] On the continent, for centuries judges and advocates

[104] Reference to the customs and ordinances in force was very infrequent. A hesitant start on teaching non-learned law was made in France by the *Ordonnance* of St Germain-en-Laye of 1679, which prescribed that a chair of French law should be established in Paris and elsewhere. The first professor of French law in Paris wrote a commentary on the *Institutes* of Loisel (see section 26 above). Cf. A. de Curzon, 'L'enseignement du droit français dans les Universités de France aux XVIIe et XVIIIe siècles', *Revue historique de droit français et étranger* 43 (1919), 209–69, 305–64 (also published separately, 1920). The order of the Consejo of Castile in 1713 to replace Roman with local law was ineffective, owing to the opposition of the faculties.

[105] In 1976 70 per cent of new solicitors and from 90 to 95 per cent of new barristers were law graduates. Around the middle of the nineteenth century virtually nothing was prescribed for legal studies in England; it is not surprising that the report of the Select Committee of 1846 which had examined the issue ended with a long list of complaints that made numerous references to the position abroad. It is therefore only since the second half of the nineteenth century that universities have begun to award degrees in law. Many eminent judges, however, opposed this innovation, and in 1904 Vaughan Williams LJ observed that the law schools would lead to codification, and so it would be better to do without them; cf. A. H. Manchester, *Modern legal history of England and Wales* (London, 1980), 54–66.

trained in practice practised alongside university graduates. In the Netherlands the latter acquired real importance only from the fifteenth century,[106] and in general the notion that a university education was indispensable for judges and advocates in the higher courts became current only in early modern times.[107] A parallel evolution took place in medicine: originally it was in the hands of surgeons and doctors trained in practice, and graduates were a minority; but graduates established themselves little by little and finally acquired a legal monopoly in the art of healing.

Each educational system – theoretical on the continent, practical in England – has its advantages and disadvantages. The continental method offered the prospect of acquiring a detailed knowledge of the principles of a rational legal system, but it was remote from actual legal practice and did not prepare graduate lawyers to practise customary law. The English method on the other hand immediately confronted the intending lawyer with daily practice and living law, but it could not offer him the theoretical and analytical approach peculiar to universities, nor familiarize him with Roman law to broaden his intellectual horizons.

Opposition to 'ius commune'

43 In the Europe of customary law, the reception given to Roman law was not always favourable. It is worth noting the main points of opposition. Like every innovation, the spread of *ius commune* disturbed conservative circles, which saw it as a challenge to their traditional interests and their manner of thinking. Feudal law was not just an abstract system of rights and obligations, but the very foundation of the landed property of numerous noble families; unforeseen innovations threatened to alter the nature of landownership completely and the rights and burdens which attached to it.

[106] At the Audience, which later became the Council of Flanders, in the course of the sixteenth century legists became ever more numerous until they obtained a monopoly. From that time almost all councillors in the superior courts had to have a legal education. At the *parlement* (1473–77) and the Great Council (1504–1794) of Malines, all the councillors were doctors or graduates in law. In the important courts of aldermen, from the fifteenth century one or two learned lawyers sat in each court, and in the eighteenth century they formed the majority. In lower courts the aldermen asked a qualified lawyer to frame an appropriate judgment.

[107] There was occasional legislation to this effect: at the Council of Brabant an ordinance of 1501 required that advocates should be graduates in Roman or canon law. H. de Ridder-Symoens, 'Milieu social, études universitaires et carrière des conseillers au Conseil de Brabant (1430–1600)', *Album amicorum J. Buntinx* (Louvain, 1981), 257–302.

Farmers were equally preoccupied. By applying the Roman law conception of absolute ownership, the learned law threatened to overturn time-honoured practices of exploiting farmland and using common lands to the profit of landowners.[108] In still other areas feudalism opposed the innovations of the learned lawyers. Thus in 1236 English barons blocked the introduction of the canon (and Roman) law principle of *legitimatio per subsequens matrimonium* because it would have had important repercussions for the traditional scheme of inheritance. Their refusal to adopt the learned law was categorical: *nolumus mutare leges Angliae*.[109] A similar reaction had already been seen in France, where in the second half of the thirteenth century the knights vigorously opposed the new 'inquest' procedure which was inspired by Roman-canonical principles and was intended to replace the traditional duel. Owing to their resistance to learned law in general, the regions of customary law retained their own character. At the Parlement de Paris, the councillors were obliged to judge appeals from these regions according to the customs of the region and not according to the learned law. In 1278 Philip III even prohibited advocates from citing Roman law in cases coming from the regions of customary law.[110] The councillors and advocates found themselves in a dilemma. Since they were educated in Roman law, they reasoned according to its categories and for their own purposes prepared their judgments or pleadings following the principles of the *Corpus iuris*, but they were prohibited from making open use of them or explicit reference to them.

The conservatism of certain circles did not provide the only support for traditional customary law: regional and local particu-

[108] See the discussion in A. Stern, 'Das römische Recht und der deutsche Bauernkrieg', *Zeitschrift für schweizerische Geschichte* 14 (1934), 20–9. The peasants' registers of grievances took particular exception to the code for Baden compiled by Zasius, probably because it altered the surviving spouse's right of succession into line with Roman law (i.e. in favour of cognates). The peasants also demanded that judges should be elected by the community, and that all the books containing 'Juristerei und Sophisterei' should be burned.

[109] Feudalism was based on primogeniture and, according to the traditional view, an illegitimate son born before the parents married was a bastard, who was excluded from all rights of succession, even if the parents subsequently married; but if he was legitimated by *legitimatio per subsequens matrimonium* he inherited the entire fief, and his younger brother born after the marriage of the parents did not.

[110] *Ordonnances des rois de France* XI (Paris, 1769), 354, art. 9, 'Li advocats ne soient si hardis d'eus mesler d'aleguer droict escrit, là où coustumes aient lieu, mais usent de coustumes' ('Advocates are not to be so bold as to cite written law where custom applies, but are to make use of customs.').

larism was another factor in its favour. In the Netherlands, among other places, local custom was valued as an element of political independence, and for the cities in particular custom constituted an obstacle to the policies of central authorities. It is typical that, when Charles the Bold conquered Lille, he abolished customary law there and replaced it with the *ius commune*, a measure revoked after his death when the Burgundian occupation ended.

Opposition to Roman law might also be inspired by considerations of national policy. This was especially so in France. Roman law, which was regarded as imperial law, awoke anxieties in the French monarchy, always eager to refute the potential claims of the Holy Roman emperors to legal supremacy. The French kings therefore always opposed the very idea of Roman law having the force of law by virtue of the authority of the German emperors. This opposition caused another dilemma: the kings appointed legists to the Parlement de Paris and included them in their governments, but refused to recognize any authority in 'imperial' law. This is the background to the bull *Super specula* pronounced by Honorius III in 1219 at the instance of the king of France: it prohibited any teaching of Roman law (but not canon law) at the University of Paris.[111]

In the sixteenth century the rise of sovereign nation states and nationalistic sentiments made its mark. In France, Fr Hotman maintained that a codified French law was needed. His was one of the first projects to aim at codification on a national level of the whole of private and public law. This was to take place in the context of a policy of nationalization and standardization of French law, and in connexion with a strong national monarchy. Hotman stressed the relative authority and the imperfections of Roman law.

It is a fact that, in spite of its intrinsic qualities, *ius commune* also presented certain disadvantages; in spite of everything lawyers found 'thorns in the garden of law'. Criticisms that learned law and procedure were beyond popular comprehension were not

[111] Although this prohibition was to some extent evaded by 'private' lessons, it remained in force until its revocation by Louis XIV in 1679. One reason (among others) alleged by the papal bull was that the study of Roman law was turning too many clerics in Paris away from their proper discipline: theology. Cf. G. Péries, *La faculté de droit dans l'ancienne Université de Paris* (Paris, 1890), 99–108; W. Ullmann, 'The prohibition of Roman law at Paris', *Juridical Review* 60 (1948), 177; S. Kuttner, 'Papst Honorius III und das Studium des Zivilrechts', *Festschrift Martin Wolff* (Tübingen, 1952), 79.

unfounded; discontent was aggravated by the secrecy and the length and expense of legal actions and appeals. The golden days of legal actions in the open air completed in a day – as prescribed by a capitulary of Charlemagne – were longingly evoked. The tendency of learned lawyers to entangle themselves in quibbles and quarrels and to contradict themselves was also a defect of the *ius commune.* The accuracy of the medieval expression *doctores certant* was too often demonstrated: for every opinion of a *doctor legum*, after a little investigation a contrary opinion could be found. The certainty of the law was at risk. Several sovereigns resorted to a *lex citandi* declaring, for instance, the exclusive authority of Bartolus over every other author. But this could only mitigate the basic weakness very imperfectly.

Commercial law

44 What of the role of merchants in the diffusion of Roman law? It might be thought that the *Corpus iuris* and its advanced law of obligations would have supported the growing international commerce of the late Middle Ages, and that merchants would have been among the most active exporters of the *ius commune.* Yet this was not the case. Commercial and maritime law developed independently of Roman law and canon law (and in opposition to the latter, so far as interest on loans was concerned). Both the *ius commune* and commercial law were international and multi-dimensional: each flourished but each pursued its own path, the first in the world of universities and the higher courts of justice, the second in the daily practice and customs of merchants and their own market and maritime jurisdictions. Roman law was suited better to jurisprudence and to administration than to commercial practice, so from the twelfth to the fifteenth centuries, a customary and cosmopolitan commercial law was developed in practice. It was dictated essentially by the needs of practice and commercial efficacy in commodity and money markets, in trade fairs, corporations, banking operations and means of insurance and credit.

Although, from the sixteenth century, there were attempts to systematize this body of rules according to jurisprudential criteria, commercial and maritime law remained connected with practice to such a degree that in the following century the author of the first general treatise on commercial law was not a lawyer but a merchant, and in France the codification of commercial law under Louis XIV was also in large part the work of a merchant.[112] Western *ius mercatorum* (commercial law) was largely shaped at the great international trade fairs, in particular those of Champagne in the twelfth and thirteenth centuries; ancient practices turned into generally recognized usages and rules, for example in the case of bills of exchange. Contributions to the formation of European commercial law were also made by the rules of merchant corporations, as well as by the two great families of maritime law, that of the Mediterranean lands, where the *lex Rhodia*[113] and the *Consulat de Mar* were observed; and that of the north of Europe, where the 'Rôles d'Oléron' and the maritime law of Damme and Wisby were followed.[114]

Merchants had their own jurisdictions, market and maritime courts (*Consulat de Mar*), in which rules of commercial law were applied, and merchants were judged by their peers. In general, commercial customs were unwritten, but compilations were made at Genoa from 1154 and in Venice under doge Ziani in 1205–29. There were also various Spanish compilations, culminating in the Barcelona version of the *Consulat de Mar* which goes back at least to 1370.[115]

The example of commercial law shows that the Middle Ages were capable by their own means of developing a new body of legal rules in response to economic demands. In the late Middle Ages practice

[112] I.e. the *Consuetudo vel lex mercatoria* of Gerard Malynes of 1622 and the *Ordonnance sur le commerce* of 1673 or Code Savary, named after the merchant Jacques Savary who had an important part in its compilation. The elements of commercial law were for a long time to be found in practical manuals, together with such miscellaneous topics as weights and measures, geodesy, mathematics, economics and so forth.

[113] Since Roman times the expression *lex Rhodia* (after Rhodes and the merchant community based there) has referred to the body of maritime customary law of the Mediteranean, of which little is known other than the citations in the *Digest*. From the eighth to the tenth centuries a written Byzantine collection was produced, which can be regarded as the point of departure for medieval maritime law. The principal concern of the ancient authors was general average, which is why the ancient law is known as the *lex Rhodia de jactu* (*jactus* meaning jettison).

[114] The 'Rôles d'Oléron' is a thirteenth-century collection of judgments of the commercial court of the island of Oléron, which lies on the Atlantic coast, on the busy sea route linking the Mediterranean with Flanders and England. Wisby was a Hanseatic town on the Swedish island of Gotland in the Baltic Sea.

[115] For a general sketch, see H. Pohlmann, 'Die Quellen des Handelsrechts' in H. Coing (ed.), *Handbuch der Quellen und Literatur der neueren europäischen Privatrechtsgeschichte*, I (1973), 801–34; L. Goldschmidt, *Universalgeschichte des Handelsrechts*, 3rd edn. I (Stuttgart, 1891); H. Mariage, *Evolution historique de la législation commerciale de l'ordonnance de Colbert à nos jours* (Paris, 1959); G. Colon and A. Garcia I Sanz, *Llibre del Consolat de Mar*, 2 vols. (Barcelona, 1981–2); M. Bottin, 'Le Développement du droit de la mer en Mediterranée occidentale du XIIe au XIVe siècles' *Recueil de mémoires et travaux des anciens pays de droit écrit* 12 (1983), 11–28.

and custom evolved an impressive legal system regulating business in general, and the organization of credit, insurance and banking in particular. This system was adequate for its time, and some of the basic principles worked out in the Middle Ages (especially fiduciary currency and bills of exchange) were preserved in the international commerce of modern times. Like the Common Law, commercial law took a fundamentally different approach from *ius commune*; the learned law, unlike Common Law and the *lex mercatoria*, had a general theory of law; it approached specific questions by setting out from general categories and concepts; and it swore by written sources (the text of the *Corpus*) and by logic, rather than by experience, precedent or practice.

LEGISLATION

The renaissance towards 1100

45 Nowadays legislation is the main source of law. The legislator abolishes existing rules and creates new ones in accordance with policy and social requirements. To legislate is to manipulate the law and society in a desired direction. In former times, it was by no means clear that law could result from deliberate and purposive intervention. Instead, law was regarded as a fixed and eternal reality, which could at most be adapted or clarified, but the main concern was to maintain the good old law. The insignificance of legislation[116] during the first centuries of the Middle Ages is explained partly by this view, and partly by the impotence of the central authorities.[117] Although the situation changed during the later Middle Ages and modern times, the importance of legislation was still very slight compared with its role in the great codifications

[116] Cf. above, section 15.

[117] This also applies to a large extent to the most important series of statutes of the early Middle Ages, the Anglo-Saxon *dooms*. Although there is an element of new law in them, whether in connexion with clerical privileges (necessarily new, after the conversion of the Anglo-Saxons to Christianity) or in connexion with the struggle against uncontrolled private feuds, these statutes also contain much traditional law, and the later *dooms*, especially the very lengthy ones of Cnut, repeat word for word a large number of provisions of the earlier ones. In the preamble to his statutes, Alfred the Great expressly states that he has repeated what was equitable in the statutes of his predecessors, and rejected or corrected other provisions, but that he would not have dared to promulgate numerous statutes which he had drafted himself. His statutes were promulgated towards the end of the ninth century, exactly at the time when the capitularies, indeed all continental legislative activity, were coming to an end.

of the eighteenth century, let alone under a legislative monopoly such as Napoleon attempted to secure.

One factor which explains the secondary role of legislation as a source of law under the *ancien régime* is competition from the *ius commune*, which made it possible to transform the old European law without legislative intervention. Yet the revival of legislation (in the sense of deliberate intervention in legal development) clearly goes back to the end of the eleventh century. From that time onwards the domain of the statute slowly but surely expanded. Even if the great national codes did not appear before the eighteenth century, or in some countries before the beginning of the nineteenth, legislation was already a fully-fledged source of old European law alongside jurisprudence and case law. During this period legislation by the church, by states and cities guided the development of law. Broadly speaking, two types of legislation may be distinguished. First, legislation by popes and secular rulers, promulgated by them and imposed on their subjects according to their policies. Second, legislation wanted by the community and implemented for the common good (hence the Dutch expressions *keur* or *willekeur*, which mean 'choice' or 'voluntary choice' and emphasize that the basis of this legislation was the free will of the community concerned). Such legislation was to be found in the cities of the later Middle Ages; this democratic form of legal development later came to an end with the rise of the absolutist state.

Popes as legislators

46 The revival of legislation within the church coincided with the Gregorian Reform. From the second half of the eleventh century, synods and reforming popes attempted to combat alleged 'abuses', that is, the traditional and customary subordination of the church to temporal power. The signal for reform was given by Gregory VII, who before his election had already played an influential part within the *Curia*. There was no chance in the revival of legislation during his pontificate; to initiate reform and suppress abuses the church authorities needed to legislate. Of this Gregory VII was perfectly aware, as is clear from his assertion 'only the pope has the right to promulgate new statutes according to the needs of the moment',[118] as

[118] Art. 7 of *Dictatus Papae*, a sort of manifesto for the Gregorian reform, dating from 1075.

well as his hostility towards custom as a source of law. The existing situation was hallowed by custom, but the pope was determined to impose new principles; he must be on his guard against custom, since the success of his policies depended on the effectiveness of his legislative initiatives. Several Roman councils promulgated new rules for the whole of the Latin church; regional councils, which were in closer touch with the people, differentiated and reinforced these principles in their respective regions and countries. But it was the popes, even more than the councils and canons, who maintained the legislative tradition from the second half of the eleventh century.[119] Constant papal legislative activity influenced western attitudes at large and illustrated that the law could be deliberately manipulated towards given social ends.

The pontificate of Boniface VIII marked the end of the great period of papal legislation and the classical age of canon law. Afterwards the principal legislative initiatives came from the councils, in two distinct periods and in very different circumstances. First came the period of conciliarist theories, from the end of the fourteenth century through the first half of the fifteenth, during which Church assemblies were dominated by attempts to organize a form of parliamentary control. This was a response to the centralist policy of the Roman *Curia*, but such interesting constitutional experiments were to have no lasting effect. The second period was that of the Council of Trent (1545–63), which was convened in order to organize the Counter-Reformation. The decisions of this council were strongly anti-protestant and firmly in favour of centralization. They shaped the church until Vatican II.

Kings as legislators in the Middle Ages

47 After a gap of several centuries, legislation by kings and territorial princes also underwent a hesitant revival and became increasingly important. Their first legislative initiatives dealt only with points or questions of detail or else did no more than abrogate a customary rule which was thought to be unjust (*mala consuetudo*). In England William the Conqueror (1066–87) regulated the organization of the judiciary, criminal law and the law of evidence; Henry II (1154–89) introduced measures to protect peaceable possession of

[119] Cf. above, section 35.

land and to generalize the use of the jury, which was intended to replace the judicial duel as a means of proof in civil matters. In Flanders, Count Baldwin IX (1194–1205) laid down rules against usury. Royal documents are extant from the Norman kingdom of Sicily which regulate feudal law and the organization of the judiciary from the twelfth century onwards. For twelfth-century France only a few scattered ordinances of the kings in criminal matters are known; more abundant legislation began only from the reign of Philip Augustus (1180–1223).[120] At the same time in the Holy Roman empire there were various statutes dealing with feudal and especially criminal law. The Germanic kings, who thought of themselves as the successors of the Roman emperors, sought to underline continuity with the imperial legislation of Antiquity by ordaining that some of their own constitutions be inserted into the *Corpus iuris*.

The first legislation on any scale (although it bears no comparison to a true codification) dates from the thirteenth century. The *Liber Augustalis* promulgated in 1231 by Frederick II for his kingdom of Sicily, and the *Siete Partidas* of Alfonso X of Castille, written in Castilian, have already been mentioned.[121] In England the reign of Edward I (1272–1307) saw a proliferation of statutes on matters of public and private law; the extent of this legislative activity was surpassed only in the nineteenth century. It appeared not in a single collection but as a succession of statutes regulating a great range of subjects. The early legislation betrays the lack of a tradition and the inexperience of legislators. Neither legislative technique nor drafting of documents was clearly established yet. Originally the new statutes were promulgated orally, and are known to us only through the chronicles or because they were confirmed at a time when writing had become customary. When, in the twelfth century, it became normal practice to set statutes down in writing, the formal aspects of this new type of publication had yet to be settled. To start with, the style was often informal: the text begins with a note of the type 'there follow the decisions of the king or count x' without an initial or final protocol, and without any formula of authenticity or mention of the date. Many important laws were typically 'granted' in the form of charters to a region or a city and, from the formal point of view,

[120] G. Giordanengo, 'Le pouvoir législatif du roi de France (XIe – XIIIe siècles), travaux récents et hypothèses de recherche', *Bibliothèque école des chartes* 147 (1989), 283–310.

[121] Cf. above, section 33.

cannot be distinguished from documents attesting the transfer of property. For example Magna Carta is a collection of constitutional principles, but was promulgated in the form of a grant by the king to his subjects. The uncertainties of the age also emerge from the various names given to these ancient statutes. The statutes were sometimes called *assisae*, particularly in England, since they were worked out and promulgated at sessions (*assisae*) of the royal court. The old identification of law and custom was entrenched to such a degree that these first statutes were sometimes called *leges et consuetudines* (statutes and customs) or even *leges consuetudinariae* (customary statutes), although to us this seems to be a contradiction in terms.

In the twelfth and thirteenth centuries in particular, the sovereign very often addressed legislation not to the whole of the country but to certain cities or villages or groups of them. This was regularly in the form of a local charter or privilege, and frequently at the request of interested parties. Sometimes it was against their will (so-called *mauvais privilège*).[122] In the Netherlands the grant of charters to cities was the method most often used for legislation. For example, count Philip of Alsace (1157–91) introduced a standard modern municipal law in the seven main cities of Flanders by granting seven individual charters, whose content is identical.[123]

Techniques and formal rules for national legislation were gradually established. In England the practice that statutes must be promulgated by the king and parliament was instituted and has not changed since the end of the Middle Ages. In France *ordonnances royales* were promulgated by the government, generally without the involvement of the Estates General. In the Netherlands it remained quite rare for the sovereign to promulgate ordinances for each or several of the provinces. Under Burgundian rule such legislation became more important,[124] but its influence ought not to be exaggerated (certainly not in the area of private law). Many of the ordinances have nothing to do with statutes proper, but are indi-

[122] E.g. the 'mauvais privilège' introduced by count Louis of Nevers in several places, especially Bruges in 1329, after the suppression of the uprising in coastal Flanders.

[123] See R. C. van Caenegem and L. Milis, 'Kritische uitgave van de "Grote Keure" van Filips van de Elzas, graaf van Vlaanderen, voor Gent en Brugge (1165–77)', *Bulletin de la commission royale d'histoire* 143 (1977), 207–57.

[124] The ordinances of the period from 1381 to 1405 have been edited by P. Bonenfant, J. Bartier and A. van Nieuwenhuysen, *Recueil des ordonnances des Pays-Bas*, 2 vols. (Brussels, 1965–74; Première serie, Comm. roy. des anc. lois).

vidual concessions, appointments or other administrative measures, or else deal only with taxation, finance or criminal law.[125]

Kings as legislators in modern times

48 Before the codification movement of the eighteenth century, national legislation in Europe in modern times was not very abundant, at least in private law. In England the Tudors passed numerous important statutes, but they regulated only political and religious questions; in the following centuries statutes were most often made up of miscellaneous provisions proposed for their own purposes by Members of Parliament. In Germany and the United Provinces legislation remained very limited; the legal system was based on the *ius commune* and *Rooms-Hollands Recht* respectively. In Spain the *recopilaciones* were no more than compilations of existing legislation. In the southern Netherlands and in France the development of law threatened to peter out after the homologation of customs. None the less in France there was a series of great royal ordinances. This was legislation of prime importance whose influence is still felt today. Although the principal ordinances were promulgated under Louis XIV and Louis XV, there is no break in continuity between the medieval and the modern. Examples are the *Ordonnance Cabochienne* (1413)[126] which was an attempt at democratic reform of political institutions. The *Ordonnance* of Montil-lez-Tours (1454) aimed at better and swifter legal procedure, and provided for the official reduction of customs to writing in order to achieve greater legal certainty. The *Ordonnance* of Villers-Cotterets (1539) extended the jurisdiction of the royal courts at the expense of that of the church courts, largely for matrimonial cases; it also regulated questions of procedure; and it contained dispositions relating to wills and the registration of donations (which are now to be found in articles 907, 931, and 939 of the *Code civil*). The *Ordonnance* of Moulins (1566) extended the jurisdiction of the royal courts still further, this time at the expense of the urban courts; it also contained

[125] On the disparate character of these ordinances see the criticism of P van Peteghem, *Revue d'histoire du droit* 48 (1980), 84–8. In criminal law, the ordinances of the Duke of Alba were most important: M. van de Vrugt, *De criminele ordonnantien van 1570. Enkele beschouwingen over de eerste strafrechtcodificatie in de Nederlanden* (Zutphen, 1978).

[126] The name refers to the riots and demonstrations which preceded the promulgation of the ordinance; the processions were often led by Caboche, who worked at the great St Jacques slaughterhouse.

a disposition requiring written proof for contracts in excess of a certain sum (repeated in article 1341 of the *Code civil*). The very extensive *Ordonnance* of Blois (1579) contained dispositions on very diverse matters: clergy (arts. 1–64); hospital management (65–6); reform of the universities (67–8); the administration of justice (89–209); the abolition of certain offices and burdens (210–55); the nobility (256–75); the army (276–320); the court (321–8); Crown estates (329–54); the police and the maintenance of highways (355–6); the guilds (357–63).

In the Middle Ages, ordinances were worked out by the royal government after consultation with the powerful secular and clerical figures of the kingdom; drafting them was generally left to legists in the service of the king. The assemblies of the Estates (the 'parliaments' of the Middle Ages) did not usually take part in this legislation (by contrast they did in England). During the second half of the sixteenth century, when the French monarchy was in a grave crisis, the Estates General were able to extend their influence, but their role diminished once more in the following century, as they were no longer convened between 1614 and 1789.

The great ordinances of Louis XIV and Louis XV

49 Some of the French ordinances were very succinct and regulated only a single question; an example is the ordinance of Louis XII in 1510 on short prescription;[127] others (as we shall see) were extensive and various, but dispositions on private and civil law were mostly infrequent. This state of affairs changed with the great ordinances of Louis XIV and Louis XV. Three ordinances were promulgated under Louis XIV thanks to the political support of Colbert, who recognized that the development of commerce and industry demanded proper administration of justice, and thanks too to the legal knowledge of Guillaume de Lamoignon (*d.* 1677) and Henri Pussort (*d.* 1697).

The *Ordonnance civile pour la réformation de la justice* (1667) was known as the *Code Louis* owing to its scale. It aimed to introduce a uniform system of civil procedure for the whole kingdom and to speed up legal process, which was to be conducted according to a written procedure. The *Code de procédure civile* of 1806 repeats this

[127] Most are repeated in the *Code civil*, arts. 2271–7.

ordinance almost in its entirety, and its influence can still be traced even in the Belgian *Code judiciaire* of 1967; other dispositions were repeated by the *Code civil* of 1804. The *Ordonnance sur le commerce* (1673) known as the *Code Marchand* or Code Savary, after its principal author, proved very durable and laid the basis for the *Code de commerce* promulgated under Napoleon. The *Ordonnance sur le commerce des mers* or *Ordonnance de la Marine* (1681) on maritime law was repeated in the second book of the same *Code de commerce.*[128]

These ordinances did not attempt to innovate, let alone to indulge in revolutionary codification. They built on existing dispositions, they harmonized the existing law, and they abrogated the rules which they did not include. This was a decisive step towards legal clarity and security. The importance attached by the young Louis XIV in 1665 to the reform of justice has to be seen in its political context; the essence of the reform was simplification and standardization.[129]

It is unfortunate that the works of the reform commission made no impression on the important fields of criminal and civil law.[130] In civil law, three partial codifications (simplifying and standardizing again, rather than innovating) were promulgated under Louis XV: the *Ordonnance sur les donations* (1731), *Ordonnance sur les testaments* (1735), and *Ordonnance sur les substitutions fidéicommissaires* (1747). The first and third ordinances applied throughout France; the second provided different rules for the regions of customary and of written law. The *Code civil* largely reiterated the principles of these ordinances. As they were in large part the efforts of the chancellor, Henri-François Daguesseau (*d.* 1751), they are also known as the *Ordonnances du chancelier Daguesseau.*[131] None the less, the monarchy did not achieve a unification and codification of civil law. It faced not merely the obstacles of ancient custom and regional tradition,

[128] The *Ordonnance criminelle*, which in fact dealt with criminal procedure, also appeared in 1670.

[129] The *Code de procédure pénale* of 1670, for example, was a logical extension of the development over the centuries of inquisitorial procedure, which had originated in Roman-canonical procedure.

[130] Guillaume de Lamoignon hoped to compile a comprehensive code of private law for promulgation by the king in a series of ordinances for the whole of France. In his compilation he made use of ordinances, case law, and above all customs, especially that of Paris. His radical unification came to nothing, although his preparatory texts, the *Arrêtés* completed around 1672, are extant. They were published as a private work in 1702 (second edition, 1783) after his death in Paris. Daguesseau was influenced by them; and the compilers of the *Code civil* were also familiar with the work.

[131] H. Regnault, *Les ordonnances civiles du Chancelier Daguesseau*, 3 vols. (Paris, 1929–65).

but also the resistance of conservative *parlements*. The political unification of France was recent in comparison with England, and in the eighteenth century still incomplete.[132]

There are several aspects to the involvement of the *parlements* in the legislative process (de Lamoignon, for example, was the first president of the Parlement de Paris), but the main one is the right of remonstrance. The *parlements*, at their head the Parlement de Paris, had the right to refuse to register new royal ordinances (that is, to inscribe the authentic text in a special register, with the legal consequence that the statute was thereby promulgated and came into force). Legal reasons for refusal had to be submitted to the king (*remontrances au roi*). The reasons might derive from divine law (which was the basis of royalty itself) or from fundamental laws of the realm, a rather vague body of customary rules which had never yet been clearly formulated and whose content seemed to be known only to the counsellors. The king then had the choice whether to accept the remonstrance and withdraw the statute or to reject the arguments of the *parlement* and ordain registration by letter of order (*lettre de jussion*). If the *parlement* persisted in its refusal, the king had a final resort to the 'couch of justice' (*lit de justice*): surrounded by his chancellor, peers and his council, he was installed on the *lit de justice* in the *parlement* and in person ordered the clerk to proceed with the registration of the statute. The frequent use of the right of remonstrance by the *parlements* (although reduced under Louis XIV) and the serious conflicts which followed seriously affected the development of French law, although more in the area of public than private law.[133]

Municipal legislators

50 Nowadays the expression 'municipal legislation' sounds contradictory: municipal authorities have the right to lay down administrative regulations about such things as traffic and highways, but legislative power in the strict sense, especially in the area of private law, is not within their competence. In an earlier period the position

[132] A distinction was drawn between the *pays d'election*, *pays d'états* and *pays d'imposition*; there were still internal customs barriers within France.

[133] S. H. Madden, 'L'idéologie constitutionnelle en France: le lit de justice', *Annales. Economies, sociétés, civilisations* 37 (1982), 32–60; S. Hanley, *The lit de justice of the kings of France: constitutional ideology in legend, ritual and discourse* (Princeton, 1983); M. P. Holt, 'The king in Parlement: the problem of the lit de justice in sixteenth-century France', *Historical Journal* 31 (1988), 507–24.

was different. In the later Middle Ages cities which gained their political independence acquired with it a legislative capacity, whose extent depended on the balance of power in that country. Where the central authorities were strong (as in England) local legislation was little more than regulatory power; but where the central authorities could assert themselves only with difficulty, and the cities were in a position of strength (as in Italy), municipal legislation was important and extensive, and might even have consequences on a European scale. In France local legislation was important in the twelfth and thirteenth centuries, during the transition from a weak monarchy and fragmented kingdom before the time of Louis VI (1108–37) to a strong monarchy and unified kingdom in the time of Philip IV the Fair (1285–1314). In the Netherlands, where the balance of power between the cities and the princes was always uncertain, municipal rules laid down by aldermen were an important element in the development of law. In Flanders in 1127 the city of Bruges obtained from the new count, William Clito, the power to 'amend' its customs. In his Great Charter, Philip of Alsace gave the great cities the right to lay down regulations under the supervision of the count, but this last restriction had already disappeared at Ypres towards 1300. An important collection of fourteenth-century legislative documents enacted by the city of Ghent is preserved; its enforcement relied on a communal system of fines.[134]

In the sixteenth century the great age of municipal legislation came to an end; the power of national monarchies and the spread of the learned law had brought it to a standstill. The cities were reduced to local subordinate administrations or were incorporated into small principalities. Custom, the *ius commune* and scholarship were the principal sources of the *Code civil*; municipal legislation was not. Yet in its heyday this legislation had had its significance for the history of European law: it was the first attempt to reform and develop law from the base of society. The content and perspective of municipal law are also interesting and quite different from that of royal legislation or the *Corpus iuris*. Within the community the policy was friendly conciliation between fellow citizens rather than repression; there, voluntary solidarity was more effective than subjection to the sovereign; it was a much more dynamic model of law than blind acceptance of the authority of ancient customs.

[134] N. de Pauw (ed.), *De voorgeboden der stad Gent in de XIVe eeuw* (Ghent, 1885).

CASE LAW

51 Case law was a source of law alongside custom, statute and scholarship, and was intimately connected with the other sources, for the origin and development of a custom is to be seen in its application by the courts; statutes (whatever some may say) cannot foresee everything, and have to be completed and interpreted by case law; while a jurisprudence which takes no interest in case law amounts to no more than an unworldly abstraction. It was often through the courts of justice, in which the legists sat and pled, that the learned law was introduced, sometimes unobserved, into practice. Owing to the case law of the Parlement de Paris, various principles of the *Coutume de Paris* came to form a French common law. And when scholarly opinion was divided, it was up to case law to determine which theory should prevail (a role which the Roman Rota often played). Not only was case law for centuries an important source of law, but for that reason it is also well documented, as the miles of archives of the European high courts of justice attest. The oldest sources of this vast judicial documentation date from around 1200 for the royal courts in England and 1250 in France. Although case law always had a role to play, its importance varied greatly from one country to another, according to the importance attached to the other sources of law. It is obvious that in the system of the Common Law, in which legislation and jurisprudence were merely secondary, case law had fundamental importance. By contrast, canon law was focused on legislation and jurisprudence and placed little weight on case law. The following is a sketch of case law from legal system to legal system and country to country.

In the classical canon law of the twelfth and thirteenth centuries, the case law of the pontifical *Curia* was eclipsed as a source of law by the decretals. When the creative energy of the decretals died out in the fourteenth century, the judgments of the supreme church court, the Roman Rota, increased in importance. The law had to develop and, when legislation was lacking, case law had the chance to take its place. During the fourteenth century court officials compiled several selections of the judgments of the Rota (*Decisiones*). Hundreds of manuscripts of these collections have been preserved, and some were printed at a very early date. Legal practice before the Rota made a major contribution to the development of the law of procedure, even in the secular courts (such as the Imperial Chamber in Germany).[135]

In England case law always occupied and still occupies an important place. From the twelfth century onwards there is an uninterrupted series of 'rolls' of the royal courts which record precedents. In legal practice, however, private anonymous collections for the use of advocates ('Year Books'[136]) were more significant. These collections, which appear from the thirteenth century, rather resemble legal journalism: they repeat the legal arguments advanced before the court, and give a vivid account of the interchanges between judges and advocates, often word for word. The Year Books report decisions in chronological order; from the fifteenth century they were reworked and were used as the basis for systematic collections ('Abridgments') which regrouped cases according to subject-matter, and which had considerable influence on the education of young lawyers.[137] The last Year Books were compiled towards the middle of the sixteenth century; their role was then taken over by the Law Reports, some of which grew into virtual commentaries.[138]

In France, too, case law was an important source of law. Authors who made use of the judgments of the Parlement de Paris and the Châtelet have been mentioned. They gathered their information by consulting the imposing series of registers covering the activities of the Parlement from the middle of the thirteenth century, and containing not only final judgments, but also interlocutors, internal discussions and even the pleadings of advocates.[139] Alongside these official sources, there were private collections compiled for the use of practitioners which contain, in addition to judgments, other sources of interest, such as notes and arguments, often borrowed from the

[135] Cf. G. Dolezalek and K. W. Nörr, 'Die Rechtsprechungssammlungen der mittelalterlichen Rota', in H. Coing (ed.), *Handbuch*, I, 849–565.

[136] From the fifteenth century, the reporters' names are sometimes known. From the reign of Henry VII (1485–1509) the Year Books were printed; a modern edition of the medieval Year Books began in the nineteenth century and is still in progress.

[137] The high point was the massive *General abridgment of law and equity*, ed. Charles Viner in 23 volumes between 1741 and 1753.

[138] E.g. the *Commentaries* of Edmund Plowden (*d.* 1585), based on the cases of the 1550s to the 1570s.

[139] M. Langlois gives a sketch of the collection in *Guide des recherches dans les fonds judiciaires de l'ancien régime* (Paris, 1958), 65–160. The judgments and appeal decisions of the county of Flanders for 1320–1521 have been edited by R. C. van Caenegem, *Les arrêts et jugés du parlement de Paris sur appels flamands conservés dans les registres du Parlement*, 2 vols. (Brussels, 1966–77; Comm. roy. anc. lois).

learned law. One such collection is the *Questiones* of Jean Lecocq, which brings together and annotates the decisions of the Parlement de Paris from 1383–98.[140] Collections of the judgments of the Parlement de Paris and the provincial *parlements* were published right through the *ancien régime*.

In principle, the task of the courts was to apply the law to actual disputes; it was for the legislator to lay down legal norms. The old courts generally kept to their judicial task. In France, however, the many *arrêts de règlement* (regulatory decisions) pronounced by the *parlements* are an exception to the rule. These decisions established general rules of law applicable to everyone, so that within the jurisdiction of the *parlement* they corresponded to a kind of legislation. They were pronounced in the course of litigation, when a new question of law arose.[141] Although they are found even in the fifteenth century, it is above all in modern times that they become important.

In the southern Netherlands case law is also to be found in the same three types of source: books of law (*rechtsboeken*) based on judgments; official series of decisions; and selections of judgments compiled and annotated by lawyers. These are some representative examples: among the medieval books of law made up essentially of judgments, the collection of the court of the Salle de Lille (from the end of the thirteenth century until the beginning of the fifteenth) is of particular interest.[142] Another important collection contains hundreds of judgments of the aldermen of Ypres for use as guidelines by their colleagues at Saint Dizier in Champagne. This city had in 1228 received the law of Ypres and for guidance turned to the aldermen of Ypres; when confronted with a new question of law,[143] they

[140] Modern edition by M. Boulet, *Questiones Johannis Galli* (Paris, 1944). From the same period there is also a collection of notes on the case law of the Parlement, gathered by an anonymous lawyer and published by Fr Olivier-Martin, 'Notes d'audience prises au parlement de Paris de 1384 à 1386 par un practicien anonyme', *Revue historique de droit français et étranger*, 4th edn, I (1922), 513–603. Cf. the edition of the *Arresta lata in parlamento* by G. Naud in *Bibliothèque de l'école des chartes* 121 (1963), 77–131.

[141] See G. Deteix, *Les arrêts de règlement du parlement de Paris* (Paris, 1930); B. Beignier, 'Les arrêts de règlement' *Droits. Revue française de théorie juridique* 9 (1989), 45–55.

[142] R. Monier (ed.), *Les lois, enquêtes et jugements des pairs du castel de Lille. Recueil des coutumes conseils et jugements du tribunal de la salle de Lille 1283–1406* (Lille, 1937).

[143] Comte Beugnot (ed.), *Les Olim ou registres des arrêts rendus par la cour du roi*, II (Paris, 1842), 718–853 (the so-called 'Tout-lieu de Saint-Dizier'); also published in L. Gilliodts-van Severen, *Coutumes des pays et comté de Flandre, quartier d'Ypres. Sources et développement de la coutume d'Ypres*, II (Brussels, 1908), 62–162 (Comm. roy. anc. lois). This series of questions and judgments extends from 1305 to 1470.

consulted them before passing sentence. The archives of the old courts of justice contain an imposing series of registers which are currently being studied. Notable among these are the archives of the Council of Flanders[144] and the Great Council of Malines.[145]

The *arrêtistes* ('case reporters') should also be mentioned. In early modern times they published collections of selected and annotated decisions. Their attention was focused principally on the decisions of the superior courts: the Great Council of Malines, the Council of Flanders, and the Council of Brabant. The titles of these collections often state that the work is made up of *decisiones*; for example, the work of Paul van Christynen (Christinaeus, *d.* 1631), advocate at the Great Council of Malines.[146] Another celebrated *arrêtiste* was Pierre Stockmans (*d.* 1671), counsellor of the Council of Brabant and author of the *Decisiones curiae Brabantiae sesquicenturia* (Brussels, 1670). This work actually consists of 150 legal essays, usually but not invariably connected with a decision of the Council of Brabant; in each essay the arguments of the parties and sometimes the reasoning of the councillors are analysed.[147]

In Germany many collections of the decisions of aldermen (*Schöffenspruchsammlungen*) were made in the Middle Ages; those of Leipzig and Magdeburg are among the best known. But in early modern times the main products of a jurisprudence which was now based on the *ius commune* were treatises and collections of opinions, and collections of case law occupied only a secondary place.[148] In Italy, from the later Middle Ages, case law paled into insignificance before

[144] The inventory of this large collection has recently been completed: J. Buntinx, *Inventaris van het archief van de raad van Vlaanderen*, 9 vols. (Brussels, 1964–79).

[145] J. T. de Smidt and E. I. Strubbe, *Chronologische lijsten van de geëxtendeerde sententiën en procesbundels (dossiers) berustende in het archief van de grote raad van Mechelen*, I, *1465–1504* (Brussels and Utrecht, 1966); J. T. de Smidt, E. I. Strubbe and J. van Rompaey, II, *1504–31* (Brussels and Utrecht, 1971); J. T. de Smidt and J. van Rompaey, III, *1531–41* (Brussels and Utrecht, 1979); J. T. de Smidt and J. van Rompaey, IV, *1541–51* (Brussels and Utrecht, 1985); two additional volumes for the period to 1580 are in preparation.

[146] *Practicarum quaestionum rerumque in supremis Belgarum curiis actarum et observatarum decisiones* (Antwerp, 1626). The work contains 1,346 judgments and essays in several volumes, following the order of Justinian's *Codex*. Christinaeus often refers to foreign collections of judgments.

[147] Cf. P. Godding, 'L'origine et l'autorité des recueils de jurisprudence dans les Pays-Bas méridionaux (XIIIe–XVIIIe siècles)', *Rapports belges au VIIIe congrès international de droit comparé* (Brussels, 1970), 1–37.

[148] H. Gehrke, *Die privatrechtliche Entscheidungsliteratur Deutschlands. Charakteristik und Bibliographie der Rechtssprechung- und Konsiliensammlungen vom 16. bis zum Beginn des 19. Jahrhunderts* (Frankfurt, 1974).

the *ius commune* and the *consilia*.[149] The absence of supreme courts of justice (a consequence of political fragmentation) was another reason why case law had little influence. In southern Italy, however, the situation was different: there a regional monarchy had established itself with its capital at Naples, and an important collection of decisions of the court of Naples was published.[150]

This short account shows that there are links between case law, legislation and jurisprudence, and that they are partly determined by political factors.[151] It is an interesting question, which will be developed in more detail later.

THE COURTS AND PROCEDURE

General considerations

52 The structure and procedure of the courts of the late Middle Ages were quite different from those of the early Middle Ages, and the modern system has retained its basic importance up to the present day. It is clear from the sources that modernization of the courts went hand in hand with that of procedure, and it is obvious that the two developments were related. But it is more difficult to say which of the developments preceded the other: were new courts created to apply new procedures, or did the new courts bring about new procedures? This (chicken-and-egg) problem can be illustrated by the example of the officialities, which were church courts created towards the end of the twelfth century. The judge was a new type of episcopal functionary, the official, who was a lawyer educated at university; the procedure of the court was Roman-canonical. It is difficult to work out what happened first: was it originally the bishops who wished to introduce specialization and delegate their own jurisdiction to a qualified clerk (who, having studied learned law, automatically applied the new canonical procedure)? Or was it the church authorities who wanted to introduce a new learned procedure (which then caused the creation of new courts and the

[149] Cf. above, section 31.

[150] The collection of the judgments of the *Sacro regio consiglio* of Naples is due to Matthaeus de Afflictis (1448–1528), and the *editio princeps* appeared as early as 1499 (the usual edition is Lyon, 1537).

[151] A general sketch of medieval sources of case law is given in P. Godding, *La jurisprudence* (Turnhout, 1973; Typologie des sources du moyen âge occidental, ed. L. Genicot, 6). For a sketch of the European collections of judgments and *consilia* in modern times, see H. Coing, *Handbuch*, II.2, 1,113–445.

appointment of new judges)? The traditional *curia episcopalis* cannot have adapted to the new system without difficulties. Although this historical problem has not yet been solved, it is at least clear that Roman-canonical procedure (and with it the first learned treatises on procedure) was established (just) before the creation of officialities.

Inevitably, one country differed from another, but the basic common trends in reform and in development of the system of courts and civil procedure can easily be identified. There is remarkable continuity between the last centuries of the Middle Ages and modern times up to the Enlightenment; in this context the traditional divide between Middle Ages and modern times around 1500 is without explanatory value. We now turn to five fundamental aspects of the history of the courts in the *ancien régime*: centralization; specialization; the movement away from democratic institutions; state control; and rationalization of the law of evidence.

Centralization

53 Centralization, which replaced the local independence of the early Middle Ages, certainly did the most to shape the court system. The decisive element in this development for both church and state was the establishment of a central court with jurisdiction over the whole of a community or principality. Several paths led to this result. Centralization was most radical in England, within the Court of Common Pleas, a central royal court which sat at Westminster. It had jurisdiction throughout the kingdom for a great number of actions at first instance, which were initiated by royal letters or writs (comparable to the Roman *actiones*). Such disputes were between free men, who all had the right to turn directly to the royal jurisdiction, and did so mostly where land rights were concerned. The emergence of a central jurisdiction under Henry II (1154–89) naturally encroached on the territory of the old feudal and seigneurial courts. This is to be explained largely by the fact that litigants had much greater confidence in the powerful royal courts. The decline of municipal courts followed, and their competence was limited to cases of little importance. It was the great strength of the kings of England, and the rapid unification of the kingdom, which made this extreme concentration of judicial activity in one central court possible. Practical inconveniences such as long journeys to Westminster were reduced by a system of circuit judges who

travelled through the country, and by the local examination of juries in the counties. An almost complete centralization has persisted in England up to the present day. Decentralization began only recently, with the creation of a system of local courts of first instance which have a jurisdiction much more extensive than that of the county courts of the nineteenth century.

In the church and in most countries, centralization was achieved by the establishment of a central court of justice, whether pontifical, royal or comital, with a limited competence at first instance (for *maiores causae*, corporations and important persons), and usually a general competence in matters of appeal. The model for these courts was the *Curia Romana* (later the *Rota Romana*) whose judicial activity from the thirteenth century onwards was particularly intensive. It was the first European court of justice, for its jurisdiction extended to legal actions from the whole of the West, from Sweden to Portugal, from Scotland to Sicily. The large number of litigants from all the countries of Latin Christendom compelled the popes to entrust many of the cases to papal judges delegate, who were charged with investigating and judging disputes in the dioceses of origin and in the name of the pope. This centralization of the church took place at the expense of local instances – bishops, archbishops, deans, archdeacons and officials – who were placed under the very strict supervision of Rome. Centralization inevitably meant a hierarchical system of justice.

So far as secular courts are concerned, the following are the main points. In France the Parlement de Paris became the supreme royal court towards the middle of the thirteenth century. It was competent at first instance for some matters and for important persons; as an appellate court its jurisdiction was general.[152] In the Netherlands councils of justice developed in different provinces: in Flanders, for example, the Audience at the beginning, and the Council of Flanders towards the end, of the fourteenth century. Under Burgundian rule, the union of Dutch provinces led to the creation of central institutions for the whole of the Burgundian Netherlands: the (itinerant) Great Council of Philip the Good gradually developed within the ducal council between 1435 and 1445; the Parlement of Malines, established there by Charles the Bold from 1473–77; the Great Council of Malines (again fixed there) from 1504 to 1794. In

[152] In later centuries the provincial *parlements* relieved the burden of the Parlement de Paris.

the German empire, the *Reichshofgericht* was replaced during the fifteenth century by the *Kammergericht* in which academic lawyers sat. On the initiative of the assemblies of Estates, the *Reichskammergericht* was created in 1495, independently of the Crown. It was intended to sustain the general movement towards unification and political reform in Germany. Originally the court was composed in equal numbers of academic lawyers and noblemen. In addition to the *Reichskammergericht*, the emperor maintained a supreme imperial council, the *Reichshofrat*.

Specialization and professionalization

54 Centralization entailed specialization among, and professionalization of, the staff of the courts. In the old feudal *curia regis*, the king had discussed the most varied matters with his great vassals. From time to time these included legal questions, although they were much less important than the political and military discussions. The vassals of the royal court were bishops, abbots, counts and dukes, who had no legal education and had acquired their experience in feudal law with age. In the new central jurisdiction the position was quite different: strict division of labour applied; the councils had specifically to ensure the administration of justice; and they were occupied full time with legal questions arising from the cases which they had to judge. These councils were fixed in one place, unlike the old *curia* which constantly followed the king on his travels.

The councillors were professional judges who, at least on the continent, had been educated at university. Later, the lower courts would also employ professional and academic judges. This general development can be seen first in the church, where the system of officialities, which developed from the end of the twelfth century, became general during the thirteenth. The officiality replaced the *curia episcopalis*, in which very varied cases had been dealt with by various (some lay) people who had no specific training. Here Roman-canonical procedure was introduced. During the first half of the twelfth century, lawyers developed a jurisprudence of procedure, based on texts from canon law and the compilations of Justinian. They ordered and commented on the elements of the canonical and Roman sources, and so formulated a coherent procedural system, whose influence over the centuries extended throughout Europe, first in the church itself (especially the officialities), and then in secular court practice. This might be either by ordinance of the sovereign or at the instigation of councillor lawyers, who modelled their own form of procedure on the learned law. The influence can be observed even in England, although not in the Common Law courts.

The *Speculum judiciale* of Guillaume Durant (first edition 1271–6, second 1289–91) offers a very detailed insight into the principles of Roman-canonical procedure. The procedure is directed by a single professional judge (or by a panel of professional judges), who both investigates and pronounces final judgment. His task therefore involves evaluating questions of fact and questions of law. The core of the procedure is the examination of witnesses or, if necessary, documentary evidence. Writing plays an important part in the procedure: the statements of witnesses are written, and a written summary of them is made available to the other party. The plaintiff initiates the litigation with a document, the *libellus*, whose main purpose is to describe his *actio*; and he presents another document containing *articuli*, that is, the allegations on which the witnesses are to be examined, and which his opponent must contest or admit. The defendant can for his part invoke various *exceptiones*. The subject-matter of the legal action was defined at *litis contestatio*, and was also set down in writing.

The law paid particular attention to the procedure for appeal, which like all other stages of procedure was regulated in detail. Examination of witnesses was secret, in order to assure them freedom of expression; broadly speaking, secrecy was characteristic of learned procedure, and the public was kept at a distance. Bureaucracy dominated the procedure, as is shown (for example) by the inquests of councillor-commissioners, whose reports were the basis for the decisions of the council.[153] The detailed rules on evidence merit their own section.[154] The diffusion of this procedural model can be followed through the late Middle Ages; there is a link between Bologna and the church courts and the Parlement de Paris, whose

[153] This characteristic became so marked that in modern times it gave rise to the expression *quod non est in actis non est in mundo* (literally 'what is not in the documents is not in the world'); the magistrates took account above all of the papers rather than the people in the case.

[154] See below, section 57.

Stylus Parlamenti inspired the procedure of the courts of justice in the Netherlands, especially the Great Council of Malines.

Movement away from democratic institutions

55 These developments had the immediate result that popular participation in the administration of justice ceased to be important. During the first centuries of the Middle Ages as well as in Germanic Antiquity, the people had taken a direct and active part in decisions; sometimes the judges had sought assistance, and the people had been asked to express agreement with, or disapproval of, the decisions proposed by the judges who had 'found' the applicable law. The procedure was completely oral and public. After the late Middle Ages this practice disappeared. It would be an exaggeration to attribute the change solely to the spread of Roman-canonical procedure, since even outside its sphere of influence the role of the people was curtailed.[155] None the less, it is clear that the example and prestige of learned procedure played a part in the decline of popular participation in the law. The people also became less and less capable of grasping the contested issues or comprehending the learned language of the courts. This alienation was exacerbated when the recruitment of magistrates was restricted to graduates, and still more by the venality of offices (that is, allocation by the Crown of seats as councillors to the highest bidder). From that time on, the magistrates formed a class of wealthy noblemen practically as exclusive as the law which they applied.

English procedure too became more esoteric. There, too, the magistracy was scarcely accessible, and legal language was unintelligible to any non-initiate, not only because of its technicality but also because the language used was not even derived from English but was a petrified form of Norman French going back to the twelfth century ('Law French'). Yet the procedure (even the civil procedure) of the Common Law did preserve one traditional institution which maintained its link with the people: the jury. Since the professional judges were obliged to explain the significance of legal principles in comprehensible terms to a jury of non-lawyers, the people were not entirely excluded from the legal system.

[155] E.g. the prohibition in the Great Charter of Philip of Alsace on contesting the judgment of a court of aldermen.

State control

56 In the course of modern times the organization of the courts was taken over by the state. Of course, other courts existed alongside the royal jurisdictions, but their competence was firmly restricted. These were the feudal and seigneurial courts, whose origins go back to the early Middle Ages, and whose jurisdiction was over vassals and the inhabitants of the great domains respectively. The jurisdiction of the feudal courts was essentially limited to law on land ownership (relating to fiefs), while that of the seigneurial courts was often restricted to cases of low justice, higher justice being administered elsewhere. These jurisdictions were also subordinate to central control by way of appeal. Even in Roman Catholic countries, the church courts lost a large part of their jurisdiction over lay people to the royal jurisdictions, while the publication of new pontifical statutes was subjected to the *placet* (approval) of the sovereign.

The municipal jurisdictions, whose competence within the walls of a city and sometimes even beyond had for centuries been total, also declined in importance; their competence was restricted and the means of appeal against their decisions extended. Yet, in spite of the superiority of the royal jurisdictions – bailiffs, seneschals (*sénéchaux*), and *parlements* – the system of courts even in the eighteenth century was not a hierarchy in the shape of a pyramid. Historical exigencies had created different networks and systems of jurisdictions, with sometimes concurrent competences. At the end of the *ancien régime* these still coexisted. The establishment of a single system was a matter for the enlightened absolutism of the eighteenth century and the French Revolution.

Rationalization of the law of evidence

57 In the early Middle Ages the law of evidence was dominated by the irrational system of ordeals. This state of affairs changed completely in the period with which we are now concerned: from the twelfth century, ordeals were abolished and progressively replaced by rational means of proof, based on critical and rational examination. This change was already apparent in the twelfth century in England, Flanders and Italy, and reached central and eastern Europe about a century later. Some residues (such as the feudal fondness for the judicial duel, and the revival of trial by water during

the witch-hunts of the sixteenth and seventeenth centuries) were still to be found at a later date, but, in general, from the thirteenth century the law of evidence in Europe employed essentially rational methods of inquiry.[156]

Roman-canonical procedure also influenced this development, but its importance must not be exaggerated. The renaissance of Roman law was not the proximate cause of the transformation. Rationalization of the law of evidence can be detected in England and Flanders from the twelfth century, and thus before Roman law penetrated into those regions, and before the church courts applied the new procedure. In England, therefore, a modern law of evidence could develop independently of Roman law based on national institutions, notably the jury. Elsewhere, where rationalization came later, it was simpler to follow the Roman-canonical method, for instance, in France in the thirteenth century. The learned law of evidence finally prevailed everywhere on the continent and became the system typical of Europe in modern times. The Common Law is the sole but important exception to this diffusion: the English system preserved the institution of the jury (and does still nowadays for criminal matters, and until recently for civil ones).

One of the most striking elements of the new procedure was the system of 'learned' or 'legal proofs'. To understand its significance, we must recall that the disappearance of the old modes of proof had created a serious gap. In the old system the irrefutable signs of Providence determined what was true or false, which party was innocent or guilty. How to replace this archaic system? By force of circumstance the judges had to rely on documents, witnesses, real evidence and so on, but it was obvious that a document could be falsified, that witnesses could contradict one another, and that evidence was sometimes unclear and misleading. Must the judges be allowed to assess the elements freely and judge on the basis of their inner conviction (as at present)? Or ought a system to be devised in which each mode of proof was assigned its own value, and in which the acceptance or refutation of various types of witnesses, and the authentication of documents, were subject to precise rules? In the

[156] Ordeals were criticized from all sides. The authorities mistrusted their ambiguousness and their potential for manipulation; the church began to see in them a challenge to God, from whom new miracles were constantly expected; the cities were against them because a merchant was inevitably at a disadvantage in a judicial duel against a knight; and the jurists were opposed to them as the *Corpus iuris* by its silence implicitly condemned them.

Common Law system the dilemma was resolved by entrusting the jury with the sovereign task of resolving questions of fact. The continent opted, on the other hand, for a system of 'learned proofs': the challenging of certain types of witness (for instance women, parents and serfs) was regulated in detail; and each element of proof (direct and circumstantial witnesses, character witnesses, real evidence, presumptions, bad reputation) was assigned a numerical probative value. In this system a full proof (*plena probatio*) corresponded to two direct corroborating witnesses. The original, and no doubt laudable, aim of this system was to safeguard the parties against any arbitrariness on the part of the judges. Jurisprudence discussing the admissibility of witnesses and the credibility of evidence certainly helped to convince magistrates of the relative value of different modes of proof. On the other hand, the system was also extremely theoretical and artificial.[157]

FACTORS

58 Without detracting from the importance of the learned lawyers, we should note some general political, intellectual and material developments which were decisive for the developments which have been described. In the first place, it must be recognized how important it was that power was concentrated in the church and in the states. The modernization of legal studies and the administration of justice fits perfectly in a policy of centralization and bureaucratization. The free cities were also in favour of a modernization of law. In the last centuries of the Middle Ages, it was these political institutions which abandoned the old feudal framework, and resolutely created new political structures.

Transformations in the law were clearly influenced by the intellectual climate in general, notably the revival of interest in ancient culture and the role of scholasticism, which attempted to combine rational criticism with faith in the absolute authority of sacred texts. Especially important was the increasingly rational character of western thought, under the influence of the works of Aristotle in

[157] Often in criminal matters it led to the use of torture: for instance when there was a single eyewitness (who counted for half proof) and a negative indication (such as running from the place of the crime, which counted for a quarter), the total was reached by declarations made under torture (worth a quarter) in order to arrive at a complete proof. G. Alessi Palazzolo, *Prova legale e pena. La crisi del sistema tra evo medio e moderno* (Naples, 1979; Storia e Diritto: studi e testi raccolti da R. Ajello e V. Piano Mortari, 6).

particular.[158] Aristotelian social analysis was a fundamental factor in the shaping of modern society. The will to understand social organization rationally and to analyse it in depth had a stimulating effect which also had a significant impact on jurisprudence.

Finally, the development of law was influenced by material factors. The revival of cities and the development of a monetary economy assured the church and the states the financial means for reorganization (salaries for magistrates and officials educated in law) and allowed them to cover the expenses of the long (not directly productive) university studies of thousands of students. The socio-economic crisis of the agrarian and feudal world caused a crisis in the legal structures and conceptions of that society. The complexity of new economic structures, which from now on had an industrial and commercial dimension, also demanded a better-adapted and more complex system of justice. In particular, commerce and the monetary system could not develop without greater contractual freedom, a better system of credit, and the liberation of landed property from feudal and family charges. These demands exceeded what the western world in the early Middle Ages could possibly supply. It could offer the interminable discussions of village leaders, and a traditional wisdom which varied from one region to another. Growth of a new economy based on rational investment and an international market now depended on a single certain system, a system that was foreseeable and predictable.

EVALUATION

59 Respect for the law, and the tireless efforts of various social groups and individuals in developing it, stand out when the old law is considered as a whole. Yet all these efforts were neither coordinated nor directed by a central authority. The old European law was the typical result of an organic and natural development, with its advantages (richness, suppleness, renewal) and its disadvantages (extreme complexity, overlapping, and lack of certainty). In that respect this period contrasts with what preceded it and what was to

[158] Cf. H. Coing, 'Zum Einfluss der Philosophie des Aristoteles auf die Entwicklung des römischen Rechts', *Zeitschrift der Savigny-Stiftung für Rechtsgeschichte* (R. A.) 69 (1952), 24–59; G. Otte, 'Die Aristotelzitate in der Glosse', *Zeitschrift der Savigny-Stiftung für Rechtsgeschichte* (R.A.) 85 (1968), 368–93; G. Otte, *Dialektik und Jurisprudenz. Untersuchungen zur Methode der Glossatoren* (Frankfurt, 1971; Ius commune Sonderhefte, 1).

follow. In the early Middle Ages the law was simple, because traditional customs dominated all legal relations. In the Enlightenment, the desire to simplify the law manifested itself in a policy of national codifications, which aimed at a uniform law set out in a clear text, certain for all. In the period we have just examined there was no true European law, although a European jurisprudence reduced the disparity between local customs and ordinances. Nor were there national codes or even (except in England) national legal systems; the position of national law, between local custom and cosmopolitan common law, was obscure and somewhat uncertain. No single legal system had a monopoly; the law was characterized by pluralism and eclecticism. Lawyers willingly drew principles and concepts from different sources of law: Roman law, canon law, custom, royal or municipal legislation, the law of the country or foreign law. Upheavals in different areas and countries led to a proliferation of authoritative sources (or so it seems to modern eyes accustomed to national legislation and a central system of justice). From modern times this proliferation was criticized; and in the eighteenth century, the tendency was reversed. In place of the old law, which was the result of organic development, the reformers advocated the introduction of codes. They were conceived as instruments of modernization and social and economic policy, and were intended to ensure clarity and legal certainty.

BIBLIOGRAPHY

60 Ahsmann, M., *Collegia en colleges. Juridisch onderwijs aan de Leidse Universiteit 1575–1630 in het bijzonder het disputeren*, Groningen, 1990; Leiden dissertation; Rechtshistorische studies, n.s. 1

Baker, J. H. (ed.), *Judicial records, law reports and the growth of case law*, Berlin, 1989; Comparative studies in continental and Anglo-American legal history, 5

Baker, J. H. and Milsom, S. F. C., *Sources of English legal history. Private law to 1750*, London, 1986

Bellomo, M., *L'Europa del diritto comune*, Lausanne, 1988

Saggio sull'università nell'età del diritto comune, Catania, 1979

Bender, P., *Die Rezeption des römischen Rechts im Urteil der deutschen Rechtswissenschaft*, Frankfurt, 1979; Rechtshistorische Reihe, 8

Bergh, G. C. J. J. van den, *The life and work of Gerard Noodt (1647–1725). Dutch legal scholarship between humanism and Enlightenment*, Oxford, 1988

Bluche, F., 'Les magistrats des cours parisiennes au XVIIIe siècle. Hiérarchie et situation sociale', *Revue historique de droit français et étranger* 52 (1974), 87–106

Caenegem, R. C. van, *The birth of the English common law*, Cambridge, 1973
'Das Recht im Mittelalter', in W. Fikentscher *et al.* (eds.), *Entstehung und Wandel rechtlicher Traditionen*, Freiburg, 1980, 609–67

Calasso, F., *Medio evo del diritto*, I: *Le fonti*, Milan, 1954

Cavanna, A., *Storia del diritto moderno in Europa. Le fonti ed il pensiero giuridico*, I Milan, 1979

Chene, C., *L'enseignement du droit français en pays de droit écrit (1679–1793)*, Geneva, 1982; Travaux d'histoire éthico-politique, XXXIX

Classen, P. 'Richterstand und Rechtswissenschaft in italienischen Kommunen des 12. Jahrhunderts', in P. Classen (ed. J. Fried), *Studium und Gesellschaft im Mittelalter*, Stuttgart, 1983; M. G. H. Schriften, 29, 27–126

Coing, H. (ed.), *Handbuch der Quellen und Literatur der neueren europäischen Privatrechtsgeschichte*, (Munich, I: *Mittelalter (1100–1500). Die gelehrten Rechte und die Gesetzgebung*, 1973; II: *Neuere Zeit (1500–1800). Das Zeitalter des gemeinen Rechts*: i: *Wissenschaft*, 1977; ii: *Gesetzgebung und Rechtsprechung*, 1976

Cortese, E., *La norma giuridica. Spunti teorici nel diritto comune classico*, Milan, 1962–4, 2 vols.

Coutumes et libertés. Actes des journées internationales de Toulouse 4–7 juin 1987, Montpellier, 1988; Recueil des mémoires et travaux publié par la Société d'histoire de droit des anciens pays de droit écrit, 14

Dekkers, R., *Het humanisme en de rechtswetenschap in de Nederlanden*, Antwerp, 1938

Elton, G. R., *English law in the sixteenth century: reform in an age of change*, London, 1979; Selden Society lecture

Engelmann, W., *Die Wiedergeburt der Rechtskultur in Italien durch die wissenschaftliche Lehre*, Leipzig, 1939

Feenstra, R., *Fata iuris romani. Etudes d'histoire du droit*, Leiden, 1974
'L'enseignement du droit à Orleans. Etat des recherches menées depuis Meijers', *Etudes néerlandaises de droit et d'histoire présentées à l'université d'Orléans pour le 750e anniversaire des enseignements juridiques*, ed. R. Feenstra and C. M. Ridderikhoff, Bulletin de la Société archéologique et historique de l'Orléanais, n.s. IX, 1985

Fowler-Magerl, L., *Ordo iudiciorum vel ordo iudiciarius. Begriff und Literaturgattung*, Frankfurt, 1984; Ius commune. Sonderhefte, 19; Repertorien zur Frühzeit der gelehrten Rechte

Fried, J., *Die Entstehung des Juristenstandes im 12. Jt. Zur sozialen Stellung und politischen Bedeutung gelehrter Juristen in Bologna und Modena*, Cologne and Vienna, 1974; Forschungen zur neueren Privatrechtsgeschichte, 21

Gilissen, J., 'Les phases de la codification et de l'homologation des coutumes dans les XVII provinces des Pays-Bas', *Revue d'histoire du droit* 18 (1950), 26–67, 239–90

Gilmore, M. P., *Humanists and jurists*, Cambridge, Mass., 1963
Godding, P., 'La formation des étudiants en droit à Louvain (fin 16e–début 17e siècle): fait-elle-place au droit coutumier et édictal de nos régions?', *Album amicorum J. Buntinx*, Louvain, 1981, 435–46
Gouron, A., *La science du droit dans le midi de la France au moyen âge*, London, 1984; Variorum reprints
Guenee, B., *Tribunaux et gens de justice dans le bailliage de Senlis à la fin du moyen âge (vers 1350–vers 1550)*, Paris, 1963
Guizzi, V., '*Il diritto comune in Francia nel XVII secolo*', *Revue d'histoire du droit* 37 (1969), 1–46
Guzman, A., *Ratio scripta*, Frankfurt, 1981; Ius commune. Sonderhefte, Texte und Monographien, 14
Hagemann, H. R., *Basler Rechtsleben im Mittelalter*, Basle, 1981–7; 2 vols.
Holthofer, E., 'Literaturtypen des mos italicus in der europäischen Rechtsliteratur der frühen Neuzeit', *Ius commune* 2 (1969), 130–66
Ius romanum medii aevi, ed. E. Genzmer, Milan, 1961–
Kan, J. van, *Les efforts de codification en France*, Paris, 1929
Kelley, D. R., *Foundations of modern historical scholarship. Language law and history in the French renaissance*, New York and London, 1970
Kisch, G., *Erasmus und die Jurisprudenz seiner Zeit. Studien zum humanistischen Rechtsdenken*, Basle, 1960
Koschaker, P., *Europa und das römische Recht*, Munich and Berlin, 1947
Legendre, P., *La pénétration du droit romain dans le droit canonique classique de Gratien à Innocent IV*, Paris, 1964
Levack, B. P., *The civil lawyers in England 1603–41. A political study*, Oxford, 1973
Luig, K., 'Institutionenlehrbücher des nationalen Rechts im 17. und 18. Jt.', *Ius commune* 3 (1970), 64–97
Maffei, D., *Gli inizi dell'umanesimo giuridico*, Milan, 1956
Martines, L., *Lawyers and statecraft in renaissance Florence*, Princeton, 1968
Meijers, E. M., *Le droit romain au moyen âge*, Leiden, 1959; Etudes d'histoire de droit, III
Milsom, S. F. C., *Historical foundations of the common law*, London, 1969
Nörr, K. W., 'Zum institutionellen Rahmen der gelehrten Rechte im 12. Jt.', *Festgabe für H. Coing*, Frankfurt, 1982, 233–44
Olivier-Martin, F., *Histoire de la coutume de la prévôté et vicomté de Paris* I; II, 1, 2, Paris, 1922–30; 3 vols.; repr. 1973 with new bibliog. by M. Boulet-Sautel
La coutume de Paris, trait d'union entre le droit romain et les législations modernes, Paris, 1925
Osler, D. J., 'Budaeus and Roman law', *Ius commune* 13 (1985), 195–212
Otte, G., 'Die Rechtswissenschaft', *Ius commune* 13 (1985), 123–42
Peach, T. 'Le droit romain en français au XVIe siècle: deux oraisons de François de Némond (1555)', *Revue historique de droit français et étranger* 60 (1982), 5–44

Pegues, F. J., *The lawyers of the last Capetians*, Princeton, 1962
Peteghem, P. van, 'De verordening van 1483 voor de Raad van Vlaanderen herzien', *Album amicorum J. Buntinx*, Louvain, 1981, 341–50
Petitjean, M., 'La coutume de Bourgogne. Des coutumiers officieux à la coutume officielle', *Mémoires de la Société pour l'histoire du droit et des institutions des anciens pays bourguignons, comtois et romands* 42 (1985), 13–20
Pissard, H., *Essai sur la connaissance et la preuve des coutumes*, Paris, 1910
Plucknett, T. F. T., *Legislation of Edward I*, Oxford, 1949
Poly, J.-P., 'Coheredes legum romanarum. La renaissance du droit romain dans le midi de la France', *Historia del derecho privado. Trabajos en homenaje a F. Valls i Taberner*, x, Barcelona, 1989, 2,909–46
Ranieri, F., 'Die Inanspruchnahme des Reichskammergerichts in den ersten Jahrzehnten seiner Tätigkeit. Versuch einer sozialgeschichtlichen Analyse der Reichsjustiz zur Zeit der Rezeption', *Zeitschrift für neuere Rechtsgeschichte* 4 (1982), 113–34
Recht und Gesellschaft im Zeitalter der Rezeption. Eine rechts- und sozialgeschichtliche Analyse der Tätigkeit des Reichskammergerichts im 16. Jt., Cologne and Graz, 1985; 2 vols., Quellen und Forschungen zur höchsten Gerichtsbarkeit im alten Reich, 17/I–II
Richardson, H. G. and Sayles, G. O., *Law and legislation from Aethelberht to Magna Carta*, Edinburgh, 1966
Ridderikhoff, C. M., *Jean Pyrrhus d'Anglebermes. Rechtswetenschap en humanisme aan de Universiteit van Orleans in het begin van de 16de eeuw*, Leiden, 1981; dissertation
Ridder-Symoens, H. de, 'De universitaire vorming van de Brabantse stadsmagistraat en stadsfunktionarissen. Leuven en Antwerpen 1430–1580', *Verslagboek vijfde colloquium De Brabantse Stad*, 's-Hertogenbosch, 1978, 21–124
Rigaudiere, A. 'L'essor des conseillers juridiques des villes dans la France du bas moyen âge' *Revue historique de droit français et étranger* 62 (1984), 361–90
Rompaey, J. van, 'Hofraad en Grote Raad in de hofordonnantie van 1-1-1469', *Album amicorum J. Buntinx*, Louvain, 1981, 303–24
Schepper, H. C. C. de, 'Rechter en administratie in de Nederlanden tijdens de zestiende eeuw', *Album amicorum J. Buntinx*, Louvain, 1981, 369–90
(ed.), *Höchste Gerichtsbarkeit im Spätmittelalter und der frühen Neuzeit. Internationales rechtshistorisches Symposium 1984*, Amsterdam, 1984; Verzamelen en bewerken van de jurisprudentie van de Grote Raad, ed. J. T. de Smidt, n.s. 9
Schott, C., 'Wir Eidgenossen fragen nicht nach Bartele und Baldele', *Festkolloquium H. Thieme*, Sigmaringen, 1983, 17–45
Schrage, E. J. H. (ed.), *Das römische Recht im Mittelalter*, Darmstadt, 1987; Wege der Forschung, 635; repr. arts. by Genzmer, Seckel, Kantorowicz, and up-to-date bibliog. on Roman law 1100–1500 by R. Feenstra

Smidt, J. T. de, 'Een verloren zaak -Grote Raad 8-5-1481', *Album amicorum J. Buntinx*, Louvain, 1981, 325–41
Smith, J. A. C., *Medieval law teachers and writers, civilian and canonist*, Ottawa, 1975
Stein, P., 'Legal humanism and legal science', *Revue d'histoire du droit* 54 (1986), 297–306
Timbal, P.-C., *Les obligations contractuelles dans le droit français des XIIIe et XIVe siècles d'après la jurisprudence du Parlement*, Paris, 1973–7; 2 vols., Centre d'étude d'histoire juridique
Troje, H. E., *Graeca leguntur. Die Aneignung des byzantinischen Rechts und die Entstehung eines humanistischen Corpus iuris civilis in der Jurisprudenz des 16. Jahrhunderts*, Cologne, 1971
Trusen, W., *Anfänge des gelehrten Rechts in Deutschland*, Wiesbaden, 1962
'Zur Geschichte des mittelalterlichen Notariats. Ein Bericht über Ergebnisse und Probleme neuerer Forschung', *Zeitschrift der Savigny-Stiftung für Rechtsgeschichte* (R. A.) 98 (1981), 369–81
Typologie des sources du moyen âge occidental, ed. L. Genicot, comprises several fascicles on the history of medieval private law:

Dievoet, G. van, *Les coutumiers, les styles, les formulaires et les 'artes notariae'*, 1986
Fransen, G., *Les décrétales et les collections de décrétales*, Turnhout, 1972
Les collections canoniques, 1973
Genicot, L., *Les actes publics*, 1972
La loi, 1977
Gilissen, J., *La coutume*, 1982
Godding, P., *La jurisprudence*, 1973

Ullmann, W., *The medieval idea of law as represented by Lucas de Penna. A study in fourteenth-century legal scholarship*, London, 1946
Vanderlinden, J., *Le concept de code en Europe occidentale du XIIIe au XIXe siècle. Essai de définition*, Brussels, 1967
Vinogradoff, P., *Roman law in medieval Europe*, Oxford, 1929; 2nd edn by F. de Zulueta
Vleeschouwers-van Melkebeek, M., *De officialiteit van Doornik. Oorsprong en vroege ontwikkeling (1192–1300)*, Brussels, 1985; Koninklijke Academie voor Wetenschappen, Verhandelingen klasse Letteren 47 nr. 117
Documenten uit de praktijk van de gedingbeslissende rechtspraak van de officialiteit van Doornik. Oorsprong en vroege ontwikkeling (1192–1300), Brussels, 1985; Koninklijke Academie voor Wetenschappen, Wetenschappelijk Comite voor Rechtsgeschiedenis, iuris scripta historica, 1
Vocht, H. de, *History of the foundation and rise of the Collegium trilingue Lovaniense 1517–50*, Louvain, 1951–5; 4 vols.
Waelkens, L., *La théorie de la coutume chez Jacques de Révigny. Edition et analyse de sa répétition sur la loi de quibus (D. 1.3.32)*, Leiden, 1984; thesis

Weigand, R., 'Romanisierungstendenzen im frühen kanonischen Recht', *Zeitschrift der Savigny-Stiftung für Rechtsgeschichte* (K. A.) 69 (1983), 200–49

Weimar, P. (ed.), *Die Renaissance der Wissenschaften im 12. Jahrhundert*, Zurich, 1981; Zürcher Hochschulforum, 2

Wieacker, F., *Privatrechtsgeschichte der Neuzeit unter besonderer Berücksichtigung der deutschen Entwicklung*, 2nd edn, Göttingen, 1976

Wiegand, W., *Studien zur Rechtsanwendungslehre der Rezeptionszeit*, Ebelsbach, 1977

Wijffels, A., 'Einflüsse der Doktrin auf die gerichtliche Argumentationspraxis in der frühen Neuzeit', *Akten des 26. deutschen Rechtshistorikertages*, Frankfurt, 1987, 371–86

'Grosser Rat von Mecheln und Hof von Holland. Zasiuszitate in den Prozessakten von 1538–71', *Ius commune* 12 (1984), 39–56

Les allégations du droit savant dans les dossiers du Grand Conseil de Malines (causes septentrionales, c. 1460–1580), Leiden, 1985; 2 vols., Rechtshistorische studies, 11

Yver, J., 'Le président Thibault Baillet et la rédaction des coutumes (1496–1514)', *Revue historique de droit français et étranger* 64 (1986), 19–42

'La rédaction officielle de la coutume de Normandie (Rouen 1583). Son esprit', *Annales de Normandie* 36 (1986), 3–36

Zorzoli, M. C., *Università dottori giureconsulti. L'organizzazione della 'facoltà legale' di Pavia nell' età Spagnola*, Padua, 1986; Publ. Univ. Pavia. Studi nelle scienze giuridiche e soziali, n.s. 46

CHAPTER 4

Enlightenment, natural law and the modern codes: from the mid-eighteenth to the early nineteenth centuries

CHARACTERISTICS

61 This short period was exceptionally important. It saw the abolition of old legal traditions, the short-lived triumph of natural law, and the more lasting emergence of a belief in codes. The period began around the middle of the eighteenth century, when criticism of Roman law and the rise of natural law began to be reflected in important codifications. By the beginning of the nineteenth century it had already ended; natural law had lost its power to inspire, and was overshadowed by positivism and the Historical School of law. None the less the legacy of this relatively brief period was lasting: faith in codes persists (albeit less fervently) to this day, and their practical importance is still considerable. In the space of a few decades, concepts and institutions which had taken shape gradually over the centuries were abolished and replaced. This was the result of a policy guided by new principles and new structures, some of which are still employed.

THE ENLIGHTENMENT

62 The renewal of the law has to be seen in the context of the Enlightenment, a European-wide movement which took a critical attitude towards the ideas and the society of the *ancien régime* in general. There was criticism especially of the following points. First, of inequality before the law, which was entrenched by the political system of Estates, with its fiscal privileges for the orders of nobility and clergy, and limited access to public office. Second, of the restraints on people and property: serfdom still existed, while various feudal and corporatist restrictions dampened down economic activity. 'Liberty' and 'equality' were therefore essential demands as

much in the political programmes of enlightened despots[1] as in the French Revolution. Third, there was criticism of unpredictable and arbitrary intervention by the Crown, and the exclusion of popular participation (in particular by the Third Estate) in political affairs. Next, there was criticism of the predominance of the church and of the religious intolerance which many considered a relic of an obsolete past. Christian revelation, through the divergent interpretations of its doctrine, had plunged Europe into religious wars, and its absolute authority was now fiercely contested. The hope – in the spirit of the Enlightenment – was that logic and science would form the new foundation of a secure learning throughout civilized Europe.

Official links between church and state were criticized. They meant that the order and government of society were subordinated to transcendental values and priorities. The new theories affirmed that the life of a society ought not to be divorced from reality, but to tend to assure the greatest (worldly) good of the greatest number of citizens. The inhumane character of many aspects of public life was criticized. Criminal law provided for the infliction of appalling capital and corporal punishments and mutilations; criminal procedure still made use of torture: these were the particular object of criticism. Argument from authority, which had dominated thinking for centuries, was now rejected. Previously an absolute value had been attributed to sacred books in different areas – religion, learning, law. The conviction was that what was old was therefore good and respectable. Now the belief was in the need for freedom from the past in order to assure a better future. Faith in progress now replaced faith in tradition.

To sum up: the old world underwent a radical renewal, which was guided by the principles of human reason and by the aim of achieving the happiness of man. The achievement of this aim now seemed to demand that the burden of preceding centuries be cast down. Applied to law, this programme meant that the proliferation of legal rules must be sharply reduced, that the gradual development of law ought to be replaced with a plan of reform and a systematic approach, and finally that absolute authority ought to be claimed

[1] This is stated expressly (e.g.) in the *Allgemeines Bürgerliches Gesetzbuch* (*ABGB*) of Joseph II from 1786 (this is the first part, known as the *Josephinisches Gesetzbuch*, of the Austrian *ABGB*: see below).

neither for traditional values such as Roman law, nor by the learned lawyers and judges who had appointed themselves 'oracles' of the law.[2] Old customs and books of authority must be replaced by new law freely conceived by modern man, and whose sole directing principle was reason. This new law would be free of all obscurantism. It would constitute a clear and certain system, comprehensible to the people, for the law from now on would also be at the service of the people. To realize this objective two conditions had to be fulfilled. The first was material: the creation of a new legal system based on a new body of sources; the second was formal: a new technique must be developed to ensure that the new law was applied in practice. The first condition was fulfilled by natural law, the second by legislation, and in particular by the national codes introduced throughout the European continent. These two aspects now demand more detailed examination.

NATURAL LAW

63 The idea of a law based on human nature is very ancient, and appears in two forms. In ancient Greece, natural law was the body of ideal unwritten norms, as opposed to the actual and very imperfect statutes of everyday life. In Rome, positive law was presented as a distortion of a primitive natural order: slavery therefore did not belong to natural law but to the *ius gentium*, as it was the consequence of wars. For the Romans, natural law corresponded to the law of nature: the coupling of animals and the marriage of human beings, for example, expressed a universal law to which men as well as animals were subject. In the Christian Middle Ages natural law had religious connotations and was identified with a divine law distinct from human laws (and which those laws could not transgress). Yet, on the other hand, many lawyers were convinced that natural law, conceived as a perfect and eternal guiding principle, was identical with Roman law, with *ratio scripta* ('written reason'). Other lawyers disagreed. They regarded the *Corpus iuris*, like other legal systems, merely as a historical product without eternal value, imperfect and capable of improvement.

So in modern times a new conception of natural law was formed.

[2] The expression is taken from J. P. Dawson, *The oracles of the law* (Michigan, 1968). It is to be found in older authors too, such as Blackstone (see below, section 68).

It still made reference to the nature of man and society, but it differed from the earlier conceptions in several respects. It rejected the conception of natural law as an ideal of justice with a significance greater than the positive legal order. On the contrary, it conceived natural law as a body of basic principles from which positive law ought to be directly derived: it was an applied natural law. The modern School of Natural Law refused to derive its principles from external systems such as divine law or the *Corpus iuris*. By means of rational study and criticism of human nature, the authors of this school searched for the self-evident and axiomatic principles from which they could deduce all other rules *more geometrico*. The title 'law of reason' (*Vernunftrecht*) is therefore more accurate than 'natural law', which has other connotations.

The first great exponent of the modern School of Natural Law was Hugo Grotius (*d.* 1645), author of *Mare liberum* (1609) and *De iure belli ac pacis libri tres* (1623). In these works Grotius attempted to find a foundation of the law of nations which would be universally recognized. He discovered it in the indispensable notion of natural law: certain basic rules had necessarily to be accepted by all men and civilized states, for those rules corresponded to principles of human nature and therefore constituted the common base shared by all men. These rules existed independently of *ius divinum* (divine law), for they were valid even if it were admitted that God did not exist. This argument enabled Grotius to defeat his religious opponents, because natural law could unite Catholics, protestants and even the devotees of a 'natural religion'. These rules were also independent of Roman law (Grotius sharply distinguished this system from Roman law) for the *Corpus iuris* recognized only the universal authority of the emperor and so could not supply the basis needed to regulate relations between sovereign states. Furthermore, these rules were independent of any legislator, for no supra-national authority could now claim to impose positive norms of law on the states of modern Europe. This formulation of the principles of a law of nations based on human wisdom and understanding already made Grotius a member of the School of Natural Law (although in the area of private law it was later authors who would develop his ideas).[3] He

[3] Grotius nonetheless did pay attention to theories of private law, in particular in property, obligations and marriage (see below, section 72).

cannot, however, be considered a true philosopher of natural law, for he was still influenced by such sources as the Bible, and various ancient texts (as a humanist he had an excellent knowledge of Latin literature), including the texts of Roman law.[4]

A decisive step was taken by Samuel Pufendorf (*d.* 1694). A chair of natural law and the law of nations was created for him at Heidelberg. Pufendorf wrote *De iure naturae et gentium libri VIII* (1672), of which he also published an abbreviated version, *De officio hominis et civis iuxta legem naturalem libri II* (1673). In these works he expounded a system which was rational and independent of all religious dogma, and which was based on deduction and observation. His works plainly show the influence of contemporary scientific thought, particularly that of Descartes and Galileo: it is necessary to set out from self-evident truths and to proceed by rigorous scientific observation. Pufendorf's general theory exerted a very powerful influence on the General Parts (*Allgemeine Teile*) which are characteristic of the modern European codes. He developed his theories above all in relation to contract and property, often taking up and building on the work of Grotius.

Christian Thomasius (*d.* 1728), a pupil of Pufendorf, continued the work of his teacher and developed his theories in a pragmatic direction, so that they could be put into practice by the legislator. He had already shown his practical sense at Leipzig, where he was the first to abandon teaching in Latin for German. He was entrusted with some of the work preparatory to Prussian legislation. Thomasius published the *Fundamenta juris naturae et gentium* (1705) whose title again asserts the link between natural law and the law of nations. He was also the author of popular works which argued that the law must be modernized. In these he criticized obscurantism, and the inhumanity of judicial torture and witch-hunts.[5] He pronounced himself resolutely in favour of new, rational legislation freed from the absolute authority of ancient (particularly Roman) law.

Christian Wolff (*d.* 1754) was a polymath who taught, among other things, philosophy, theology and mathematics. His main legal

[4] Not until the eighteenth century did respect for Roman law decline and even turn to open criticism. Leibniz (*d.* 1716), for instance, still treated the *Corpus iuris* as the basis for his projects of codification.

[5] *Dissertatio de tortura e foris christianis proscribenda* (1705); *Dissertatio de crimine magiae* (1701).

work was entitled *Jus naturae methodo scientifica pertractatum* (8 volumes, published between 1740 and 1748). The title declares a programme, for Wolff had already advanced the view that the principles of law must be established by modern scientific method.[6] It is characteristic of Wolff's work that axioms of natural law are elaborated by means of detailed concrete examples, and that scientific method is used to deduce all rules of law strictly according to the principles of geometric proof (Spinoza had provided the model for this). As the author himself put it in 1754, 'all obligations are deduced from human nature in a universal system'.[7] It was Wolff's work which served as the point of orientation for later authors of the School of Natural Law. It was his method which influenced the judgments of courts into employing logical deduction from fundamental norms and general concepts, rather than the example of precedents. The practice of law in continental Europe today is still shaped by Wolff's conception of law as a discipline and as a closed logical system.[8]

The work of these German lawyers was known throughout Europe. Their works were regarded as authoritative particularly in France, although the School of Natural Law produced few French authors. The most important was Jean Domat (*d.* 1696), nephew of the philosopher, mathematician and physician Pascal. His work is an ambitious attempt to structure the law according to Christian principles as well as rational criteria, and so to achieve a system valid for all time and all peoples. In fact his work *Les lois civiles dans leur ordre naturel* was original in form (a new organization and new system) but not in substance, for the substance remained that of Roman law, although the order was different from that of the *Corpus*.[9] Broadly speaking, the authors of the School of Natural Law borrowed from the principles of Roman law whenever they needed to formulate concrete rules for specific questions.[10] Their intention was not to reject the traditional rules of law as a whole. That would hardly have been realistic. It was instead to modernize

6 An abridged version, *Institutiones juris naturae et gentium*, appeared in 1750 and was translated into German in 1754.

7 Cited by Wieacker, *Privatrechtsgeschichte*, 319–20.

8 Especially in Germany, where the expression *Begriffsjurisprudenz* was actually used in the nineteenth century.

9 M. F. Renoux-Zagame, 'Domat, le salut et le droit', *Revue d'histoire des facultés de droit et de la science juridique* 8 (1989), 69–111.

10 See below, section 71.

legal method and to free jurisprudence from the restrictions imposed by ancient authority.

Montesquieu's *Esprit des lois* was not a treatise on natural law, but a philosphical and comparative study of the role of legislation and types of public institutions. Montesquieu attached particular importance to national character, and to climate and geography as factors determining the diversity of legal systems.

In the Republic of the United Provinces there were also lawyers who reacted against the absolute authority of the *Corpus iuris*. Their concern was largely with the contradictions and excessive subtleties of the civilians, and with the consequent lack of legal clarity and security: there was no longer a Roman legislator in a position to promulgate binding norms, and even the *communis opinio* of scholars (so far as it existed) had no binding force. Thus, Willem Schorer (*d.* 1800), who was in favour of a codification of the law of the provinces of the Netherlands, and wrote annotations to, and produced a new edition of, Grotius' *Inleidinghe*, made violent criticisms of the traditional learning of Roman law, especially in his treatise 'on the absurdity of our current system of legal doctrine and practice' (1777), which caused an animated controversy.[11] The jurist himself, who was president of the Council of Flanders at Middelburg in Zeeland, did not mince his words: according to him, Roman law was packed with 'insipid subtleties, unwarranted cavillations and useless fictions'; its sources were 'a *corpus ineptiarum*, commonly known as a *corpus iuris*'; and the author regretted that the 'written law', which he described as a wandering star, had struck Europe like a bolt from the blue.[12]

In the Austrian Netherlands a typical representative of the law of the Enlightenment was Goswin de Fierlant (*d.* 1804), who campaigned in particular for a more humane criminal law. J. B. C. Verlooy (*d.* 1797) should also be mentioned among the partisans of the Enlightenment and social progress (which led him to collaborate with the French occupying forces), although he was first and foremost a specialist in old Brabancon law.[13]

[11] *Vertoog over de ongerijmdheid van het samenstel onzer hedendaagsche regtsgeleerdheid en praktijk.*

[12] L. P. van de Spiegel, *Verhandeling over den oorsprong en de historie der Vaderlandsche Rechten* (Goes, 1769), and H. Cohen Jehoram, *Over codificatie. Van Portalis tot na Meijers* (Deventer, 1968), 2.

[13] See Jan van den Broeck, *J. B. C. Verlooy, vooruitstrevend jurist en politicus uit de 18e eeuw* (Antwerp and Amsterdam, 1980).

THE CODES OF THE ENLIGHTENMENT

64 Legislation, and national codes in particular, were the means of putting the conceptions of the law of reason into practice.[14] Two different political regimes were responsible for promulgating modern codes: government by enlightened despots, and the French Revolution. For the first, modernization was the deliberate policy of emperors, kings, and high officials won over to new ideas. From time to time their policy of modernization came up against the conservatism of the people, and prevailed only through the efforts of a cultivated and progressive official elite. In the Austrian Netherlands, the rational reforms of Joseph II actually provoked a national conservative uprising, known as the Brabançon Revolution. Policies of modernization were conducted in Germany, Austria, Tuscany, in Naples, Russia, Portugal, and in the Scandinavian countries, as well as in the southern Netherlands. Yet in France the Enlightenment produced philosophers, but it did not produce any enlightened kings. There it was a revolutionary people which broke with the *ancien régime*, and it was with popular support that modern ideas were imposed. In either case the result was the same: the promulgation of great codes composed by small groups of eminent lawyers. They would dominate the middle-class society of the nineteenth century.[15]

Like Pope Gregory VII in the eleventh century, the modern reformers counted on legislation to achieve their political ends; and they were hostile to rival sources of law, such as custom and case law. In their view the public good depended entirely on codes, and reliance on custom betrayed a lack of confidence in social progress. Judges, they believed, ought not to compete with the legislator, and ought not to apply statutes restrictively on the pretext of respecting fundamental unwritten principles. The role of the judge was deliberately reduced to acting as the 'mouth of the law'. Otherwise all efforts at codification would have been in vain; and the aim of legal certainty would have been endangered by judges making decisions

[14] Case law played a very small part, since the courts followed a very conservative line. As we shall see (section 65), the role of universities was also limited.

[15] This is clear for the codes of absolutism, although the people were sometimes consulted, but also for the *Code civil* of 1804. It was the work of a general who had dictatorial power, and a small group of experienced and learned lawyers; institutions representative of the nation had no real opportunity to contribute or participate in its composition.

according to personal convictions.[16] Competition from jurisprudence was also not tolerated: there must be an end to subtleties and quibbles, which could only confuse the perfect clarity of the codes and make them, in the end, incomprehensible to the citizens. Emperors and kings were happy to pronounce prohibitions on commentaries on the codes, or other restrictive measures. Legislation, on the other hand, was elevated to the rank of 'science'.[17]

The first important code of the period was the *Codex Bavaricus civilis* of the Elector Max Joseph III of Bavaria, which was promulgated in German in 1756. It was the work of W. A. von Kreittmayr (*d.* 1790), who had studied in Germany and the Netherlands and had practised in the imperial chamber of justice. The Bavarian code was a substantial codification, but still followed the tradition of according a supplementary role to the *ius commune*. Codifications in Prussia and Austria went further: every disposition outside the codes was abrogated, and conversely judges could not refuse to apply new dispositions on the ground that they had not previously been in force. (This was stated expressly in the letters patent which ordered the publication in 1721 of a revised version of the old Prussian law, entitled *Verbessertes Landrecht des Königreiches Preussen.*)

In 1738 Frederick William I had ordered the preparation of a general book of laws for Prussia. It was to be based on Roman law (*Allgemeines Gesetzbuch gegründet auf das römische Recht*). In 1746, however, Samuel von Cocceji (*d.* 1755) was entrusted by Frederick II the Great, a friend of Voltaire, with compiling 'a general codification of German law based solely on reason and on national laws' (*bloss auf die Vernunfft und Landesverfassungen gegründetes Teutsches Allgemeines Landrecht*). This was a fundamental change of direction, as is confirmed by a pejorative reference to 'uncertain Latin-Roman law' and by an express prohibition on all commentaries, in order to prevent any interpretation by professors or advocates.[18] Cocceji was

[16] Francis Bacon (*d.* 1626), who in the early seventeenth century had declared himself in favour of a codification of English law, foresaw that the judge must not become a legislator, for *si iudex transiret in legislatorem, omnia ex arbitrio penderent* (quoted in *Handwörterbuch zur deutschen Rechtsgeschichte* II, col. 915). The famous expression 'mouth of the law' is from Montesquieu's *Esprit des lois* XI.6: 'the judges of the nation are merely the mouth which pronounces the words of the law, inanimate beings who cannot moderate either its force or rigour'.

[17] G. Filangieri, *La scienza della legislazione* (Florence, 1764; French trans., Paris, 1821).

[18] In the *Vorrede* (foreword) to the project of the *Corpus Juris Fridericiani* of 1749–51 entrusted to Cocceji, it is stated that 'all doubtful points of law which arise in Roman law or have been found by the doctors' must be decided once and for all, and a *Jus certum et universale* must be promulgated for all Crown provinces.

unable to fulfil his task,[19] but his work was continued by J. H. C. von Carmer (*d.* 1801) and C. G. Svarez (*d.* 1796), lawyers whose views were still closer to natural law and all the more remote from Roman law. Their labours finally culminated in the promulgation of the Prussian *Allgemeine Landrecht* in 1794. This massive and exhaustive code covered not only civil law, but also commercial and public law, church law, and criminal and feudal law. The code went into (or lost itself in) cases in extraordinary detail, in the vain hope of foreseeing and regulating all possible cases. Every extension or even interpretation of law by precedent, commentary or learned distinction was forbidden; in case of doubt clarification was to be sought from an official *Gesetzcommission* (legislative commission). The influence of Wolff, and through him Pufendorf, on the system of this code is obvious.

In Habsburg territory, important and progressive work towards codification was able to commence, since the Empress Maria Theresa and in particular her son Joseph II (a true reformer) were favourable towards the Enlightenment. A commission was appointed in 1753 to produce a draft based on common law (in order to correct and supplement it) and on the law of reason. The draft was completed in 1766 but was rejected by the Council of State, which thought it had its merits as a collection of rules, but that it was incomprehensible and too vast to be used as a code (it consisted of eight folio volumes). A new text was to be drawn up which was to aim at simplicity and natural equity; it was not to be a textbook, but concise, clear, free from the absolute authority of Roman law, and based on natural law. The first part of this code was promulgated under Joseph II in 1786 (*Josephinisches Gesetzbuch*), but it was not until 1806 that F. von Zeiller (*d.* 1828), a professor of natural law and one of the leading figures of the Austrian *Aufklärung*, completed the project. The *Allgemeines Bürgerliches Gesetzbuch* was therefore promulgated in 1811, initially for the old hereditary German lands of the Habsburg empire, and later for other lands under their rule. It was of course more modern than the Prussian code, which, for example, still attached much importance to the inequality of subjects before the law, and which still respected in full the privileges of the nobility. The Austrian code excluded all existing

[19] Only a fragment, known as the 'Projekt des Corpus Juris Fridericianum' was completed and published in 1749, according to Cocceji a *jus naturae privatum*.

and even future customary law (art. 10). Analogy or, failing that, natural principles were to be used to fill potential gaps.

The Prussian and Austrian codes remained in force for a long period. Only in 1900 was the former replaced, by the *Bürgerliches Gesetzbuch*; the Austrian Code, with the exception of some pandectist modifications in 1914–16, remains in force to the present day. Each of these codes subjected different peoples to a uniform law: the political aim was to promote the cohesion of the scattered, disparate territories united under the Crowns of the king of Prussia and the Austrian emperors.

The circumstances of the codification of French law have already been outlined. During the years of intermediate law, codes were not the work of enlightened sovereigns but expressed the will of a revolutionary people. Yet the contrast between legal development under monarchic and under revolutionary regimes should not be exaggerated. The codes of intermediate law got no further than drafts; and the Napoleonic codes reflect above all the political will of a powerful statesman and the work of educated, philosophically cultivated legal officials. They belonged to just the same social classes as the professors, magistrates and officials who were members of the codification commissions in Prussia and Austria.

FACTORS

65 The codification movement was carried along by strong social currents. First, there was the political factor. Sovereigns regarded the promulgation of national codes as an essential component of their policies of unification. The principle 'one state, one code' fitted perfectly with such policies. This was particularly clear in the case of the Danubian monarchy, which ruled a state made up of heterogeneous ethnic groups; but in France too the 'single and indivisible Republic' had every interest in establishing a single code for the whole country. The nationalization of law was at the expense both of the cosmopolitan *ius commune* and of particular local customs.

National codifications have had their place in a general evolution of law since the Middle Ages: the universal authority of the pope and the emperor was now replaced by the sovereignty of nation states which, large or small, set out their own legal order in national codes. Countries whose political unity came late were also the last to acquire their national codes: Italy acquired its *Codice civile* only in

1865, and Germany its *BGB* in 1900. National governments hoped that national codes would give them firm control on legal development: that had always been obscure and elusive, but central authorities were now in a position to take charge. The new legal order spelt the end for the diverse sources of law as well as for the various jurisdictions (the special competence of the church courts, for instance, which had been recognized in certain cases by the secular authorities).

Another significant political development was that the task of the state was now regarded as being to ensure the common good of its citizens, not the glory of God, the protection of the church or the power of dynasties. In countries governed by enlightened despots, this task was reserved to the sovereign (hence the adage 'everything for the people, nothing by the people'). This conception stands out particularly clearly in the *Josephinisches Gesetzbuch* of 1786 (I.1): 'Every subject expects that his sovereign will assure him security and protection. It is thus the duty of the sovereign to lay down the rights of his subjects clearly, and to order their actions for the sake of the common and the individual good.' So in Germanic lands the citizens were the product of the law, whereas in France the law was the product of the citizens, for there the law derived not from a sovereign but from the *volonté générale* ('common will').[20] The authorities now had the political will to give the people the rights which it had lost through the intervention of learned lawyers and their proclivity for treating legal affairs *in camera*.

Economic considerations also played an important part. Modern codes responded to the demands of a confident and enterprising middle class: demands such as individual freedom and responsibility, the abolition of feudal barriers and discrimination (restrictions on alienation of land, corporatism, privileges of the 'orders', mortmain). The economic premisses of some legal arguments can also be easily identified. So, for instance, Holland in the seventeenth century was a small nation whose prosperity depended above all on commerce with overseas countries. It was no coincidence, then, if Grotius concluded that freedom of the seas was a principle of natural law.[21]

[20] 'La loi est l'expression de la volonté générale': *Déclaration des droits de l'homme et du citoyen* of 1789, repeated in art. 6 of the Constitution of 1791. See also t. III art. 2 of this Constitution, 'The State, from which alone all powers derive, cannot exercise them by delegation' and art. 3 'There is no authority in France above that of the law.'

[21] Grotius was prompted to write his *Mare liberum* (1609) by Spanish and Portuguese claims to a monopoly of colonial commerce. Portugal was from 1581 to 1640 a dependency of Spain.

John Selden (*d.* 1654), an English lawyer at a time when England was beginning to assert its maritime hegemony, defended the opposite thesis in his *Mare clausum* of 1653. This was two years after Cromwell's Act of Navigation, which restricted commercial traffic to England to the English fleet. Another example is the abundant legislation on land and mortgages which was introduced at the instance of the Third Estate during the first years of the French Revolution, and aimed to free feudal and church land and so permit its use within the system of credit.[22] It would, however, be inaccurate to suggest a direct link between the great French codes and the Industrial Revolution, since that reached the continent long after the first attempts at codification, and even after the codes had already been promulgated. None the less, the law of these modern codifications proved itself to be perfectly adapted to the needs of the capitalist, middle-class economy of the nineteenth century.

Finally, it is worth noting the importance of intellectual factors. The philosophy of the Enlightenment rejected old dogmas and traditions (especially religious ones) and placed man and his well-being at the centre of its concerns. The change of attitude was partly caused by the influence of modern science: its new conception of a universe dominated by measurable elements, and laws of physics which could be logically proved, had replaced the old cosmology with its spirits and celestial circles. The eighteenth-century method of natural law is characterized by precise and exact deduction from set axioms, just like mathematics. The approach was clearly inspired by Descartes's *Discours de la méthode* (1637), the *Philosophiae naturalis principia mathematica* of Newton (1687) and Spinoza's *Ethica more geometrico demonstrata* (published posthumously in 1677).[23] According to the new conceptions, man and society were part of an intelligible universe ruled by the laws of nature. The idea of a being created in the image of God and placed above nature was now excluded from scientific discourse.

The universities played only a secondary role in this period,

[22] In the Decree of 5–12 June 1791, art. 1 of the *Code rural*, t.1 s.1 states that 'the territory of France in its entire extent is free like the people who inhabit it'. See the volume *La Révolution et la propriété foncière* (Paris, 1958) in M. Garaud, *Histoire générale du droit privé français* (from 1789 to 1804).

[23] D. von Stephanitz, *Exakte Wissenschaft und Recht. Der Einfluss von Naturwissenschaft und Mathematik auf Rechtsdenken und Rechtswissenschaft in zweieinhalb Jahrtausenden. Ein historischer Grundriss* (Berlin, 1970; Münsterische Beiträge zur Rechts- und Staatswissenschaft, 15), 52–100, 120–33.

except in Germany, where some were specially founded in the spirit of the *Aufklärung* (Halle in 1694, Göttingen in 1737), and where natural law was taught with enthusiasm. In France in particular the faculties of law made virtually no contribution to the legal developments of the eighteenth century. Of course, some lawyers knew the doctrines of Pufendorf, Thomasius and Wolff, and some professors exerted a considerable influence on the codification, but the decline of the universities continued. The case of Orléans is typical: one of the most influential jurists of the time, Pothier, taught there; but the university (which was in any case no more than the pale shadow of the brilliant school it had once been) was obliged to close its doors in 1793 for want of students. In the eighteenth century universities were also in decline in many other countries, and their suppression at the time of the French Revolution hardly took contemporaries by surprise. Science and modern philosophy had taken shape outside university institutions; and the universities had been discredited by granting degrees to candidates without serious examination, or even simply selling them to those whose only merit was to have taken the trouble to make the journey to the university city. The fate of university reputations and the value of their degrees can readily be imagined.[24]

THE COURTS AND PROCEDURE

General aspects

66 The courts and their procedure did not escape the criticism levelled at the learned law of the *ancien régime*. It was directed mainly at the random confusion of courts which had grown up. It also struck out at the role of the judges in developing the law, which sometimes tended to shade into true legislative power, as in the case of the *arrêts de règlement*.[25] Particular exception was taken to the learned Roman-canonical procedure: it was incomprehensible for the vast majority of the people; it was written, and therefore long and costly; and it caused still greater offence because it was secret and bureaucratic. The general trend of reforms proposed by partisans of the Enlighten-

[24] The following anecdote of the university of Pont-à-Mousson shows that the professors had at least their sense of irony, if not learning. A student who had acquired a law degree wanted to buy one for his horse too; to which the Faculty replied that 'it could grant degrees to asses but not to horses'.

[25] See above, section 51.

ment is therefore easy to imagine. They were driven by revolutionary zeal and inspired by their confidence in the natural goodness of man (under the influence especially of Rousseau). Some actually went so far as to advocate the abolition of all formal judicial procedure: the good citizens estranged by a dispute would be reconciled by arbiters or justices of the peace, without any of the formalities and rigorous procedural rules of the *ancien régime*. Various experiments were undertaken in the regime of intermediate law, but of these only the preliminary of conciliation survived,[26] and even it turned out to be a mere formality without much practical value, since in practice people turned to the courts only when their disputes could not be resolved amicably. Most of the reformers took the view that courts and the administration of justice were indispensable, but that they had to be fundamentally modernized. Their proposals for reorganization of the courts were these.

The labyrinth of tribunals, courts of justice and *parlements* with their overlapping jurisdictions had to be abolished and replaced nationally and for the citizens as a whole by a rational and uniform hierarchy of courts. This was what Joseph II attempted in the Austrian Netherlands: the abolition of a situation inherited from the Middle Ages and its replacement with a new 'pyramidal' system of courts.[27] Similarly the whole court structure was abolished at the beginning of the Revolution in 1790–1 and replaced with one which has constituted the basis of court organization in France and Belgium to the present day. In private law jurisdictions (apart from the commercial courts) the system provided for one justice of the peace for each canton; one court of first instance for each *arrondissement*; a court of appeal for each of twenty-seven jurisdictions; a single Cour de Cassation, to see that the laws were uniformly applied. No international, European or universal authority superior to the system of national courts was envisaged.

Legal practice had to become more democratic: if justice was not to be entrusted to the people, it must at least be brought closer to them. The most radical method was to elect judges under a temporary mandate (a system still in use in some states of the United States of America) and to abandon all qualifications for judicial office, in particular the requirement for a law degree. For a very short period, the French Revolution employed such a system (Con-

[26] Code de Proc. civ. II.i, arts. 48–50. [27] See below, Section 68.

stitution of 1791, III, 2 and 5) but the popular courts were suppressed under Napoleon. The Constitution of Year VIII (13 December 1799) readopted the traditional conservative system of professional judges, who had been educated in law and appointed for life by the first consul. The unpopular system of selling judicial appointments had evidently been abandoned earlier.[28]

Statute: the sole source of law

67 The monopoly of statute as a source of law had to be ensured: judges were given instructions to keep strictly to their task and to refrain from all legislative intervention. This is to be understood in connexion with the doctrine of separation of powers, as defended by Montesquieu.[29] Robespierre would actually have been happy to see the term 'case law' disappear from the French language, since 'in a state having a constitution and legislation, the case law of courts is nothing other than statute'. Article 5 of the *Code civil* of 1804 provides: 'Judges are prohibited from pronouncing general regulatory dispositions in cases submitted to them.' The subordination of judges to statute can also be seen in the requirement that they give reasons for, and the statutory basis of, their decisions.[30] In the old law, by contrast, the judge who gave reasons for his decisions (as Wielant had observed) was considered a fool. But what if the text of a statute was obscure? Was each judge to be left the freedom to interpret the statute according to taste? The reformers thought not: their preferred solution would have been to reserve necessary interpretation to the legislator himself.[31] But the procedure adopted by the Constituante of 1790, *référé au législatif* ('referral to the

[28] Statute of 16–24 August 1790 on the court system, t.II art. 2, 'The sale of judicial office is abolished for ever, judges shall do justice freely and shall be paid by the state.'

[29] Art. 16 of the *Déclaration des droits de l'homme et du citoyen* of 26 August 1789 reads, 'Any society in which there is no guarantee of rights and no separation of powers has no Constitution.' The separation of powers has also to ensure the independence of the judiciary from the executive. J. P. A. Coopmans, 'Vrijheid en gebondenheid van de rechter voor de codificatie', *Rechtsvinding. Opstellen aangeboden aan prof. dr. J. M. Pieters* (Deventer, 1970), 71–109; K. M. Schönfeld, 'Montesquieu en "la bouche de la loi"' (Leiden, 1979; doctoral thesis); H. Hübner, *Kodifikation und Entscheidungsfreiheit des Richters in der Geschichte des Privatrechts* (Königstein, 1980; Beiträge zur neueren Privatrechtsgeschichte der Universität Köln, 8).

[30] Constitution of Year III, art. 208; Belgian Constitution of 1831, art. 97.

[31] The statute of 16–24 August 1790 required the courts to approach the legislature at any time when they thought it necessary to interpret a statute.

legislature'), was less radical. A single Tribunal de Cassation[32] was created, to nullify judgments which had misapplied the law and remit them to another court of the same instance. Where three tribunals persisted in judging to the same effect, the Tribunal de Cassation had to submit the question to the legislative assembly to obtain a legislative statute, which was then imposed on the judiciary at large. This system was also introduced into Belgium, and was confirmed after the revolution of 1830 by the organic law of 1832 which created the Belgian Cour de Cassation. Referral to the legislature was abolished only in 1865, when it was replaced by the current system under which, when two lower courts have given judgments to the same effect but their judgment has each time been annulled, the lower court to which the case is then remitted must follow the decision in law of the Cour de Cassation. This system finally brought judicial powers of statutory interpretation under control.

The modern codes

68 Reforms were also advocated in civil procedure. The rules of procedure were to be codified to ensure certainty and clarity, qualities which were completely lacking in the weighty and obscure volumes of Roman-canonical procedural jurisprudence.[33] The new codes made substantial changes in procedure, which brought justice closer to the citizens or, in other words, gave the administration of justice a more humane appearance. Procedure had to be public (apart from the judge's deliberations) and oral, which reduced both length and costs. Secret examination of witnesses was to be abolished. The excessively theoretical and complicated system of legal proofs was abolished, at least in criminal cases; now the judge decided according to his own conviction, reasonably based on the evidence before him (*conviction intime*). Justice was to be made democratic by abolishing the profession of advocate, since the citizen, properly informed by the codes, would from now on be

[32] This court, which was set up by decree dated 27 November – 1 December 1790 to annul all formally defective procedure and all judgments contrary to the law, had antecedents in the *ancien régime* in the case law of the Conseil du Roi for which rules had already been made in 1738.

[33] The 'Code Louis' (see above, section 49) was a notable exception in the European law of procedure.

perfectly capable of defending his own interests.[34] Juries on the English model were to be introduced, so that every citizen would be judged by his fellow citizens.[35]

The abolition of advocates was very short-lived. The proposal for a jury in civil cases was rejected by the Constituante after intervention by Tronchet, who maintained that in civil cases questions of fact could not be distinguished from questions of law. But the reformers were almost unanimous in defending the old *Verhandlungsmaxime*.[36] The exception to the rule was Frederick the Great who, as an enlightened despot, thought it the duty of the court to seek out the truth, even if this involved the judge in investigation beyond the submissions made by the parties. His divergent view of procedure rested on the principles of the *Instruktionsmaxime* and the *Offizialmaxime*, in which the *officium iudicis* is the guiding principle of civil procedure. The task of the judge is to protect the citizen, and to convince himself on the merits of the case, independently of the allegations of parties, even if they say nothing or make mistakes. Cases are investigated by an *Instruent* appointed by the court, who may be compared with the *juge d'instruction* of criminal law. These principles are set out in book 1 (*Von der Processordnung*) of the *Corpus Juris Fridericianum* (1781), which also abolished advocates chosen and paid by the parties and replaced them with officials attached to the courts (*Assistenzräte*).[37] As in France, however, so in Prussia: the profession of advocates rapidly re-established itself, and the experiment undertaken by Frederick the Great was transitory. Yet in the twentieth century similar notions about the role of the judge and judicial assistance have again attracted attention.

The principal codes of civil procedure of the time were the code of

[34] This was one of the reforms of the *Déclaration des droits de l'homme* as well as of the Constitutions of 1791 and 1795. The abolition of advocates was part of the struggle against the revival of the privileges of the *ancien régime*. It did not last long: the Ordre des Avocats was re-established by Napoleon in 1804, with the requirement that its members be graduates in law.

[35] In 1790 E.-J. Sieyès had already proposed to the Constituante that all civil and criminal cases should be decided by jury. His proposal had met with results in practice only in criminal law. As Robespierre observed to the Convention in 1793, the difference between juries and non-professional judges was merely one of name.

[36] i.e. where procedure is in the hands of the parties, and the decision of the court is based on the submissions of the parties and the witnesses they have cited.

[37] Traditional advocates were regarded as mercenaries.

Frederick II in Prussia,[38] that of Napoleon in France, and in Austria the *Allgemeine Gerichtsordnung* of Joseph II, which was promulgated in 1781 for the territories of central Europe under Habsburg rule and was also important for the Austrian Netherlands. The *Gerichtsordnung* was a systematic and comprehensive codification of procedural law. It was also a statutory modernization of the law in the spirit of the Enlightenment. Where it preserved traditional procedures, the *Gerichtsordnung* was a codification of Roman-canonical procedure, while its modern characteristics derived from comparison with other European systems, from the ideas of the authors of the Enlightenment, and from the work of Montesquieu, who was often quoted by the codification commission. Some of the new experiments with oral procedure were developed more systematically in later legislation. But radical reform of the Austrian law of procedure came only around 1895, with the introduction of the *Zivilprozessordnung* prepared by Professor F. Klein. In the Netherlands, Joseph II attempted a complete reform of the court system, by abolishing the existing courts in 1787 and replacing them with a single pyramidal court structure. His reform envisaged sixty-three regional courts of first instance, two courts of appeal, at Brussels and Luxembourg, and a single sovereign council sitting at Brussels. The courts of appeal were to hear appeals, while the sovereign council would be competent to review judgments. This system already foreshadowed the contemporary one. In the time of Joseph II, however, this direct assault on tradition and vested interests provoked the Brabançon revolution in October 1789, and the authorities found themselves compelled to reinstate the old jurisdictions, which survived until the French occupation in 1794.

As part of his policy, Joseph II had in Brussels in 1786 promulgated a *Règlement de procédure civile*. This contained 451 articles and was close to the Austrian model. It provided in particular that only graduates in law could practise as advocates. Judges were to apply the dispositions of the *Règlement* strictly: they were prohibited from diverting from it by appealing to the 'spirit of the law', 'praetorian equity', 'contrary custom' or 'any other pretext whatsoever'. A judge who allowed a case to languish for long had to pay damages and

[38] This was largely composed by von Carmer and Svarez, who have already been mentioned. It was revised by the *Allgemeine Gerichtsordnung für die preussischen Staaten* (1793) of Frederick-William II and an ordinance of 1799. Ordinances of 1843 and 1846 took up again with traditional practice.

interest. Where there was a gap in a statute, the court was to judge by analogy or, failing that, to address itself to the sovereign council of justice which was to be set up in Brussels. The preparatory work for the *Règlement* had been done in Brussels from 1782, but the draft worked out in the Netherlands was rejected by the Viennese authorities and replaced by a more 'enlightened' code, which was already in use in the Habsburg territories in North Italy. To the government of Joseph II, the draft which was rejected was too traditional and still too attached to local customs.[39]

In conclusion it should be recalled that the procedural codes of the Enlightenment, or at least those which lasted some time, were decidedly conservative. In France the codification reiterated the essential elements of the *Ordonnance* of 1667, which had shown itself to be practical and had managed to avoid the excesses of Roman-canonical doctrine. The *Gerichtsordnung* of 1781 preserved the essence of 'common procedure' (*gemeiner Prozess*), although it revised some aspects in a modern light. Yet in some regions new ideas initially had no effect on procedure. In Spain, justice continued to be administered according to the medieval learned procedure; and England maintained its medieval common-law procedure.

ENGLISH LAW IN THE ENLIGHTENMENT

Lord Mansfield and William Blackstone

69 On the European continent the legal world was face to face with a series of upheavals, or at least a wide-ranging movement of new ideas and reform. But English law steadfastly steered its traditional course. The best expression to sum up the history of English law in the second half of the eighteenth and the beginning of the nineteenth centuries is 'all quiet on the English front'. There was no modernization, revolutionary or otherwise. Far from it: in this period of extreme conservatism the existing system was actually consolidated. The Common Law was, and it remained, the basis of

[39] Joseph II's reforming zeal can be observed, among other things, in nearly a thousand ordinances which he promulgated in the Austrian Netherlands in the course of his ten-year reign. See R. Warlomont, 'Les idées modernes de Joseph II sur l'organisation judiciaire dans les Pays-Bas autrichiens', *Revue d'histoire du droit* 27 (1959), 269–89; P. van Hille, *De gerechtelijke hervorming van Keizer Jozef II* (Tielt, 1972). Joseph II also upset Belgian legal circles by abolishing torture: E. Hubert, *La torture aux Pays-Bas autrichiens pendant le XVIIIe siècle* (Brussels, 1896).

English law. Equity, the case law of the Court of Chancery, was more restrictive than ever and had degenerated into a mass of rules of positive law which bore no relation to the natural equity from which, some centuries earlier, it had arisen. The powerful 'Prerogative Courts'[40] had collapsed in the course of the Puritan revolution, and the courts which applied Roman or canon law were only marginal. So the Common Law remained what it had always been: a body of unwritten rules, thought to be based on ancient customary law, whose definition and interpretation was in the hands of the judges, in particular the twelve judges who sat in Westminster Hall. Legislation, especially private-law legislation, was not significant. Statutes were rare and, even if the courts did not adopt the extreme position of Sir Edward Coke,[41] they still allowed themselves great latitude in interpreting statutes. At times this came close to judicial control of statutes according to the fundamental principles of the Common Law.[42]

Judges were not just the (conservative) guarantors of the law in force.[43] They could also contribute actively, by means of constructive precedents, to the development of English law. William Murray, Earl of Mansfield (*d.* 1793) was notable in this respect. Lord Mansfield was of Scottish descent (hence his familiarity with continental and Roman law), and after a political career in the House of Commons, from 1756 to 1784 he occupied the position of Lord Chief Justice in King's Bench, one of the Common Law courts at Westminster. At the same time he still sat in the House of Lords and took part in political affairs. His fundamental lasting contribution was to integrate English commercial law firmly into the system of Common Law. The antecedents of commercial law were in continental, especially Mediterranean, practice. In constructive, sometimes bold

[40] These were courts based on the royal prerogative, and of an absolutist character; the most important was the Star Chamber.

[41] In *Bonham's Case* in 1610 it was maintained by Coke (*d.* 1634) that old law books showed that 'in many cases the Common Law will control Acts of Parliament and sometimes adjudge them to be utterly void: for when an Act of Parliament is against common right and reason or repugnant, or impossible to be performed, the Common Law will control it and adjudge such Act to be void'.

[42] Only in 1871 did the Bench expressly reject this notion and declare that the judges as 'servants of the Queen and the legislature' had to accept the authority of Parliament, for 'the proceedings here are judicial, not autocratic, which they would be if we could make the laws instead of administering them', *Lee* v. *Bude* L. R. 6 C. P. 576, 582 *per* Willes J.

[43] At the beginning of the nineteenth century, two judges in particular were notoriously conservative, Lord Ellenborough in the King's Bench (1802–18) and Lord Eldon in Chancery (1801–6, 1807–27).

judicial opinions, Lord Mansfield developed this commercial law into an instrument suited to modern commercial and financial demands (credit, bills of exchange, insurance, banking), and is therefore regarded as the founding father of English commercial law. The development of the law was accomplished in collaboration with London merchants: they sat in the civil juries, and were asked detailed questions about the scope and meaning of their professional practices.

The role of legislation was merely ancillary. According to Blackstone (see below), *lex non scripta* (the uncodified Common Law) had to be distinguished from *lex scripta* (Acts of Parliament or – strictly speaking – of the Crown and the Houses of Lords and Commons). Statutes were merely complementary to the Common Law. They were declaratory, since they made explicit a particular point of Common Law, and they were remedial, since they were intended to correct deficiencies in the Common Law. Furthermore, there was a presumption that the intention of the legislator was never to modify or abrogate a rule of the Common Law, unless this intention was expressly declared. According to Blackstone, where there was no statute the task of the judges, who were regarded as living oracles and repositories of the laws, was to resolve all doubtful cases, and thus the Common Law was and remained a creation of case law.

Scholarship played an even more modest part than legislation. Law faculties and the teaching of law in general had lost all importance. The Inns of Court completely abandoned teaching and became purely social clubs for lawyers. At Oxford the creation of the Vinerian Chair of English Law was the first tentative step in university teaching of law. Blackstone was the first to occupy it, from 1758, and he did so with distinction. After him, it deteriorated into mediocrity and became a sinecure.[44] The legal system and procedure remained trapped in their medieval moulds.

Such inertia seems surprising against the background of the continental Enlightenment, whose inspiration – paradoxically – was largely British. It is even more surprising in the perspective of the Industrial Revolution, which reached its high point at precisely the time when the English legal world was at its most lethargic. It is a paradox of English legal history that this social and economic upheaval could take place under a legal system which came straight

[44] H. G. Hanbury, *The Vinerian Chair and legal education* (Oxford, 1958).

from the Middle Ages, as if the nation's entire energy had been mobilized for the economic miracle, and the institutional framework had been totally ignored.

The age of reason, however, was not wholly without influence on English law, or at least English legal thought (which was in any event far removed from practice). Two eminent but very different jurists stand out at this time: one as the last great author of the classical Common Law, the other the critic of that same Common Law and the initiator of the reforms of the nineteenth century. Sir William Blackstone (*d.* 1780) was the author of the *Commentaries on the laws of England* (1765–8; several editions and adaptations), a comprehensive account and analysis of English law. Although he has his critical observations to make, his general appraisal of English law is positive. His aim was to consolidate the English legal system and, in the spirit of the Enlightenment, to demonstrate its rational character and reveal its fundamental principles. The elegant language and style of the author favourably surprised his public, since most authors wrote in unintelligible and rebarbative jargon. Proper English replaced Law French and Latin only from 1731.

Jeremy Bentham

70 Jeremy Bentham (*d.* 1832) was quite a different matter. He confronted the status quo directly, and throughout his lifetime was a vigorous and eloquent apologist for the principle of codification. The point of departure for Bentham's critique of the English system (which in his day was still substantially medieval) was not continental natural law[45] but instead an entirely original idea: the principle of utility. Bentham did not formulate axioms and deduce rules of law from them; instead he questioned the utility of each legal rule and concept, and the practical purpose it served for contemporary man and society. Many traditional values failed this test, and so had to be replaced by new ones. In particular they had to be replaced by a codification compiled under the watchword 'utility': Bentham called his doctrine 'utilitarianism'. In his view, codes had to ensure the 'cognoscibility' and the certainty of law, and legislation and case law

[45] 'Continental' in the sense that it was there that natural law had particular success and a marked influence on legal practice. This does not mean that English thought made no contribution to natural law; think of Hobbes.

must aim at the 'greatest happiness for the greatest number' (the slogan was J. Priestley's, *d.* 1804).

Among Bentham's works are *A Fragment on government* (1776), which attacked Blackstone's *Commentaries*; *Principles of morals and legislation* (printed in 1780, published in 1789), which was a plea for radical legislation as the source of modern law, and *Codification proposals* (1823). He also wrote a *Theory of legislation* (which appeared only in 1931).[46] Bentham's time was dominated by conservative ideas; any call for change at that time summoned up the spectre of the French Revolution and the Terror. As a result Bentham's work, which advocated fundamental reform of the existing system, did not meet with success. After his death, however, Parliament, which had been substantially modernized by the Reform Act of 1832, did begin to carry out his programme, owing largely to the efforts of Lord Brougham, a fervent reformer and, as a politician, more adept than Bentham.[47]

It is a paradox that the greatest European theoretician and exponent of codification – who actually coined the expression 'codification' – came from England. Right to the present day England has kept its distance from codification; its legal system is still based partly on the unwritten customary law of thousands of precedents, and partly on a vast collection of statutes which are chronologically ordered in imposing volumes and range from the Middle Ages to the present. The greatest prophet of codification was rejected in his own land.[48]

There are several reasons for these divergent developments in England and continental Europe, and for the astonishing sterility of English law during this period. On the continent, the great codes were the work of enlightened despots or generals who had dictatorial powers. But England experienced neither of these regimes. The continental codes aimed particularly to reinforce the unity of the nation state, but there was no such need in England, where local legal peculiarities were unknown and the Common Law was the

[46] Many of Bentham's works were translated into French by his pupil E. Dumont, and read assiduously on the continent.

[47] The signal for fundamental reform was given in 1828, when Brougham made a six-hour speech in the House of Commons on the Common Law, and two Royal Commissions were appointed. As Lord Chancellor from 1830 to 1834 Brougham was in a position to urge reform. He was one of the founders of the Law Amendment Society in 1844.

[48] As an exponent of codification, Bentham had a brilliant but equally unfortunate precursor in Francis Bacon (*d.* 1626), the lawyer, politician and philosopher of science.

oldest national law of Europe. The very fervour with which codification was carried out on the continent aroused the mistrust of many of the English. For them the continent evoked the political regimes which they most abhorred: absolutism and revolutionary radicalism. In addition, the objectives of the continental reformers had partly been achieved in England already. For instance, in France land was still held by religious establishments in mortmain, or kept off the market by medieval customs; but in England the monasteries had been dissolved and their lands confiscated under Henry VIII (1509–47), and vast tracts of land had re-entered the economic system. The numerous Enclosure Acts of the eighteenth century had also lifted medieval restrictions on common lands and property rights. Consequently large areas of agricultural land were now open for economic exploitation.

EVALUATION OF THE LAW OF REASON

71 A balance sheet of the successes and failures of the law of reason may be helpful. Some of its basic objectives were achieved. It had a liberating effect, since it led to the abandonment of the constricting system of the *auctoritas* of ancient texts. Admittedly, even in medieval thought *auctoritas* (authority) had to be subject to *ratio* (reason), but of the two it had been *auctoritas* which prevailed. Now *ratio* had become the guiding principle. The antiquity of a rule of law was no longer thought to guarantee its superiority. Some authors even adopted the opposite thesis and affirmed that each legal innovation necessarily represented progress.

The primacy of statute (especially codified statute) was now accepted. On the continent this was hardly challenged again, while some of the earlier extremism had now been abandoned, such as the statement by J.-J. Bugnet (*d.* 1866) that 'I do not know the civil law, I teach the Code Napoléon alone.' Since their homologation, customs had in any case come close to being statute in disguise, but were now relegated to a marginal role. Legal scholarship had no binding authority. Only case law maintained an important place in legal practice. The result, however, was much less radical than the supporters of statute as the unique source of law had (somewhat naively) imagined, and the attempt to prevent lawyers writing doctrinal commentaries was as vain as the hope of providing for every case in the codes. Yet the priority of statute over all other sources of law did bring about a marked simplification: henceforth, knowledge and application of the law were incontestably clearer and more certain. Natural law was an essential element in the triumph over old customary law and the (still prestigious) Roman law. Only a still more universal law, or rather a truly universal law, was in a position to mount a challenge to the quasi-universal authority of Roman law. If the *Corpus iuris* was the law of the Roman empire and of the western world, natural law was that of all humanity; if Roman law was the work of the greatest people of lawyers in history, then natural law was the very expression of reason. So at the beginning of the eighteenth century it was possible to argue that the Roman rule *alteri stipulari nemo potest* was obsolete, since by virtue of natural law principles every agreement could give rise to a legal action. According to one author of the period 'most, or at least the better, lawyers recognize that on this question it is proper to follow not the subtleties of the Romans but the simplicity of natural law'.[49]

The natural law method was to deduce concrete rules of positive law from general concepts and axioms. This systematic approach (*Begriffsjurisprudenz*) still exercises an influence today. It replaced the old method, the principal task of which had been exegesis of individual texts of the *Corpus iuris* in order to harmonize them. The modern, more abstract method deliberately followed that of the exact sciences, for the aim of the lawyers was to realize a universal science based on demonstrable propositions. Even today this aim represents an insuperable obstacle to all attempts to reconcile English and continental legal thought. The conviction and the ambition were trenchantly expressed by the civilian Fr. Laurent, professor at the University of Ghent (*d.* 1887): 'Law is a rational science.' The notion that law is purposive, that it can be used to direct social policy or even to bring about a certain kind of society, is also part of the legacy of the age of reason. The law of reason saw law in a political context, utilitarian or philosophical. This led to law becoming ideological, and it allowed governments to tighten their control on their peoples. This had previously been unthinkable. The eighteenth century also made a start on

[49] Augustin Leyser (*d.* 1752), an important figure of the *Usus modernus*; see K. Luig, 'Der Einfluss des Naturrechts auf das positive Privatrecht im 18. Jahrhundert', *Zeitschrift der Savigny-Stiftung für Rechtsgeschichte* (G. A.) 96 (1979), 41.

humanizing the law, mainly, although not exclusively, the criminal law.[50]

The secularization of the law, its removal from the authority of theology and divine laws, was an objective of the Enlightenment which was largely attained. Civil marriage and divorce were introduced, and religious discrimination, especially against 'dissident' Christian sects and Jews, was abolished. At one time a distinction had been made between the *civitas Dei* and the *civitas terrena*, the superior divine order and the temporal order subject to it. Now the temporal order was emancipated. It could set its own goals, and means to achieve them.

In several respects, however, the ambitions of the law of reason were frustrated. Natural law itself, although it was greatly in vogue in the Enlightenment, had only a short life ahead of it. By the beginning of the nineteenth century, it had lost all real importance as a guiding principle and source of inspiration for the law. It had completed its task of mounting a challenge to the ancient order and inspiring the codes. It could disappear, like the revolutionary masses, with which nineteenth-century generals and citizens had nothing to do. Once the revolutionary codes were promulgated and the civil order of the nineteenth century was established, natural law amounted to no more than a suspect source of criticism and opposition. In the Constitution of the Year VIII, the consuls, the senior of whom was Bonaparte, had proclaimed that the Revolution had ended. Natural law as a discipline in the syllabuses of the law faculties crumbled away without any proper scholarly discussion. It was not conquered or exiled, but merely faded away. Although the term 'natural law' was retained in several syllabuses, the material taught covered everything but natural law (legal theory, sociology of law, legal statistics, philosophy and so on). In the middle of the nineteenth century, Windscheid observed 'Der Traum des Naturrechts ist ausgeträumt' ('The dream of natural law is at an end'). Natural law was now no more than a purely academic subject without practical significance. For an advocate to resort to natural law, his case must already be desperate.

[50] Imprisonment for debt was abolished by a decree of 12 March 1793 which stated that 'it is not even permitted to contract for it'. None the less it reappeared in the *Code civil*; it had already been revived by a law of 14 March 1797 on the basis that the purpose of its abolition had been merely 'an attack on property'. Only in 1867 in France, and in 1871 in Belgium, was it abolished (in 1980 in criminal cases).

THE LAW OF REASON AND THE HISTORICAL SCHOOL

72 The two great schools of thought which took over from natural law at the beginning of the nineteenth century were the Exegetical School and the Historical School. Members of the Exegetical School believed that law was identical with the codes and that, since statute was now the sole source of law, scholarship had to confine itself to the exact interpretation (or 'exegesis', the term used for interpretation of biblical texts by theologians) of statutes in general, and above all the codes. Such an approach inevitably excluded any philosophical system such as natural law.[51] The Historical School was launched by the work of its founder, F. C. von Savigny (*d.* 1861), *Vom Beruf unsrer Zeit für Gesetzgebung und Rechtswissenschaft* (1814), and had its own periodical, the *Zeitschrift für geschichtliche Rechtswissenschaft* founded in 1815. The name ('Journal for Historical Jurisprudence') proclaimed the programme: jurisprudence should be historical, and the historical experience of a people ought to be the true source of inspiration for its legal practice.[52] This school believed that law was a natural, organic expression of the life of a people. It could not be codified at a given stage of development, any more than a language could.[53]

At first sight the complete failure of natural law is surprising. Yet it is connected with the great political and social changes of the time (which will be examined at length), and also with its intrinsic impotence as a school of thought. Its claim was to establish objective and universal certainties, which were valid for humanity at large. But these ambitions were not realized. What seemed just in all the circumstances to one scholar, people, age or civilization did not seem so to others. The axioms of natural law were in fact subjective, and so they had no value as the basis of a universal human system. The few general principles on which unanimity could be achieved (such as the duty to be honest and sincere, to keep promises and respect agreements) were so vague that they could scarcely solve the real problems of daily life. Natural law was too often inadequate

51 The Exegetical School (see also the following chapter) in fact dealt with the *Code civil* as the glossators had in their day dealt with the *Corpus iuris*.

52 Savigny's *Vom Beruf* was a polemical work aimed at A. F. Thibaut (*d.* 1840), the exponent of codification. The polemic between the two was one of the most celebrated of the nineteenth century.

53 Like Savigny, who was mainly interested in ancient and medieval Roman law, the scholars K. Eichhorn (*d.* 1854) and J. Grimm (*d.* 1863), who were both interested in the Germanic and German past, belonged to the historical movement.

precisely where a legal rule was most needed. Grotius' views on family law illustrate how unfocused and non-universal the 'certain' principles of natural law could be: he states that polygamy is not incompatible with natural law, whereas polyandry and marriage between ascendant and descendant are contrary to it. This doctrine is shored up by very dubious propositions.[54] Grotius also believed that natural law supported his very traditional views on the legal status of women. These views – especially that the husband is the natural head of family, and his wife submits to him by marriage – nowadays appear totally illegitimate. The partisans of natural law inevitably had to turn in large part to Roman law, in order to be able to state the rules required by practice in more precise and concrete terms. It is also significant that the codes of intermediate law, which were inspired by natural law, were a failure and had to be replaced by the Napoleonic codification, whose authors drew largely on ancient law.[55]

Savigny and the Historical School had a similar experience. Although they declared that the *Volksgeist* and the traditions of a nation were the sources of law *par excellence*, it very soon became clear (in particular in Savigny's own work) that their formulation of concrete, practical rules derived to a large extent from the *Corpus iuris*. The paradoxical result was that Savigny was the leader of the Historical School and at the same time the precursor of the German study of the Pandects (*Pandektistik*), a nineteenth-century doctrine wholly based on Roman law and entirely unconnected with the German *Volksgeist*.

It was, therefore, only in times of crisis that discontent with, and criticism of, positive law crystallized around natural law. Once the crisis was over and a new equilibrium had been established, natural law had played its part, and the new system (the *Code civil* or the *Pandektenrecht* of the nineteenth century) could claim that it represented the desired legal order and the ideal law. The School of Natural Law was equally unable to realize its universal vocation. The hope had been to set out from reason, and so to work out a universal (or at least a European) law which would put an end to the

[54] Marriage between ascendant and descendant was ruled out, as the intimate relations between spouses are incompatible with the respect due by a child to a parent. There was disagreement even on the question of the legal nature of marriage: for Grotius it was a corporation, while for many others (including Roman law) it was a contract.

[55] See above, section 4.

absurdity denounced by Pascal: 'Three degrees of latitude overturn all case law, a meridian decides the truth; it is a strange justice which stops at the first river!'[56]

In reality the triumph of national codes brought about the nationalization of legal systems which was characteristic of nineteenth-century legal development. The law of reason and the cosmopolitan Roman law had to give way to different national legal orders based on national codes and national administration of justice. The development went along with that of sovereign states in the same period, as well as with various intellectual currents. In France, Montesquieu had already emphasized the necessity of adapting the law to the 'spirit' of peoples, and numerous German jurists of the late eighteenth and nineteenth centuries were convinced that each people must live by its own laws, adapted to its particular needs. So the School of Germanists (which opposed that of Romanists) looked in ancient law for elements which could shape a Germanic law adapted to the needs of the German people.[57] It was not a question of raising legal barriers between peoples, but at least legal unity had been achieved within states. The geographical frontiers of customary regions had disappeared, or would do in the course of the nineteenth century, and many old corporatist and social barriers (such as the 'Estates') had been suppressed.

BIBLIOGRAPHY

73 d'Amelio, M., *Illuminismo e scienza del diritto in Italia*, Milan, 1965

Baudelot, B., *Un grand jurisconsulte du XVIIe siècle: J. Domat*, Paris, 1938

Bernard, P. P., *The limits of enlightenment. Joseph II and the law*, Urbana, Chicago, London, 1979

Bussi, E., 'Meditazioni sullo "Allgemeines Landrecht für die preussischen

[56] *Pensées*, II, 3, I. The author continues, 'The brilliance of true equity would have subdued all peoples, and legislators would not have taken as a model the fantasies and caprices of the Persians and the Germans instead of this constant justice . . . It would be implanted in all States of the world and in all times, instead of which there is nothing just or unjust which does not change its quality when the climate changes.' And Pascal concludes, 'Truth this side of the Pyrenees, error on the other side . . . nothing, following reason alone, is just in itself; everything changes with time.'

[57] G. Beseler (*d.* 1888) was the most prominent representative of the Germanist school and at the same time very active in national politics. His most important work was *System des gemeinen deutschen Privatrechts* (1847–55). His *Volksrecht und Juristenrecht* (1843) was a fundamental assault on the *Corpus iuris*, which he denounced as a foreign body parasitic on the German nation; the reception was described as a national disaster, the blame for which fell squarely on the learned jurists.

Staaten" ', *Historia del derecho privado. Trabajos en homenaje a F. Valls i Taberner*, x, Barcelona, 1989, 2,981–99

Caroni, P., 'Savigny und die Kodifikation. Versuch einer Neudeutung des Berufes', *Zeitschrift der Savigny-Stiftung für Rechtsgeschichte* (G. A.), 86 (1969), 97–176

'Savigny's "Beruf" und die heutige Krise der Kodifikation', *Revue d'histoire du droit* 39 (1971), 451–76

Coing, H., 'Zur Vorgeschichte der Kodifikation im 17. und 18. Jahrhundert', in *La formazione storica del diritto moderno in Europa* II, Florence, 1977, 797–817

Die Bedeutung des Systemgedankens in der Rechtswissenschaft, Frankfurt, 1956; rectoral address

'Commémoration du quatrième centenaire de la naissance de Grotius', *Académie de droit international, recueil des cours*, vol. 182 (1983), IV, The Hague, 1984, 371–469

Denzer, H., *Moralphilosophie und Naturrecht bei Samuel Pufendorf. Eine geistes- und wissenschaftsgeschichtliche Untersuchung zur Geburt des Naturrechts aus der praktischen Philosophie*, Munich, 1972

Dubischar, R., *Theorie en praktijk in de rechtswetenschap. Van Friedrich von Savigny tot Niklas Luhmann*, Antwerp and Amsterdam, 1981

Dufour, A., 'L'influence de la méthodologie des sciences physiques et mathématiques sur les fondateurs de l'Ecole de Droit naturel moderne', *Grotiana* I (1980), 33–52

Ebel, F., *200 Jahre preussischer Zivilprozess. Das Corpus iuris Fridericianum vom Jahre 1781*, Berlin and New York, 1982; Schriftenreihe der juristischen Gesellschaft zu Berlin, 71

d'Entrèves, A. P., *Natural law. An historical survey*, 2nd edn, London, 1970

Eysinga, W. J. M. van, *Huigh de Groot*, Leiden, 1945

Gans, E., *Naturrecht und Universalrechtsgeschichte*, ed. and intr. by M. Riedel, Stuttgart, 1981; Deutscher Idealismus, 2

Hall, W. van, 'Friedrich Carl von Savigny als Praktiker. Die Staatsratsgutachten (1817–42)', *Zeitschrift der Savigny-Stiftung für Rechtsgeschichte* (G. A.) 99 (1982), 285–97

Hufteau, Y. L., *Le référé législatif et les pouvoirs du juge dans le silence de la loi*, Paris, 1965

Jansen, C. J. H., *Natuurrecht of Romeins Recht. Een studie over leven en werk van F. A. Van Der Marck (1719–1800) in het licht van de opvattingen van zijn tijd*, Leiden, 1987; doctoral thesis

Kern, B.-R., *Georg Beseler. Leben und Werk*, Berlin, 1982; Schriften zur Rechtsgeschichte, 26

Lieberwirth, R., *Christian Thomasius. Sein wissenschaftliches Lebenswerk*, Weimar, 1955

Loschelder, M., *Die österreichische allgemeine Gerichtsordnung von 1781. Grundlagen und Kodifikationsgeschichte*, Berlin, 1978; Schriften zur Rechtsgeschichte, 18

Luig, K., 'Der gerechte Preis in der Rechtstheorie und Rechtspraxis von Christian Thomasius (1655–1728)', in *Diritto e potere nella storia europea. Atti in onore di Bruno Paradisi*, II, Florence, 1982, 775–804

'Wissenschaft und Kodifikation des Privatrechts im Zeitalter der Aufklärung in der Sicht von Thomasius', *Festschrift H. Coing*, Munich, 1982, 177–202

Mohnhaupt, H., 'Potestas legislatoria und Gesetzesbegriff im ancien regime', *Ius commune* 4 (1972), 188–239

Neusüss, W., *Gesunde Vernunft und Natur der Sache. Studien zur juristischen Argumentation im 18. Jahrhundert*, Berlin, 1970

Nourrison, P., *Un ami de Pascal: Jean Domat*, Paris, 1939

Pauw, F. de, *Grotius and the law of the sea*, Brussels, 1965

Petit, J.-L., 'Joseph de Crumpipen (1737–1809). Les idées d'un haut fonctionnaire et magistrat des Pays-Bas autrichiens sur la justice de son temps', *Revue d'histoire du droit* 54 (1986), 127–48

Pick, E., *Aufklärung und Erneuerung des juristischen Studiums. Verfassung, Studium und Reform in Dokumenten am Beispiel der Mainzer Fakultät gegen Ende des Ancien Regime*, Berlin and Munich, 1983; Historische Forschungen, 24

Salmonowicz, S., 'Die neuzeitliche europäische Kodifikation (16.-17. Jt.). Die Lehre und ihre Verwirklichung', *Acta Poloniae historica* 37 (1978), 29–69

Samuel von Pufendorf 1632–1982. Ett rättshistorisk symposium i Lund 15–26 Jan. 1982, Stockholm, 1986; Skrifter utgivna av Institutet för rättshistorisk forskning, serien II; Rattshistoriska Studier, 12

Schwinge, E., *Der Kampf um die Schwurgerichte bis zur Frankfurter Nationalversammlung*, Breslau, 1926; thesis

Stoll, A., *Friedrich Karl von Savigny. Ein Bild seines Lebens*, Berlin, 1927–39, 3 vols.

Strakosch, H. E., *State absolutism and the rule of law*, Sydney, 1967

Tarello, G., *Le ideologie della codificazione nel secolo XVIII*, I, Genoa, 1971

Thieme, H., *Naturrecht und europäische Privatrechtsgeschichte*, 2nd edn, Basle, 1954

Vanderlinden, J., *Le concept de code en Europe occidentale du XIIIe au XIXe siècle. Essai de définition*, Brussels, 1967

Wagner, W. (ed.), *Das schwedische Reichsgesetzbuch (Sveriges Rikes Lag) von 1734. Beiträge zur Entstehungs- und Entwicklungsgeschichte einer vollständigen Kodifikation*, Frankfurt, 1986; Ius commune Sonderheft, 29

Welzer, H., *Die Naturrechtslehre Samuel Pufendorfs*, Berlin, 1958

Wolf, E., *Das Problem der Naturrechtslehre. Versuch einer Orientierung*, 2nd edn, Karlsruhe, 1964

World of Hugo Grotius (1583–1645), The. Proceedings of the international colloquium organized by the Grotius committee of the Royal Netherlands Academy of Arts and Sciences 1983; Amsterdam and Maarssen, 1984

CHAPTER 5

The nineteenth century: the interpretation of the Code civil and the struggle for the law

FRANCE

74 The years from 1789 to 1804 had been troubled but also very creative: suddenly everything – even the boldest and most improbable innovations – seemed possible. The Napoleonic codes brought this brief period to an end and inaugurated a century of stability. From a legal point of view, it was also a century of sterility. The codes now existed; they suited the mentality and the interests of the citizens, and there was no reason to question them. Judges had only to respect them and apply them strictly; authors had merely to interpret the articles of the codes faithfully. It was out of the question now for case law or scholarship to attempt to innovate or play a creative role. Law had merged with statute, the statute was the work not of professors or magistrates, who had no mandate to act in the name of the nation, but of the legislator, the sole representative of the sovereign people.

During the Revolution the universities of the *ancien régime*, and their law faculties in particular, had been abolished. Some years later, schools of law were founded again, and in 1808 university teaching of law recommenced, although on a very different basis. The new system provided for a single Imperial University comprising twelve faculties of law, which were of identical standing and were under the direction of a central administration. Teaching and the subjects taught were strictly supervised by five inspectors-general. In 1809 a vice-rector was actually appointed in order to oversee the dean of the Paris faculty. This system was not operated in its full rigour,[1] but it did for long influence the French university world profoundly. It is scarcely surprising, in an atmosphere of extreme

[1] There are cases of professors who had criticized statutes being accused of inciting disobedience; even a Roman law textbook was impounded by the censor.

subordination to statute, and mistrust of both case law and scholarship, that what the dominant school of thought practised was literal interpretation of the codes; it is for that reason known as the Exegetical School.[2] Rarely in history has a single movement been predominant for so long and so totally as was this school in nineteenth-century France and Belgium. That was in part because of the stability of the legislative texts commented on: for, while the Constitutions of France rapidly succeeded each other, the *Code civil*, like a rock in a tempest, remained immovable.

At the beginning of the nineteenth century, however, there were still some lawyers educated under the *ancien régime* who devoted their studies to the new codes, but continued to make use of the sources from which the *Code civil* had drawn so much, Roman and customary law. Philippe Antoine, count Merlin de Douai (*d.* 1838), was certainly among the most learned lawyers of his day and, as political circumstances changed, he pursued a turbulent political career, during which he made an important contribution to the development of intermediate law, and acted as Napoleon's personal adviser at the time of the compilation of the *Code civil*. His works amount virtually to an encyclopaedia of French law ancient and modern, whose aim was to explain the new legislation with the aid of the old law. He published a *Répertoire universel et raisonné de jurisprudence*[3] and a complementary *Recueil alphabétique des questions de droit*.[4] Jacques de Maleville (*d.* 1824), who has already been mentioned as one of the compilers of the *Code civil*,[5] from 1805 published an *Analyse raisonnée de la discussion du Code civil au Conseil d'Etat*, which is both an account of the works preliminary to the codification and a doctrinal commentary. The German jurist, K. S. Zachariae (*d.* 1842), who was a professor in Heidelberg, is a special case. He came from the Rhineland, which at that time was under French rule, and in 1808 published the first proper commentary on the *Code civil*. His *Handbuch des französischen Civilrechts* (2 vols., Heidelberg, 1808, 2nd edn 1811–12) is a treatise on the *Code civil* which follows the order and method of *gemeines Recht* (that is, Roman law as applied in Germany). It had

[2] The name was suggested by E. Glasson who, on the occasion of the centenary of the *Code civil*, spoke of 'civil lawyers who have formed a sort of school which might be called the School of Exegesis'.

[3] Paris, 1807–8, 4 vols. (the 3rd edn is in fact a revised version of an older work; 4th edn, 1812–25, 17 vols.; 5th edn, 1827–8, 15 vols.).

[4] Paris, Year XI–XII, 7 vols.; 4th edn, 1827–30.

[5] See above, section 4.

a great influence in France, since it was the model for a celebrated and authoritative commentary (on which see below) by two professors of the university of Strasbourg, C. Aubry (*d.* 1883) and F.- C. Rau (*d.* 1877).

These lawyers, who had been educated and had sometimes practised in the eighteenth century, represent a transitional phase. After them, the legal scene was dominated by true exegetes, to whom ancient law was no more than an object for historical study. Among the major jurists of this new generation pride of place must go to A. Duranton (*d.* 1866), professor in Paris and the first French author of a complete commentary on the *Code civil* (*Cours de droit français suivant le Code civil*, 21 vols., 1825–37). The career of this first 'pure exegete' was also characteristic of the new generation: by contrast with the sometimes dangerous professional quarrels of his predecessors of the revolutionary period, Duranton managed to occupy his university chair without incident for thirty-six years, which enabled him to publish regular successive volumes of his *Cours*. Another exegete was R. Troplong (*d.* 1869), who was a magistrate and president of the Cour de Cassation. He started to publish his work *Le droit civil expliqué suivant les articles du Code* in 1836. It finally reached twenty-seven volumes. A third influential jurist was J.- C.- F. Demolombe (*d.* 1887), who taught civil law for half a century (which itself testifies, and contributed, to the great legal stability of the period). His *Cours du Code Napoléon* in thirty-one volumes was published between 1841 and 1876.[6] Finally, G. Baudry-Lacantinerie should be mentioned. Some of his works were of high authority: *Précis de droit civil* (3 vols., Paris 1882–4, 1889–92) and *Traité théorique et pratique de droit civil* (Paris, 1895 and many editions).

The Strasbourg professors Aubry and Rau, who have already been mentioned, occupy a special place in the French School of Exegesis. They were familiar with German systematic jurisprudence in general and the work of Zachariae in particular. Initially, their commentary on the *Code civil* was so close to Zachariae's *Handbuch* that they published their own work as an adaptation of it: *Cours de droit civil français traduit de l'allemand de C. S. Zachariae ... revu et augmenté* (1838). In the third and fourth editions of 1869 and 1879, however, the commentary is no longer presented as a translation. While the *Cours* was (or at least became) a complete and original

[6] The many editions of these classic works also show the stability of the regime. Demolombe's *Cours*, for instance, reached its fifth edition in 1874–9.

French work, owing to German influence it occupies a place apart in legal literature. The subject-matter was not in the order of the code, but arranged according to a system of general concepts which had been particularly popular in Germany since the days of the School of Natural Law.[7] German influence also explains why the authors make a distinction (unusual in France) between theoretical and practical civil law. Although this idiosyncratic approach was criticized and was not followed, numerous lawyers have recognized the work as one of the masterpieces of French scholarship.

Criticism of the School of Exegesis made little headway before the end of the nineteenth century. At that time criticism was directed not just at the method followed by the school and at its positivistic concept of law, but also at some of the principles of the *Code civil*: excessive individualism, the lack of an adequate regulation of employment, exaggerated respect for freedom of contract, absolute rights of property, the role of the paterfamilias, and so forth. All these themes have taken on still greater importance in the course of the twentieth century. Here the following names deserve mention: Fr Geny (*d.* 1959), author of a *Méthode d'interprétation et sources du droit privé français* (1899); M. Planiol (*d.* 1931), who in 1899 published the first volume of his *Traité élémentaire de droit civil*; and A. Esmein (*d.* 1913), founder in 1902 of the *Revue trimestrielle de droit civil.*

The essential theses of the School of Exegesis were that law and statute were identical, and the other sources of law – custom, scholarship, case law, natural law – had only secondary importance. To understand the exact meaning of the codes, it was necessary to set out from the text, from the text alone, and not from its sources. Scholarship and case law had therefore to resist going back beyond the codes, for that would inexorably lead to uncertainty. The legislator had chosen between different possibilities ancient and modern and, if his choice was not observed, the law would sink back into the diversity and uncertainty of the old sources, and so into the very faults for which the old law had been criticized. This approach (fairly described as 'fetishism for written statute') also ruled out any recourse to natural law or 'general principles of law'. Demolombe asserted that 'clear law' required no commentary, and that the law 'ought to be applied even when it does not appear to conform to general principles of law or equity'.[8]

[7] See above, sections 63 and 65.
[8] The same is said by many others, Cf. Bouckaert, *Exegetische school*, 124, 454 n. 104.

According to Laurent, authors who invoked the 'spirit of the statute' to mitigate its literal meaning were guilty of trying to revive the ancient supremacy of scholarship and to seize a creative role in the development of law; guilty, in other words, of usurping the function of the legislator. The task of scholarship was 'not to reform but to explain statute'; it was equally irrelevant to invoke the need to adapt the law in line with social development. Laurent did not hesitate to take his thesis to extremes: 'Statute', he claimed, 'even if it were a thousand times absurd, would still have to be followed to the letter, because the text is clear and formal.'[9]

Considerations of equity were also irrelevant, since they were individual and subjective. The situation where a judge might be called on to make a ruling as a 'minister of equity', owing to the silence of statute, 'was so rare that it may be left aside for the purposes of our discussion'.[10] The right of disobedience also had to be rejected, since even an unjust statute must be observed. It would be for the lawyers to point to unjust measures, in the hope that the legislator would wish to remedy them. In any case, unjust statutes would be rare because the codes, the nineteenth-century lawyers believed, would correspond to the ideal image of law, for they fused statute, law, and natural equity. This general complacency is one of the most striking characteristics of the School of Exegesis.

Some authors so resolutely refused to recognize custom as a source of law that they would not even admit its existence and applicability when statute referred to it expressly. And the obsession with the statutory text led scholarship to invent purely hypothetical situations which might fall under one article of the code or another, instead of considering the real cases encountered in case law. It was an attitude which led to abstract theoretical discussion, and which alienated jurisprudence from case law.

BELGIUM AND THE NETHERLANDS

75 In 1795 the French Republic annexed the Austrian Netherlands and the principality of Liège, which as a result became subject to French law and to the Napoleonic codes in particular. The

[9] Cited by Bouckaert, *ibid.*, 127.

[10] Again, according to Laurent (Bouckaert, *ibid.*, 159), who asks himself 'where will the judge find the rules of natural law which are completely unwritten?' (185). Hence a vicious circle, since natural law is precisely the eternal and supreme *agraphoi nomoi*.

Republic of the United Provinces (from 1795 the Batavian Republic) initially went through several different legal systems: the French occupiers made the country into a satellite kingdom, and Louis Napoleon, the emperor's younger brother, was imposed on it as sovereign (1806–10). In 1810 France also annexed the kingdom of Holland, which briefly formed part of French territory. Under Louis Napoleon, a *Wetboek Napoleon ingerigt voor het Koningrijk Holland* (Napoleonic code for the kingdom of Holland) was introduced on 1 May 1809. It was an adaptation of the *Code civil* which incorporated elements of old Dutch law. The code was extremely short-lived, since on 1 March 1811 the French codes, including the *Code civil* of 1804, came into force in Holland. Shortly afterwards, the French withdrew, and in 1815 Belgium and the Netherlands were amalgamated into the kingdom of the Netherlands under William I.

One of the first questions for the new state to answer was what to do about the existing French codes. A solution was swiftly reached in principle, although in practice it required time to implement: the new kingdom would have new national codes. The decision was only to be expected, since codifications were *à la mode*, and each sovereign state was supposed to have its own codified national law. In April 1814, even before the union of Belgium and the Netherlands, William I set up a commission for national legislation (*Commisie tot de nationale wetgeving*) to prepare new codes appropriate to the customs of the people of the Netherlands, and inspired by the traditional doctrine of the Netherlands. After 1815 efforts were made in Belgium as well as Holland to carry out the project. For various reasons, however, the compilation of a common civil code for the north and south proved extremely problematic: French law had established itself better in Belgium than in the Netherlands, and many Belgians preferred to retain the French codes; nationalistic enthusiasm for having a Netherlandish codification was scarcely felt in Belgian circles favourable to the French regime; and, from the seventeenth century, the development of the law in the northern and southern Netherlands had been very different. In the southern provinces (homologated) customary law prevailed, while in the northern provinces Roman or Roman-Dutch law was more important; in the north jurisprudence was also closer to German legal science and political philosophy.

In spite of these difficulties, and in spite of personal opposition between the rather doctrinaire Dutch jurist Johan Melchior Kemper (*d.* 1824) and the Belgian magistrate and practitioner Pierre Thomas Nicolaï (*d.* 1836), the preparatory works did manage to arrive at acceptable results, and by 1829 four codes were complete, including the *Code civil*, which was a decided compromise between north and south.[11] They were intended to come into force on 1 February 1831, but the Belgian revolution disrupted the plan. Its result was that in Belgium the Napoleonic codes were maintained, and in 1838 the Netherlands promulgated their own civil code, which was essentially the 1804 *Code civil* adapted on the basis of the work done by Kemper and Nicolaï.

The new kingdom of Belgium felt obliged, however, like all other kingdoms, to promulgate its own codes, and this was actually set down as a principle in the Constitution (art. 139). But a new Belgian civil code was never realized, all the attempts at wholesale revision of the French *Code civil* having failed. This is why five-sixths of the original *Code civil* are still in force in Belgium.[12] In spite of frequent recent changes to the *Code*, particularly in the areas of family law, matrimonial regimes and succession, there is no such thing as a new Belgian civil code.[13] In the Netherlands, on the other hand, it was decided after the Second World War to introduce a new civil code. The drafting of a new code in outline was entrusted to the civilian and legal historian E. M. Meijers (*d.* 1954), professor at the university of Leiden. Meijers' draft comprised an introductory title and nine books, the first four of which he completed; he also completed a large part of book v and set out the broad lines of books vi and vii.[14] Books i and ii were promulgated on 1 October 1971 and came into force on 26 July 1976; the introduction of the new civil code as a whole has not yet been completed.

For Belgium, the effect of this development on legal scholarship can easily be summed up: Belgium was a colony of the French School of Exegesis. The Belgian exegetes are distinguished only by their extremism, and by the fact that they adhered to the exegetical method much longer than the French themselves. The dominant

[11] The other codes were of commerce, civil procedure, and criminal procedure.

[12] By 1976 about 400 of the 2,281 articles of the 1804 *Code civil* had been changed.

[13] In 1976 more than 200 new articles were introduced by the statute of 14 July on the rights and duties of spouses and on matrimonial regimes. New criminal (1867) and judicial (1967) codes have, however, been produced.

[14] The nine books deal with: i, the law of persons and the family; ii, legal persons; iii, the law of property in general; iv, succession; v, real rights; vi, obligations in general; vii, particular contracts; viii, sea, river and air rights; ix, intellectual property.

figure in nineteenth-century Belgian jurisprudence, and the only Belgian jurist of repute in France and internationally, was François Laurent (*d.* 1887), a professor at Ghent. As a lawyer, historian and politician, he was deeply involved in the problems of his time. Politically, he was a liberal and fiercely anti-clerical.[15] In 1836 he was appointed to the chair at Ghent, where he taught a remarkable range of legal subjects for forty years. His principal work, *Principes de droit civil*, appeared in thirty-two volumes between 1869 and 1879; an abridged version for the use of students was published under the title *Cours élémentaire de droit civil* (1878). The introductions to these works set out the programme of the School of Exegesis in all its vigour. Laurent completed a draft Belgian *Code civil* in 1883 but, owing to a change in the political climate, it was not adopted.

It was also in Belgium, and in Ghent in particular, that the School of Exegesis survived the longest. Thus the very successful *Beginselen van Burgerlijk Recht* ('Principles of civil law') by the Ghent professor A. Kluyskens (*d.* 1956) still bears the clear stamp of exegesis,[16] which is all the more remarkable as a new method (the 'Scientific School') had grown up in France around 1900 and had also spread into Belgium. This was largely due to the work of the Brussels professor H. de Page (*d.* 1969) who wrote a very influential *Traité élémentaire de droit civil*, which appeared from 1933, latterly in collaboration with R. Dekkers (*d.* 1976), a professor in Brussels and Ghent. One of the first Belgian authors to attack the exegetical method was Edmond Picard (*d.* 1924), a progressive advocate and socialist senator who regarded law as a 'social phenomenon' which must be studied without 'pedantic erudition' (*Le Droit pur. Cours d'encyclopédie du droit*, 1899). Professor Jean Dabin (*d.* 1971) was another lawyer who reacted against the School of Exegesis, more on ideological than sociological grounds.[17]

In the Netherlands, the School of Exegesis never acquired the

[15] His *Histoire du droit des gens*, later entitled *Histoire de l'humanité* (18 vols., 1850–70), was so anti-Catholic that it was put on the *Index librorum prohibitorum* in 1857.

[16] I, *De Verbintenissen* ('obligations'; 1925, 5th edn 1948); II, *De Erfenissen* ('succession'; 1927, 5th edn 1954); III, *De Schenkingen en Testamenten* ('gifts and wills'; 1930, 4th edn 1955); IV, *De Contracten* ('contracts'; 1934, 2nd edn 1952); V, *Zakenrecht* ('property'; 1936, 4th edn 1953); VI, *Voorrechten en Hypotheken* ('ranking and securities'; 1939, 2nd edn 1951); VII, *Personen- en Familierecht* ('persons and family law'; 1942, 2nd edn 1950); VIII, *Het huwelijkscontract* ('the contract of marriage'; 1945, 2nd edn 1950).

[17] See his *Philosophie de l'ordre juridique positif* (1929) and *Technique de l'élaboration du droit positif* (1935).

doctrinal near-monopoly which it had had in Belgium. In any case, jurisprudence in the Netherlands was not influenced exclusively by French thought: German thought, especially the Pandectist and Historical Schools (which went more or less unnoticed in Belgium), had a greater influence there.

GERMANY

76 The German empire acquired its code only in 1900. There were various reasons for the delay. Political events were of course decisive: the political conditions necessary for the introduction of a national code were not satisfied while Germany remained fragmented into kingdoms, principalities and free cities. Some regions – such as the kingdom of Saxony in 1863 – promulgated their own codes. Other, more westerly, regions retained the French codes. There were those in favour of introducing the French codes throughout German territory, in order to provide a modern, common law. (This had been done in Russia, where the *Code de procédure civile* of 1806 was introduced.) Yet political objections prevailed against the introduction of the codes of France, the old enemy and occupier, against which the whole German nation had so patriotically conducted its war of independence.[18] When Germany was unified in 1871, although the old states did not disappear, political circumstances were distinctly more favourable, and there was a pronounced feeling that the new empire should have its own codes. In 1877 a code of civil procedure (*Reichscivilprocessordnung*) was completed, and came into force on 1 January 1879. It took longer to work out a civil code: that was promulgated in 1896 and came into force in 1900. For economic reasons it had already been necessary to unify commercial law: in 1862 the principal states had adopted a general statute on German commerce, which was extended to the union of northern Germany in 1869, and in 1871 became general to the German empire.

The problems were not only political. There were ideological problems too, especially the objections of principle raised by

[18] Savigny had stipulated that, if a German code was to be compiled, it must originate from the German people, and not be adopted from a nation which had shortly before threatened the ruin of Germany. For similar national and political reasons, the intended adoption of the *Code civil* in Russia was prevented by the Tsar.

Savigny's Historical School.[19] The polemic between the proponents and opponents of codification (like that between Romanists and Germanists) divided German legal practice throughout the nineteenth century. Even if the principle of German codification was accepted, the question still remained what sources should be employed in such a codification. It immediately became clear that the codes of the new German empire would not be innovative, let alone revolutionary: they would be traditional, and not much orientated towards the future. The next question was on what past and what tradition they should be based. The influence of the Historical School managed to rule natural law out of order, and only a legal system which had actually been in force in Germany came into consideration. There were two possibilities. The first was the learned law as 'received' in Germany from around 1500: this was Savigny's choice. It had been greatly developed and systematized by the School of Pandectists under Bernhard Windscheid, which could point to the facts that over the centuries *gemeines Recht* had become completely integrated into Germany, and that its system was intrinsically superior.

The second possibility was ancient Germanic or German law. In the nationalistic spirit of the time, this had been rediscovered and had been the object of important scholarly studies. K. F. Eichhorn (*d.* 1854)[20] and J. Grimm (*d.* 1863)[21] were the leaders of the Germanists. They regarded old Germanic law as the only possible basis for a true national law of the German people (a *Volksrecht* rather than a *Professorenrecht*). The dispute was essentially a political one which, in the face of any academic rationality, divided German legal historians in the nineteenth century into two opposed camps. German public opinion was nationalistic or even xenophobic: it favoured the Germanists. But the Romanists could plead that *Pandektenrecht* was much more sophisticated and more modern than the law of Germanic antiquity or the Middle Ages.

It is not altogether surprising that the code which eventually resulted bore clear signs of pandectist method, although these had been even more marked in the first draft. It is unnecessary to enter

[19] See above, section 72.

[20] Author of a *Deutsche Rechts- und Staatsgeschichte* (1808) and of an *Einleitung in das deutsche Privatrecht* (1823).

[21] Author of *Deutsche Rechtsalterthümer* (from 1823). He was a distinguished linguist and one of the founders of German philology.

the labyrinth of all the commissions whose works from 1873 onwards contributed to compilation of the *Bürgerliches Gesetzbuch*. Suffice it to note that the final text was adopted by the *Reichstag* and promulgated in 1896, and that it came into force on 1 January 1900. Some non-lawyers, people of distinction in politics and economics, had been asked to join the commissions, but the *BGB* was above all the work of professional lawyers (their views readily prevailed over those of the lay members), and still more the work of academic lawyers rather than judges. The main academic contributor to the preparatory works to the *BGB* was the eminent pandectist Bernhard Windscheid.[22]

The *BGB* is a very systematic and theoretically coherent code, entirely in the spirit of the pandectists, as its important *Allgemeiner Teil* ('General Part') shows. It was the work of academic lawyers addressing themselves to learned judges; their aim was not to disseminate knowledge of the law among the people, although that did not prevent a lively popular interest in the code. An example of the systematic structure of the *BGB*, and the manner in which it moves from general principles to specific rules, is provided by the contract of sale. First it is necessary to consult the *Allgemeiner Teil* (art. 116 and following, art. 145 and following), then the articles on the general principles of obligations (art. 275 and following), next the general principles of contractual obligations (art. 305 and following), and finally the articles on the contract of sale in particular (art. 433 and following).

The *BGB* is typical of the nineteenth century; the fact that it came into force in the last year of that century is symbolic. It is a code which bears the stamp of individualism: its family law is patriarchal (the husband is head of the family including his wife, and he alone is responsible for administering family property); freedom of contract is absolute,[23] and so is the right to private property.[24] In spite of that, and in spite of Nazi intentions of introducing a *Volksgesetz-*

[22] Windscheid was the lynch-pin of the first commission (1881), which published a first draft in 1887. It aroused vigorous criticism from O. von Gierke among others, who published an *Entwurf eines bürgerlichen Gesetzbuchs und das deutsche Recht* in 1888–9. Gierke is best known for his *Das deutsche Genossenschaftsrecht* (4 vols., Berlin, 1868–1913).

[23] N.B. the omission of the *laesio enormis* of Roman and (continental) common law.

[24] The socially conservative tendency of the civil law aroused protest from the Viennese professor of civil procedure A. Menger (*d.* 1906), among others, in his *Das bürgerliche Recht und die besitzlosen Volksklassen* (1890); cf. his *Uber die sozialen Aufgaben der Rechtswissenschaft* (1895).

buch,[25] the *BGB* has proved to be a stable code, and its outstanding professional craftsmanship has secured it great influence abroad.[26]

In the nineteenth century German jurisprudence reached its zenith, both in the development of legal doctrine and in the history and philosophy of law. Its influence was felt in all countries and all areas of law. The technical quality and range of German learning were admired: the advances made by Romanists in the nineteenth century completely transformed understanding of ancient law; the pandectists developed *gemeines Recht* to an unequalled degree of systematization; at the same time pioneering work in medieval Germanic law was carried out, which is still of value today. Legal scholarship had a profound influence on the practice of law. Since no single code applied throughout German territory, scholarship was the principal means of interpreting the learned law, mainly by the issue of binding opinions (*Gutachten*) by the faculties of law to the courts.[27]

German civilian doctrine was fundamentally different from the French School of Exegesis in substance as well as method. But the traditional middle-class lawyers of the two countries shared an essentially conservative and text-orientated approach. It was precisely this which provoked a violent reaction in Germany in the second half of the nineteenth century. The revolutionaries who called the prevailing doctrine into question did not see law as an academic exercise consisting of elaborating and refining legal concepts. They saw it as a struggle between opposing forces and interests. For them, law was above all a social product and a tool for

[25] On this see J. W. Hedemann, *Das Volksgesetzbuch der Deutschen. Ein Bericht* (Berlin, 1941); *Volksgesetzbuch. Grundregeln und Buch I. Entwurf und Erläuterungen*, edited by J. W. Hedemann, H. Lehmann and W. Siebert (Munich and Berlin, 1942); *Zur Erneuerung des bürgerlichen Rechts* (Munich and Berlin, 1944; Schriften der Akademie für deutsches Recht. Gruppe Rechtsgrundlagen und Rechtsphilosophie, 7); H.-R. Pichinot, *Die Akademie für deutsches Recht. Aufbau und Entwicklung einer öffentlich-rechtlichen Körperschaft des dritten Reiches* (Kiel, 1981); H. Hattenhauer, 'Das NS-Volksgesetzbuch', *Festchrift R. Gmür* (Cologne, 1983), 255–79; W. Schubert, W. Schmid and J. Regge (eds.), *Akademie für deutsches Recht. Protokolle der Ausschüsse 1934–44* (Berlin, from 1986); D. le Roy Anderson, *The academy of German law* (London, 1987); M. Stolleis and D. Simon (eds.), *Rechtsgeschichte im Nationalsozialismus. Beiträge zur Geschichte einer Disziplin* (Tübingen, 1989; Beiträge zur deutschen Rechtsgeschichte des 20. Jts., 2).

[26] The Swiss code of 1907, which was mainly the work of Eugen Huber (*d.* 1922), is clearly influenced by the *BGB*. Further afield, the main follower of the *BGB* was Japan, which hesitated for years between the French and German codes but finally adopted the *BGB* in 1898, before it had even come into force in Germany. The *BGB* also influenced the Chinese code of 1929, and others too numerous to mention. The ascendancy of the *BGB* brought an end to the monopoly of the *Code civil*, which until then had served as the international model.

[27] See above, section 31.

social action, rather than the privileged domain of learned jurists; their doctrine is known as *Interessenjurisprudenz*, as opposed to the traditional *Begriffsjurisprudenz*.[28] It was necessary therefore to establish what social objectives were to be achieved with the aid of the law: hence the title of the radical work by Rudolf von Jhering (*d.* 1892), *Der Zweck im Recht* (1877)[29] and its motto 'Purpose is the creator of all law.' Von Jhering had himself begun as a traditional Romanist, but he became dissatisfied with abstract logical reasoning and involved in the social problems of his time, and this led him to develop his own concept of law. His evolution can be followed through the various editions of his outstanding *Geist des römischen Rechts auf den verschiedenen Stufen seiner Entwicklung* (1852–65),[30] in which a sociological approach to ancient law becomes increasingly prominent. His *Der Kampf ums Recht* (1872)[31] caused a sensation by presenting law explicitly as the object of a struggle for collective interests and for power, and so, ultimately, as the result of political forces. This analysis was an inevitable conclusion from legal positivism: for, if statute was the sole source of law (and all reference to a superior order such as natural law had been disposed of), it necessarily followed that law was the instrument of the forces which dominated the state and its legislative organs.[32]

CONSERVATIVE ENGLAND

77 A continental lawyer who crosses the Channel enters another world. Exegesis of a civil code is unknown, since English law is not codified. Academic *Begriffsjurisprudenz* is also unknown, since until recently there were no law faculties and even nowadays the role of scholarship in legal practice is very modest. As a result, case law is the main source of law, closely followed by legislation, which has steadily gained ground over the years. At the beginning of the nineteenth century, English law was old and out of date, and many of its basic structures and concepts went straight back to the Middle

[28] P. Heck, 'Interessenjurisprudenz und Gesetztreue', *Deutsche Juristenzeitung* (1905), col. 1140–2; *idem.*, 'Was ist diejenige Begriffsjurisprudenz die wir bekämpfen?', *ibid.* (1909), col. 1019–24.

[29] 'The purpose of law.' Jhering's work was translated into French by O. de Meulenare, this particular work as *L'évolution du droit* (Paris, 1901).

[30] 'The spirit of Roman law at different stages of its development.'

[31] 'The struggle for law.'

[32] Here the influence of the sociologist Auguste Comte is clear, and his rejection of any metaphysical principle in favour of observation and experience.

Ages. It is a paradox that the most economically and socially advanced nation in the world had only a medieval legal system. Modernization of the law came late and did not alter the basic characteristics of the Common Law, in spite of Jeremy Bentham's virulent attacks on it. So civil law was not codified, but remained what it had been for centuries, a system based on custom and thousands of cases, and progressively developed by case law. The dichotomy between Common Law and statute was maintained.

The role and prestige of judges remained very significant, and the authority of their judgments considerable. It even came – temporarily – to the absurd point that the supreme court declared itself bound by its own precedents, an effective recipe for fatal immobility.[33] But this has now been abandoned. The judiciary has also recognized the primacy of statute and expressly abandoned any pretensions to controlling the validity of statute by reference to the general principles of the Common Law. Yet case law has taken sometimes surprising liberties in the application of statutes whose text seemed clear.[34] It is still a widely held view that statute constitutes a sort of derogation from the Common Law and ought therefore to be interpreted restrictively, as if the Common Law were the rule and statute the exception. A remark by Stallybrass, who taught law at Oxford, on the law syllabus at that university is typical: he congratulated the Oxford law school for having the good sense to exclude 'those branches of the Law which depend on Statute and not on precedent'.[35]

Universities and law professors played a modest part, and their prestige was low. Although they have now risen from a low point in the nineteenth century, the secondary importance of universities is characteristic of the English legal world. University teaching of law (at least English law) began late, at Oxford, Cambridge and London in the second half of the nineteenth century, and in the provincial universities only after the First World War. The delay was partly due to the attitude of the universities, which considered the teaching of law barely respectable, and thought its place was not in an

[33] The House of Lords in *London Street Tramways* v. *LCC* (1898).

[34] e.g. the judgment of the House of Lords in *Roberts* v. *Hopwood* (1925): the statute allowed local authorities to fix the salaries of their staff as they thought appropriate, yet when a local authority fixed a minimum weekly salary of £4 this was held by the House of Lords to be unreasonable and inspired by 'eccentric principles of socialistic philanthropy'.

[35] W. T. S. Stallybrass, 'Law in the universities', *Journal of the Society of Public Teachers of Law*, n.s. 1 (1948), 163.

academic context but in professional or technical education. The professional organizations too were partly responsible for the delay, since their preference was to found practical law schools, and they did in fact found several. Finally, in the courts there was a deep-seated mistrust of academic and theoretical legal education. Traditional judges favoured a general university education, for instance in history or politics, followed by a professional education in the Inns of Court or the schools of the Law Society. Talented young people who wanted to embark on a legal career were therefore advised to study a more 'respectable' discipline at university: anything but law.[36] Leading figures openly expressed their doubts about the appropriateness of university teaching of law. Professor A. V. Dicey (*d.* 1922) even devoted his inaugural lecture at Oxford to the (unrhetorical) question, 'Can English law be taught at the universities?' (1883), fully expecting that lawyers would at once answer, 'no'. It is therefore hardly surprising that university teaching and university degrees in law began only cautiously during the second half of the last century.

The role of scholarship was (and still is) of little importance. In 1846 Brougham summed up this trait of English law in the caustic remark that 'not only does it have no professors, but it does not even have books to replace them with'. Yet England did produce authors of international distinction, particularly in the nineteenth century and in the areas of legal philosophy and international law. The following deserve mention: John Austin (*d.* 1859), the positivist author of *The province of jurisprudence determined* (1832) and *Lectures on jurisprudence* (posthumous edition, 1863); Sir Henry Sumner Maine (*d.* 1888), *Ancient law* (1861); F. W. Maitland (*d.* 1906), author, with F. Pollock, of *History of English law before the time of Edward I* (1895); A. V. Dicey (*d.* 1922), *Introduction to the study of the law of the Constitution* (1885) and *Digest of the law of England with reference to the conflict of laws* (1896); Sir Thomas Erskine Holland (*d.* 1926), *Elements of jurisprudence* (1895–1924) and *Studies on international law* (1898). But there were no great commentaries on English civil law in the manner of the great continental *traités*, *cours* and *Lehrbücher*; and the great names

[36] See A. Philips, *The credentials of a law faculty* (Southampton, 1958). Most judges were students at Oxford or Cambridge but virtually none had studied law. Even in 1963 a prominent figure such as Lord Shawcross, who had taught law at Liverpool, could advise intending lawyers not to study law at university; and Lord Cross, who had been a professor at one of the Law Society's schools, praised judges who had taken degrees in subjects other than law.

of English law are not those of scholars or professors, but of celebrated judges such as Lord Denning, Lord Shawcross, Lord Gardiner or Lord Devlin.

INNOVATION IN ENGLAND

78 For the time being, the basic structures of English law had been preserved, but from the early nineteenth century the system underwent several important transformations. Most were due to the legislature taking a grip on the old and often elusive Common Law and replacing it with clear and precise statutes. In England, to do this was to explode the myth of the traditional law.

In the first instance, the legislature attempted to extricate itself from the extraordinary profusion of statutes, which had been promulgated without any coordination since the Middle Ages; they sometimes contradicted one another, and a clear overview of them was impossible. A commission of the House of Commons calculated in 1796 that a thousand statutes which were no longer applied were still officially in force.[37] In the nineteenth century, above all after Brougham's speech to the House of Commons in 1828 and the relative democratization of the House by the Reform Act of 1832, a considerable effort was made to abolish many statutes and institutions which were either feudal or simply out of date (e.g. the judicial ordeal) and to establish an authentic modern collection of statutes in force. For this purpose Parliament published lists of obsolete statutes and promulgated Repeal Acts. Even Magna Carta was sacrificed on the altar of modernization,[38] although some conservative authors maintained that ancient statutes could not be abrogated, even if their actual or potential utility could be neither demonstrated nor even guessed at.[39] This modernization, pursued in accordance with the principles of utilitarianism, represented Bentham's posthumous revenge.

The abolition of obsolete texts was a substantial project, but it did not involve codification; it merely allowed the compilation of a vast

[37] One of the results was the publication between 1810 and 1822 of nine folio volumes of statutes going back to 1713. This was at the same time a practical collection, an edition of historical sources, and the point of departure for the nineteenth-century reform movement.

[38] A. Pallister, *Magna Carta. The heritage of liberty* (Oxford, 1971), examines this point in detail.

[39] G. Sharp, *A declaration of the people's natural right to a share in the legislature* (London, 1774), 202–3: 'This glorious charter must ever continue unrepealed and even the articles which seem at present useless must ever remain in force.'

repertory of the statutes still in force. The great volume of the Acts could be appreciated when they were brought together in 1870 in an official collection of no fewer than eighteen volumes.[40] Many ancient statutes had been abrogated, but many had been preserved, and the 'old law' as such was never abolished, as it had been in France at the time of the Revolution. In any case, the notion of 'old law' is quite meaningless for English law, which is characterized precisely by its continuity. Old statutes and cases are to be found side by side with recent statutes and precedents, as the index of sources at the beginning of any English legal work will show.

The work of Parliament was not limited to abrogation of antiquated statutes; it also produced positive results. In no area was this more spectacular than in the court system and in civil procedure. It must be emphasized that in Common Law any important modification in procedure inevitably involved a change in substantive law. The Common Law had developed as a system based on the 'forms of action', each form being initiated by a particular writ and each following its own rules. This system remained essentially in place until the nineteenth century so that an action, like a Roman *actio*, could not be initiated unless the appropriate writ existed. Over the centuries, new writs had been created and others had fallen into disuse, giving a total, around 1830, of nearly seventy writs. When the legislature abolished the forms of action, it therefore overturned the procedural basis of Common Law. At the same time the rather disorderly system of courts and tribunals which had developed since the Middle Ages was replaced by a more systematic hierarchy of higher and lower courts. The main elements of the court reform were the following.

In 1846 county courts were created for minor cases. For the more important cases, the various courts of medieval origin (including the church courts) were replaced by a central High Court of Justice sitting at first instance, and a Court of Appeal. Both courts were in London. The old distinction between Common Law and Equity and their separate courts were abolished. It was also intended that the jurisdiction of the House of Lords should be abolished, and in fact the Judicature Act 1873 provided for its abolition. That provision, however, was repealed in 1875, and so the Court of Appeal is still

[40] This was the starting-point for further revision, which continued into the twentieth century. But revision does not mean reduction: the third edition of *Statutes revised* (1950) is in thirty-two volumes.

subordinate to the House of Lords, which operates not as a *cour de cassation* but instead as a second court of appeal (this double appeal is a peculiarity of the English legal system). By the Appellate Jurisdiction Act 1876 the judicial activity of the House of Lords was restricted to those members who were professional lawyers (Law Lords). There was a fundamental modernization of the law of procedure. The old forms of action were abolished,[41] and replaced by a single, less formal, procedure. Henceforth process was initiated by a uniform writ, which stated the claim simply, in terms which were neither prescribed nor technical. The difference between the procedures in Equity and in Common Law also disappeared. The new procedure made use of elements of both systems, but the principles of Equity were decisive. It is true that the jury in civil cases was taken from the Common Law, but its role was sharply reduced until it eventually became non-existent in practice. The 1875 Act also made it possible to codify the rules of procedure, by means of detailed regulations made by the courts themselves (*Rules of Court*).

The democratic significance of these reforms is obvious, since the procedural rules were extremely technical and one of the areas of English law least accessible to the public. Intellectual democratization, however, was not accompanied by any financial democratization, and the expenses of process remain exorbitant. This is why many cases go to arbitration or conciliation. Only litigants of great means (in particular large companies) can pursue their cases to the very end, in the hope of obtaining a precedent. The result is that a very small number of cases is dealt with by a very small number of highly qualified and highly authoritative judges in the central courts in London.

The great reforms of the nineteenth century also introduced a modern appeal procedure for the first time. This was of the Roman and continental type, which allowed a new inquiry into the facts. Prior to this Common Law had provided only a restricted procedure for revision of an error committed at first instance.

Reform of the civil law also began, but on a much more modest scale. The new legislation dealt only with specific areas which had somehow engaged public attention. One example is the statutes of 1870 and 1882 providing that the income and personal property of a

[41] The main steps were the Uniformity of Process Act 1832, the Civil Procedure Act 1833, the Real Property Limitation Act 1833, which reduced the sixty real and mixed actions to four, and the Common Law Procedure Acts 1842, 1854 and 1860.

woman acquired before or during her marriage should revert to her personally. Another is divorce, which had previously been possible only by virtue of an extremely costly private Act, but which was now within reach of everyone and followed the rules of ordinary procedure.[42] Debtors' prison for the insolvent was abolished in 1869. Few areas of civil and commercial law were codified.[43] Until the creation of the Law Commission in 1965, no official initiative was taken towards codification of the civil law.[44] The only branch of the law which was to be codified in the nineteenth century was criminal law, but a draft prepared by Sir James Fitzjames Stephen, author of the *Digest of criminal law* of 1877 was abandoned, even though codification had been announced in 1882 as one of the government's projected reforms. The practice of law in England today is of course affected by the lack of any significant codification. The rules and principles of English law are still to be found in more than 3,000 Acts of Parliament going back to the first half of the thirteenth century and in some 350,000 reported cases.[45]

BIBLIOGRAPHY

79 Abel-Smith, B. and Stevens, R., *Lawyers and the courts. A sociological study of the English legal system 1750–1965*, London, 1967

Algra, N. E., *Rechtsafgang*, Groningen, 1973

Arnaud, A.-J., *Les juristes face à la société du XIXe siècle à nos jours*, Paris, 1975; Coll. SUP. Le juriste, section dir. J. Carbonnier, 7

Atiyah, P. S., *The rise and fall of freedom of contract*, Oxford, 1979

Baert, G., 'François Laurent', *Nationaal biografisch woordenboek* 5, Brussels, 1972, col. 502–12

Baums, T. (ed.), *Entwurf eines allgemeinen Handelsgesetzbuches für Deutschland (1848–49). Text und Materialien*, Heidelberg, 1982

Bellefroid, P., 'Het Nederlandsch Burgerlijk Wetboek van 1838 en Napoleon's Code civil', *Rechtskundig weekblad* (1937–8), col. 1,473–84

Björne, L., *Deutsche Rechtssysteme im 18. und 19. Jahrhundert*, Ebelsbach, 1984; Münchener Universitätsschriften, Jur. Fakultät. Abhandlungen zur rechtswissenschaftlichen Grundlagenforschung, 59

[42] For the time being divorce was available only for adultery, desertion or cruelty (although the last of these was interpreted rather broadly). Only in 1969 did the Divorce Reform Act introduce divorce by consent.

[43] Bills of Exchange Act 1882, Partnership Act 1890, Sale of Goods Act 1893.

[44] The parliamentary brief for the Commission states expressly 'all the law . . . with a view to its systematic development and reform, including in particular the codification of such law . . .'.

[45] G. Wilson, *Cases and materials on the English legal system* (London, 1973), 271.

Nordische Rechtssysteme, Ebelsbach, 1987; *ibid.*, 67
Bonnecase, J., *L'école de l'exégèse en droit civil*, 2nd edn, Paris, 1924
La pensée juridique française de 1804 à l'heure présente, Bordeaux, 1933
Bouckaert, B., *De exegetische school. Een kritische studie van de rechtsbronnen- en interpretatieleer bij de 19e eeuwse commentatoren van de Code civil*, Antwerp, 1981
Broeck, J. van den, 'De Belgische rechtsleer en de Duitse rechtshistorische school in de 19e eeuw', *Liber amicorum J. Andriessen, A. Keersmaekers and P. Lenders*, Louvain and Amersfoort, 1986, 309–22
Caroni, P. (ed.), *Das Obligationenrecht 1883–1983. Berner Ringvorlesung zum Jubiläum des schweizerischen Obligationenrechts*, Berne and Stuttgart, 1984
Privatrecht. Eine sozialhistorische Einführung, Basle and Frankfurt, 1988
Le Code civil. Livre du centenaire, Paris, 1904; 2 vols.
Coing, H. (ed.), *Handbuch der Quellen und Literatur der neueren europäischen Privatrechtsgeschichte*, III, 3: *Das 19. Jahrhundert: Gesetzgebung zu den privatrechtlichen Sondergebieten*, Munich, 1986
Vorträge zum 200. Geburtstag von F. C. von Savigny, Frankfurt, 1979; Ius commune 8
Coing, H. and Wilhelm, W. (eds.), *Wissenschaft und Kodifikation des Privatrechts im 19. Jahrhundert*, Frankfurt, 1974–82, 6 vols.; Studien zur Rechtswissenschaft des 19. Jahrhunderts
Coppens, C., 'Het tribunal civil du departement de l'Escaut en de rechtbank van eerste aanleg te Gent. Een bijdrage tot de studie van de burgerlijke rechtspraak in de periode 1796–1830', *Revue belge d'histoire contemporaine* 14 (1983), 1–52.
Dabin, J., 'Individu et société. Les transformations du droit civil du Code Napoléon à nos jours', *Bulletin Acad. royale des sciences de Belgique*, 5th ser. 44 (1958), 176–98.
Dahlmanns, G. J., *Der Strukturwandel des deutschen Zivilprozesses im 19. Jahrhundert*, Aalen, 1971
Dannreuther, D., *Der Zivilprozess als Gegenstand der Rechtspolitik im deutschen Reich 1871–1945. Ein Beitrag zur Geschichte des Zivilprozessrechts in Deutschland*, Frankfurt, 1987; Rechtshistorische Reihe, 53
Dekkers, R., '150 jaar Burgerlijk Wetboek', *Rechtskundig weekblad* 18 (1954–5), col. 737–46
Derine, R., *Grenzen van het eigendomsrecht in de 19de eeuw. Bijdrage tot de geschiedenis van het modern privaatrecht*, Antwerp, 1955
Dievoet, E. van, *Het burgerlijk recht in België en in Nederland van 1800 tot 1940. De rechtsbronnen*, Antwerp and The Hague, 1943
Dievoet, G. van (ed.), *Tweehonderd jaar notariaat. Het kantoor Hollanders de Ouderaen te Leuven (1783–1983)*, Louvain, 1983; Acta falconis, 83/6
Dilcher, G. and Kern, B.-R., 'Die juristische Germanistik des 19. Jahrhunderts und die Fachtradition der deutschen Rechtsgeschichte', *Zeitschrift der Savigny-Stiftung für Rechtsgeschichte* (G. A.) 100 (1984), 1–46
Dufour, A., 'Savigny, la France et la philosophie allemande. Etude critique

à propos de deux ouvrages récents sur Savigny', *Revue d'histoire du droit* 55 (1987), 151–64

Duguit, L., *Les transformations générales du droit privé depuis le Code Napoléon*, 2nd edn, Paris, 1920

Duman, D., *The judicial bench in England 1727–1875: the reshaping of a professional elite*, London, 1982; Royal Historical Society

Ebel, F., *Savigny officialis*, Berlin and New York, 1987; Schriftenreihe der juristischen Gesellschaft zu Berlin, 104

Erauw, J. and Bouckaert, B. (eds.), *Liber memorialis François Laurent 1810–87*, Brussels, 1989

Gaudemet, J., 'Histoire et système dans la méthode de Savigny', *Hommage à René Dekkers*, Brussels, 1982, 117–33

Gilissen, J., 'Codifications et projets de codification en Belgique au XIXe siècle (1804–1914)', *Revue belge d'histoire contemporaine* 14 (1983), 203–8

Godding, P., 'Les contrats de mariage dans la première moitié du 19e siècle: fidélité à la coutume ou adoption sans réserve du Code Napoléon', *Revue belge d'histoire contemporaine* 14 (1983), 91–114

Grimm, D., 'Methode als Machtfaktor', *Festschrift H. Coing*, I, Munich, 1982, 469–92

Hedemann, J. W., *Die Fortschritte des Zivilrechts im XIX Jt. Ein Uberblick über die Entfaltung des Privatrechts in Deutschland, Osterreich, Frankreich und der Schweiz* I, II, 1, 2, Berlin, 1910–35

Heyse, M., 'Edmond Picard', *Nationaal biografisch woordenboek* 6, Brussels, 1975, col. 773–7

Hofmeister, H. (ed.), *Kodifikation als Mittel der Politik*, Vienna, 1986; Wiener rechtsgeschichtliche Arbeiten XVI

Holthofer, E., 'Zivilgesetzgebung nach dem Code civil', *Vorträge zur Geschichte des Privatrechts in Europa. Symposium in Krakau 9–12 okt. 1979*, Frankfurt, 1981; Ius commune Sonderhefte Texte und Monographien, 15, 123–49

Jakobs, H. H., 'Der Ursprung der geschichtlichen Rechtswissenschaft in der Abwendung Savignys von der idealistischen Philosophie', *Revue d'Histoire du Droit* 57 (1989), 241–73

Wissenschaft und Gesetzgebung im bürgerlichen Recht nach der Rechtsquellenlehre des 19. Jts, Paderborn, 1983; Rechts- und staatswissenschaftliche Veröffentlichungen der Görres-Gesellschaft, n.s. 38

Janssen, A., *Otto von Gierkes Methode der geschichtlichen Rechtswissenschaft. Studien zu den Wegen und Formen seines juristischen Denkens*, Göttingen, 1974; Göttinger Studien zur Rechtsgeschichte, ed. K. Kroeschell, 8

Kelley, D. R., *Historians and the law in post-revolutionary France*, Princeton, 1984

Kiralfy, A. K. R., *The English legal system*, 4th edn, London, 1967

Kop, P. C., *Legisme en privaatrechtswetenschap. Legisme in de Nederlandse Privaatrechtswetenschap in de negentiende eeuw*, Deventer, 1982; Rechtshistorische cahiers, ed. G. C. J. J. van den Bergh and R. Feenstra, 3

Lecocq, P. and Martinage, R., 'Les magistrats et la politique au XIXe siècle. L'exemple des commissions mixtes de 1852', *Revue d'histoire du droit* 50 (1982), 19–48

Lehner, O., *Familie, Recht, Politik. Die Entwicklung des österreichischen Familienrechts im 19. und 20. Jahrhundert*, Vienna and New York, 1987

Maitland, F. W., *The forms of action at Common Law. A course of lectures*, ed. A. H. Chaytor and W. J. Whittaker, Cambridge, 1909

Manchester, A. H., *A modern legal history of England and Wales 1750–1950*, London, 1980

Sources of English legal history. Law, history and society in England and Wales 1750–1950, London, 1984

Marini, G. (ed.), *A. F. J. Thibaut – F. C. Savigny. La polemica sulla codificazione*, Naples, 1982

Motte, O., *Savigny et la France*, Berne, 1983

Nörr, K. W., *Reinhardt und die Revision der allgemeinen Gerichtsordnung für die preussischen Staaten. Materialien zur Reform des Zivilprozesses im 19. Jahrhundert*, Frankfurt, 1975; Ius commune Sonderhefte, 4

'Wissenschaft und Schrifttum zum deutschen Zivilprozess im 19. Jt', *Ius commune* 10 (1983), 141–99

Ogorek, R., *Richterkönig oder Subsumtionsautomat? Zur Justiztheorie im 19. Jahrhundert*, Frankfurt, 1986; Rechtsprechung: Materialien und Studien. Veröffentlichungen des Max-Planck-Instituts für europäische Rechtsgeschichte, 1

Ogris, W., *Die Rechtsentwicklung in Osterreich 1848–1918*, Vienna, 1970

Piret, R., 'Le Code Napoléon en Belgique', *Revue internationale de droit comparé* 6 (1954), 753–91

Postema, G. J., *Bentham and the common law tradition*, Oxford, 1986; Clarendon law series

Radcliffe, G. and Cross, G., *The English legal system*, 6th edn, by G. J. Hand and D. J. Bentley, London, 1977

Rotondi, M. (ed.), *Inchieste di diritto comparato 6: la scienza del diritto nell'ultimo secolo*, Padua, 1976

Royer, J.-P., *La société judiciaire depuis le XVIIIe siècle*, Paris, 1979

Rubin, R. R. and Sugarman, D. (eds.), *Law, economy and society. Essays in the history of English law 1750–1914*, Abingdon, 1984

Rückert, J., *Idealismus, Jurisprudenz und Politik bei Friedrich Carl von Savigny*, Ebelsbach, 1984

Rumble, W. E., *The thought of John Austin: jurisprudence, colonial reform and the British constitution*, London, 1985

Savigny e la ciencia juridica del siglo XIX. Anales de la cátedra Fr. Suarez, 18–19, Granada, 1978–9

Schröder, H., *Friedrich Karl von Savigny. Geschichte und Rechtsdenken beim Ubergang vom Feudalismus zum Kapitalismus in Deutschland*, Frankfurt, Berne, New York, 1984

Schubert, W., Schmiedel, B. and Krampe, C. (eds.), *Quellen zum Handelsge-*

setzbuch von 1897 I: *Gesetze und Entwürfe*; II, 1, 2: *Denkschriften, Beratungen, Berichte*, Frankfurt, 1986

Schwartz, E., 'Die Geschichte der privatrechtlichen Kodifikationsbestrebungen in Deutschland und die Entstehungsgeschichte des Entwurfs eines Gesetzbuchs für das Deutsche Reich', *Archiv für bürgerliches Recht* I (1899), 1

Spanoghe, E. and Feenstra, R. (eds.), *Honderdvijftig jaar rechtsleven in België en Nederland 1830–1980*, Leiden, 1981; Leidse juridische reeks, xv

Stewart, R., *H. B.: the public career of Henry Brougham 1778–1868*, London, 1985

Thibaut und Savigny. Ein programmatischer Rechtsstreit, Darmstadt, 1959

Tripp, D., *Der Einfluss des naturwissenschaftlichen, philosophischen und historischen Positivismus auf die deutsche Rechtslehre im 19. Jahrhundert*, Berlin, 1983; Schriften zur Rechtsgeschichte, 31

Verdam, P. J., *Nederlandse rechtsgeschiedenis 1975–1795* [*sic*], Alphen a. d. Rijn, 1976

Victor, R., *Een eeuw Vlaamsch rechtsleven*, Antwerp, 1935

Warlomont, R., *François Laurent juriste, homme d'action et publiciste*, Brussels, 1948

Wieacker, F., *Rudolf von Jhering. Eine Erinnerung zum 50. Todestage*, Leipzig, 1942

CHAPTER 6

Statute, case law and scholarship

THE QUESTION

80 The preceding chapters have said a good deal about the various sources of law, especially statute, case law (which is often closely associated with custom) and scholarship (which can be regarded as the creator of natural law). What is needed now is a systematic examination of the role and significance of each of these three great creative forces. What are the merits of each source? What social forces make use of which source? The aim of the chapter is to demonstrate historically that the use of these sources is not random or accidental; they are the basic options open to society when faced with the phenomenon of law. And if law is an instrument of social control, then it matters who controls the sources of law; this fundamental question is far more important than technical or scholarly problems. The origins of legislation and case law are very different: but with what interest groups in society are they associated? And what views of society are expressed by legislator, judge and scholar?

ADVANTAGES AND DISADVANTAGES

81 Each of the three sources of law and legal development has its own advantages and disadvantages. Legislation has the advantage of being able to set out clear rules, and the authority necessary to ensure that they are respected. It is true that case law and scholarship have sometimes gone to extreme lengths to adapt, or even through interpretation to nullify, statutes which they considered outdated or unjust. None the less there is a limit to what free interpretation can do, and it does appear that no other source is as well able to assure legal certainty as the clear and express rule of the

legislator. When statutes have been codified, there is the additional advantage of a coherent, accessible and also limited body of legislative material.

But legislation has its defects too. A statute cannot provide for or regulate all the cases which might arise in practice; the German codes which aimed at exhaustive regulation soon lost themselves in endless enumerations of cases. Individual statutes (not codes) can be promulgated or abrogated quickly and easily, more or less according to the will of the legislator in power, in order to seize opportunities or make temporary provisions. Such manipulation inevitably affects the legal stability essential to the good working of society,[1] and in excess can even lead to lawlessness. But the idea that the authorities can decide that what was at one point law is now no longer so (or vice versa) is relatively recent, and quite unknown in many civilizations. It gives rise to the idea that there must be a counterpart to excessive or arbitrary legislation, a body of superior, unwritten and eternal rules – 'natural' or 'divine' law – independent of positive law and sometimes in opposition to it. The difficulty with codes, however, is quite the opposite: a well-conceived codification makes such great claims to permanence and to logical coherence that it tends to resist change and to lose its normative significance only very gradually. Historical instances of the complete abrogation or replacement of a code are in fact very rare.

Jurisprudence has the ability to explain statutes and judgments, to make criticisms which may lead to reforming legislation, and above all to give a rational basis to the study of law. This demands theoretical reflection, close attention to general principles and the coherence of the system as a whole, as well as an interest in legal philosophy and the purpose of law. But scholarship too has its difficulties. It often has a tendency to become lost in formulating abstract concepts or working out systems which have nothing to do with legal practice. Authors often contradict one another, and contradictory opinions threaten the certainty of the law. In any case scholarly opinions always remain private opinions without power to bind the courts, unless (exceptionally) they have been collected in a

[1] Promulgation and abrogation of statutes was sometimes so casual that judges, and even the legislator, could not be sure what was currently in force. Thus, under Queen Victoria an Act was passed to repeal statutes of Queen Anne and George II which had already been repealed at the beginning of Victoria's reign; and in *Reg.* v. *Great Western Railway* (1842) the court of Queen's Bench considered a statute of Edward VI which had been repealed fourteen years earlier; C. K. Allen, *Law in the making*, 442.

code and promulgated as statute, or a law of citations has given the opinions of one author or another the force of law.

The advantage of case law is that it remains in close touch with reality. Judges invariably give their opinions in concrete cases. As society progresses and is confronted with new situations and new problems, case law has to resolve the questions which arise. As a result the courts cannot afford to develop theories which disregard everyday reality. Precedents do not, admittedly, have the authority of statute, but they have greater weight than scholarly opinions and can therefore offer greater legal certainty. The main disadvantage of case law is that it is made from case to case: it therefore never formulates a general theory which would give an overview of the structure and purpose of the law. In addition, when judges do not give reasons for their decisions, it becomes practically impossible to retrieve rules of law from a mass of specific judgments.[2] The flexibility of judge-made law contrasts with academic or official law, since academics aim precisely to give general accounts and set out basic principles in detail.

A weakness of case law is that it runs the risk of stagnation, particularly when it has excessive regard for its own precedents. A striking example of this is to be found at the beginning of the French Revolution, when the Parlement de Paris was required to decide on the voting method of the newly elected Estates General. The question was whether voting should be by counting heads or by Estates. It was a question which had enormous political significance, since the Third Estate was numerically superior, and would have dominated the assembly in the event of voting by counting heads; indeed, its claim to do so was not unfounded, given its qualitative and quantitative importance within French society. On the other hand, voting by Estates (that is, one vote for the Third Estate, one for the nobility and one for the clergy) would have allowed the two old classes of privilege to predominate, even though their sociological importance was far less than that of the Third Estate: this solution would therefore have given preference to the minority. The question was apparently just a procedural one, but it in fact concealed a crucial political problem. The Parlement de Paris,

[2] See the blunt statement of Chief Justice Fortescue in 1458 (Year Book 36 Henry VI, folio 35 verso to 36): 'The law is what I say it is, and it has been since law existed, and we have a system of procedural forms which are regarded as law and applied for good reasons, although we may not know what those good reasons are.'

however, ignored the political aspect (perhaps in a deliberate attempt to evade the contemporary political trend) and dealt with the question from a purely technical point of view. In its judgment, the Parlement simply followed the precedent of the previous meeting of the Estates General in 1614. The Third Estate revolted against this attempt in 1789 to follow the principles of 1614 without further ado, and proclaimed itself an Assemblée Nationale. The days of the Parlement de Paris were numbered.

LEGISLATORS, JUDGES AND PROFESSORS: COMPETITION

82 Historically, it is clear that representatives of each source of law were firmly convinced of the importance of their own contribution compared with other sources. Some examples will illustrate the point. Savigny's attitude towards statute is instructive. He remarked disdainfully of the Prussian *Allgemeines Landrecht* that it would have to be 'ennobled' by jurisprudence based on Roman law.[3] Although he was not in favour of natural law, Savigny did not go so far as to advocate repeal of the codes inspired by the School of Natural Law. But he did think that they ought to be subject to a jurisprudential revision which would have sharply curtailed their practical importance. He regarded the codes simply as elements of *gemeines Recht*, and thought that the task of jurisprudence was, by appropriate interpretation and correction, to eliminate codified principles which were contrary to Roman law ('pandectization' of the codes). Savigny, who belonged to a family of the old nobility, was frankly hostile to the French revolutionary codes, and feared that the new legislation was the death-knell for the social standing of the upper classes in general and lawyers in particular.

According to Savigny's theory, law develops from a nation's innate sense of justice and from a people's historical and traditional attitudes and values; law is therefore the result of a nation's entire past, and cannot arbitrarily be imposed by the authorities of the present day. Thus to the crucial question: who was qualified to discover and expound the rules of law which the people had developed? Savigny's answer was quite clear: this was a task neither for legislators nor politicians, but for lawyers. They were the legitimate representatives and spokesmen of the people and of the

3 For this purpose Savigny held five lectures on the *Allgemeines Landrecht* in Berlin between 1819 and 1832.

Volksgeist (the same *Volksgeist* which restricted the freedom of the legislator).[4] In Savigny's view, it was the professional class of lawyers which could best secure the development of living customary law, which was the true agent of progress. Resort should therefore not be had to codification, which was the fashion of an age of declining moral standards, but instead to the sound law of the people, expounded with the aid of 'professors, faculties of law, courts, scholarly commissions and judges of the higher courts'.[5] The hostility of the scholar towards the legislator, who with a stroke of the pen could sweep away the most cherished doctrinal constructions, is not at all difficult to understand.[6]

In countries in which case law was of high authority, there was no shortage of judges who took a critical approach towards legal doctrine, including professors and law faculties. The acerbic remarks of some eminent English judges with regard to academic lawyers have already been mentioned. This situation was exactly the opposite of that obtaining in nineteenth-century Germany. The origin of the *BGB* is in fact a case study in the power of legal doctrine, both in the sense that judges remained under the influence of their university education throughout their careers, and in the sense that the non-legal members of the parliamentary codification commissions deferred to the views of the scholars and so made few original contributions to the preparatory works.[7]

The legislator himself was not immune from judicial criticism, even when his projects of reform were both obvious and reasonable. A clear instance is the case of Lord Raymond, Chief Justice of England (*d.* 1733), who in the House of Lords forcefully opposed the plans of the House of Commons to replace Law French with the

[4] Since it was lawyers who had accomplished the *Rezeption*, Savigny acquitted it of the charge of being a foreign product foisted on the German national spirit; cf. 'Atti del seminario internazionale su Federico Carlo di Savigny, Firenze 27–28 ott. 1980', *Quaderni Fiorentini* 9 (1980)); G. C. J. J. van den Bergh, *Wet en gewoonte. Historische grondslagen van een dogmatisch geding* (Deventer, 1982; Rechtshistorische cahiers, 5).

[5] See Wesenberg, *Neuere deutsche Privatrechtsgeschichte*, 142–3; Gerbenzon and Algra, *Voortgangh*, 257.

[6] See the sarcastic remark of Julius von Kirchmann (*d.* 1884) in his lecture of 1848 entitled *Die Werthlosigkeit der Jurisprudenz als Wissenschaft* ('the worthlessness of jurisprudence as a discipline'): 'three correcting words by the legislator, and whole jurisprudential libraries become waste-paper'; quoted by Wieacker, *Privatrechtsgeschichte*, 415.

[7] See Wieacker, *Privatrechtsgeschichte*, 473, who observes that the chairs of law never exercised such great influence on the higher judiciary as in the first half of the nineteenth century, during which most of the lawyers of the *BGB* commissions studied: these conscientious practitioners were not bold or presumptuous enough to free themselves from their teachers.

obligatory use of English in the practice of law and in the courts. In his eyes, the abandonment of the traditional language of the law opened the way to the most capricious innovations; this policy might even lead to the Welsh demanding the power to proceed in Welsh. In spite of his speech, a statute of 1731, which came into force on 25 March 1733, permitted the anglicization of justice.[8]

It is not surprising that politicians confronted with such undemocratic and reactionary obstructions did not allow themselves to be influenced by the 'oracles of the law' of the superior courts. Instead, so far as it seemed necessary, they devoted all their energies to binding the courts to strict observance of the statutes promulgated by the political assemblies.[9] A striking example of the latent opposition between legislative and judicial powers is the judicial control of statutes, in particular in the United States. Judicial review is one of the fundamental institutions of the United States, although it is not a principle expressly recognized by the Constitution, but was introduced and developed by the case law of the Supreme Court from 1803. As a result the American judiciary, and in particular the Supreme Court, has the power to declare a statute promulgated by the legislative bodies (Congress and the President) unconstitutional and to prevent it from being applied.

In Great Britain, on the other hand, where there is no written constitution and where the sovereignty of Parliament is a fundamental principle, judicial review is unknown. The Belgian Constitution makes no mention of it, and the Cour de Cassation has to the present day held firm to its case law going back more than a hundred years and refused to control the constitutionality of statutes. Judicial control exists only in a few legal systems.[10] The principle of a control on the constitutionality of statutes can scarcely be challenged, and if it is accepted that Parliament is bound to respect the Constitution, and that in doubtful cases the judiciary is the power most competent to pronounce on the constitutionality of a statute, then judicial review is the most logical solution. There is, however, the legal objection that the representative assembly of the people expresses the will of the sovereign nation 'from which all powers derive' and so

[8] D. Mellinkoff, *The language of the law* (Boston and Toronto, 1963), 133.

[9] Recall Robespierre's remarks: above, section 67.

[10] See M. Cappelletti, *Processo e ideologie* (Bologna, 1969), 477–510; *idem.*, 'Quelques précédents historiques du contrôle judiciaire de la constitutionnalité des lois', *Studi in memoria di Tullio Ascarelli*, v (Milan, 1969), 2,781–97; *idem.*, *Judicial review in the contemporary world* (Indianapolis and New York, 1971).

cannot be subordinate to the will of another institution; the corollary of this is that, if Parliament violates the Constitution, there is no sanction, but this is generally accepted as a necessary consequence. In Belgium the refusal of the Cour de Cassation, even in its recent case law, to run the risk of judicial review is no doubt partly to be explained by a concern that this would involve the judiciary in political and social conflict. Yet now that the problem of judicial control and the role of the Cour de Cassation has arisen, it is a topical issue in legal and political circles in Belgium.[11]

In France the sovereignty of the legislature is firmly established, and judicial control of the constitutionality of statutes is a recent development. There is a long tradition of administrative law, which is applied by the *Conseil d'Etat*, but constitutional law, which is the province of the *Conseil Constitutionnel*, is a more recent innovation. Since the creation of the *Conseil Constitutionnel* by the Constitution of the Fifth Republic in 1958, development has proceeded apace; and since 1971 the *Conseil Constitutionnel* has assumed responsibility for handing down completely impartial judgments on the constitutionality of statutes, and for supervising parliamentary legislation which might infringe fundamental rights. This trend was reinforced by a constitutional statute of October 1974, which allowed parliamentary minorities to attack legislation before the *Conseil Constitutionnel*. The situation in France has therefore now come close to that in other European countries. Yet, although judicial control is obligatory for organic laws (as defined by the Constitution) and optional for ordinary laws, it is still subject to important restrictions. Individuals cannot address the *Conseil*, as only groups of at least sixty deputies or senators and a small number of the highest political officials have any standing to do so. And a statute can be attacked only in the short period between adoption of its text by Parliament and promulgation. Once a statute is in force, no judge can abrogate it by declaring it contrary to the Constitution.[12]

Legal scholars in favour of law reform also attacked the 'tyranny

[11] The question whether statute was to be interpreted by the legislature or the judiciary has already been dealt with in connexion with the founding of the Cour de Cassation.

[12] M. Cappelletti, 'Repudiating Montesquieu? The expansion and legitimacy of "constitutional justice"', *Catholic University Law Review* 35 (1985), 17–18; L. Favoreu, 'Actualité et légitimité du contrôle des lois en Europe occidentale', *Revue du droit public et de la science politique en France et a l'étranger* 5 (1984), 1,147–201; C. Debbasch, *Droit constitutionnel et institutions politiques*, 2nd edn (Paris, 1986), 503; J. Gicquel and A. Hauriou, *Droit constitutionnel et institutions politiques*, 8th edn (Paris, 1985), 910.

of judges'. Bentham, for instance, was violently critical of a judiciary which on its own authority decided what was the law, referred only to precedents and a vague body of customary rules, and was guided only by unwritten tradition. According to Bentham, lawyers would always defend unwritten law, since it was the source of their power; only the primacy of statute and the power of Parliament to legislate freely would put an end to the despotism of the lawyers.[13] Laurent fulminated just as fiercely against judges (although for quite different reasons) and reproached them for not recognizing the supremacy of the code and for usurping the prerogatives of the legislature. In this dispute, advocates were not lined up on one side or the other. On the European continent they were independent of the legislature, the courts and the universities. In England they had traditional links with the judiciary which were formed at the beginning of their professional lives, when they learned their law as apprentices in the courts. The judges themselves were recruited from among the most successful barristers; a seat on the Bench was an honourable end to a career at the Bar. In England it sometimes also seems that judges and barristers have a common sense of belonging to a group initiated into a rather mysterious, almost religious heritage, which is inaccessible to other men.

LAW AND THE *VOLKSGEIST*

83 From time to time, especially in connexion with Montesquieu and Savigny, reference has been made to theories that law is a product of the life of a nation, and the expression of the national spirit. On the other hand there are the theories that law is or ought to be supra-national and related to human nature, and that a law confined within national frontiers is scandalous or even absurd (Pascal). What can legal history teach us about these two contrasting conceptions?

The classic philosophical discussion of the *Volksgeist* is to be found in Hegel. For him, all the cultural manifestations of a people – its religion, institutions, morality, law, customs, science, art and crafts – are merely visible expressions of a central reality, the *Volksgeist*. Any serious study in any area will sooner or later reveal this central element of the national nature. In the nineteenth century this

[13] See his *General view of a complete code of laws* and his *Book of fallacies*, in *Works*, ed. J. Bowring, II, III (New York, 1962).

conception was very popular, and it is clearly linked with the rise of the nation state, especially in Germany where, under French occupation, nationalistic sentiments developed rapidly. Yet theories about the national character of law are open to criticism. In the Middle Ages and early modern times, the idea that law had a national aspect was virtually unknown. The Roman and canonical models of law were supra-national or even universal; and, in spite of many local variations, the feudal law of all western countries also had a common basis. The prevailing view was therefore of a common law subject to local variation. In practice, national legal systems hardly existed in the Middle Ages, although they are to be found in England and Hungary. In early modern times there was a trend towards national laws, but its results were very incomplete, as is shown in particular by the case of France. The correlation between nation and law was so undeveloped that at the end of the *ancien régime* France still had two great legal zones which were fundamentally different. From the time of the homologation of customs onwards, it was clear that in law the geographical unit was the region rather than the nation.

The speed with which national law developed depended on the individual political circumstances of each country. The strong monarchy in England favoured the very early development of a national law. By contrast Germany, which was divided from the thirteenth century, arrived at a national code only with unification at the end of the nineteenth century. France lies between these two extremes, since it was unified later than England, but earlier than Germany; still, the development of a national French law was slow and halting. A closer inspection of England reveals that the Common Law which developed so early has little to do with a *Volksgeist*, a 'national spirit' or whatever it may be called. The 'typically English' system is in fact nothing other than a continental feudal law, which was imported by the Norman conquerors, and has nothing to do with ancient traditions of the English people or Anglo-Saxon law. The developments in Germany and in Scotland in the sixteenth century also show how little the national law need have to do with the customs of a nation: both of these countries introduced the *ius commune* as their national law in order to make up for the deficiencies of custom.

Here it is also appropriate to consider the development of law in France and in Belgium. The *Code civil* of 1804 was a French code through and through, so the question arises whether, in the Belgian regions in which it was introduced, it represented a foreign element and a break with the national past.[14] The answer is quite clearly no: French law (especially in the north) and 'Belgian' law had developed from common origins and over the centuries had followed parallel courses. Until the sixteenth century most of the county of Flanders was legally part of France. All the essential (Germanic and Roman) ingredients – local and regional customs whether homologated or not, canon law, Roman law, the 'books of law' – were part of a common patrimony. The same applies to the political structures, which in both countries developed from the same feudal, urban and monarchical institutions. The introduction of the *Code civil* into Belgium was therefore not the abrupt imposition of a completely foreign legal system; Belgium was at the same stage of development, and codification was among the ideas of the Enlightenment which were being diffused throughout Europe.[15] Of course, not all rules of the *Code civil* corresponded to old Belgian customs, and it is interesting to note that recently in Belgium there have been occasional steps back to the customary law which the *Code* supplanted. The rights of the surviving spouse, for example, were much more extensive in the old law than under the *Code civil*, and modern Belgian legislation in this area represents a return to ancient custom.[16]

[14] See the commentary in van Dievoet, *Burgerlijk recht in België en Nederland*, 8–11.

[15] See the similar conclusion for the Netherlands in J. van Kan, 'Het burgerlijk wetboek en de Code civil', *Gedenkboek burgerlijk wetboek 1838–1938*, ed. P. Scholten and E. M. Meijers (Zwolle, 1938), 276.

[16] P. Godding, 'Lignage et ménage. Les droits du conjoint survivant dans l'ancien droit belge', *Famille, droit et changement social dans les sociétés contemporaines* (Brussels, 1978; Bibliothèque de la Faculté de droit de l'Université catholique de Louvain, xi), 296; J. P. Levy, 'Coup d'œil historique d'ensemble sur la situation patrimoniale du conjoint survivant', *Etudes offertes à René Rodière* (Paris, 1982), 177–96.

CHAPTER 7

Factors

INTRODUCTION

84 There are two kinds of factor in legal history. The main legal traditions and methods of formation of the law are one kind of factor which has affected the development of law in Europe. This is the sense in which T. F. T. Plucknett used the term in discussing the theme of 'some factors in legal history',[1] where he dealt with five elements: Roman law, canon law, custom, legislation, and precedent. All these can be called 'technical' factors, since they are sources of law in the strict sense, sources of the rules formulated and laid down by lawyers. There are other kinds of factor, however, which may be called 'social'; they encompass broad political, socio-economic and intellectual developments and disputes. These affect society as a whole, and through it the law. Although it is plain that social factors do have an impact on the evolution of law, their influence is much harder to trace than that of technical factors, which can sometimes be identified in the sources themselves, for instance when a text states expressly that a rule is adopted from Roman law or refers to the *ratio scripta*;[2] or where the part played by a particular source is easily identified because – to take the example of Roman law again – the terminology has clearly been lifted from the *Corpus iuris*.

The situation is more complicated if a Roman legal principle is found in a medieval text, but the text does not make use of the Roman terminology. This applies, for instance, to article 9 of Magna Carta of 1215, which provides that the guarantors of a debtor cannot

[1] In Part 3 of the first book of his fundamental work on the Common Law, *A general survey of legal history*.

[2] On this term, which first appeared in the form *razons escricha* in the custom of Alais of 1216–22, and the shifts in its meaning in the following centuries, see A. Guzman, *Ratio scripta* (Frankfurt, 1981; Ius commune Sonderhefte, Texte und Monographien, 14).

be pursued so long as the principal debtor is solvent and in a position to pay his debts. The rule corresponds to the Roman *beneficium excussionis*, but is it a borrowing from Roman law? The timing makes this possible since, in the time of King John, English legal, and particularly church, circles were acquainted with the new learning of Bologna.[3] The example of Archbishop Stephen Langton, who played an important part in Magna Carta, makes this especially clear. But it is also possible that the same measures were taken in different times and places, for equitable or practical reasons, without there necessarily being any direct influence. Thus, the barons in 1215 may well on their own account have eliminated a practice which was not favourable to them, without being aware of Justinian's law. It is a difficult question, which has hardly been studied; yet it is no doubt significant that Magna Carta, unlike other old English legal texts, contains no Roman terminology.[4]

It is clear that a legal historian has to consider what factors have influenced his area of research, and this means not merely technical factors, but social factors too. After all, the small world of lawyers, courts, faculties and government advisers is only a microcosm of the diverse interests and ideas in the world at large.[5]

CHANGE IN LAW

85 The shifting of these interests and ideas means that society, and as a result the law as well, is constantly changing. The appearance at certain historical periods of a stable and immutable law is misleading; and so are the beliefs held by the people of the time. Even in the early Middle Ages, when the predominant view was that the law was unchanging, and when there were in fact fewer attempts at deliberate manipulation of the law than in later periods, pressure groups were still active, and still managed to turn to their own account institutional structures which had been set up for other purposes. Take an example from feudal law: originally the basic principles of the feudal bond, and the interests of the lord, prevented fiefs from being inherited: the fief was granted as the counterpart of personal

3 R. C. van Caenegem, *Royal writs in England from the conquest to Glanvill. Studies in the early history of the common law* (London, 1959; Selden society, 77), 360–90.

4 e.g. Glanvill's *Tractatus de legibus et consuetudinibus regni Angliae* of 1187–9, ed. G. D. G. Hall (London, 1965; Medieval texts).

5 Cf. S. Reynolds, 'Law and communities in western Christendom c. 900–1140', *American Journal of Legal History* 25 (1981), 205–25.

military service which the vassal had to offer; when he died the contract was dissolved and the fief returned to the lord, who could again feu the same property to another vassal (without any obligation to choose the son of the deceased, who might not be so talented or so trustworthy). Vassals, however, were eager to provide for the material well-being of their own line of descendants and, under pressure from them, the principle of inheriting fiefs was recognized in the Frankish kingdom during the ninth century. This is a very clear example of the evolution of customary feudal law.[6] The lords at least managed to preserve their entitlement to *relevium*, the tax due to the feudal lord by the heir when he took possession of the fief. Yet this again aroused a conflict of interests which was to have legal repercussions. Lords were themselves eager to determine the amount of reliefs, according to the heir's circumstances and financial means. But vassals were anxious to avoid arbitrary impositions and called for a fixed scale for reliefs. In England they obtained this scale in article 2 of Magna Carta. This was a reversal of the policy of King John, who had been guilty of imposing arbitrary and exorbitant *relevia*.

Although law is constantly changing, the rate of change varies from one period to another, and periods of stagnation alternate with periods of rapid change. This constant movement occurs whatever the predominant source of the law may be, whether custom, precedent, legislation or scholarship. The shifts in customary feudal law have just been illustrated, and earlier an account was given of the creation of English commercial law through the bold case law of Lord Mansfield.[7] Likewise, several illustrations of the influence of scholarship have been given, while that of legislation is obvious. Yet whatever the means of change in the law, innovation is usually the result of the collective pressure of interests or ideas, and the efforts of groups in society aiming at emancipation or power. For centuries it was possible to justify (and to impose) one particular conception of the law by appealing to the notion of a return to the 'golden age'. During the *ancien régime*, however, opposition to the established order was rife, and argument in favour of a new order widespread; return to the 'good old days' was treated as a notion which had been corrupted by certain self-seeking social groups. But until the seventeenth century, innumerable insurrections and peasant revolts

[6] F. L. Ganshof, *Qu'est-ce que la féodalité?*, 5th edn (Brussels, 1982), 218.
[7] See above, section 69.

marched under the banner of a return to the past. In seventeenth-century England, nationalistic motives provided another reason for this; there the good old law was Anglo-Saxon law, which had been corrupted by the continental law imposed by the Normans under the tyrannical William the Conqueror (the 'Norman yoke'). Only in the eighteenth century did reformers have their eyes fixed resolutely on the future. The old law had lost its prestige as 'good' law.

IDEAS AND POLITICAL POWER

86 To emphasize the role of social movements and conflicts of powers and interests is not to misunderstand the influence of ideas, which are themselves historical facts. Even the best and the most just of ideas, however, can assert itself only when social forces are disposed to adopt it. Without the political will, legal principle has little prospect of success. From the Middle Ages onwards, numerous projects for a supra-national order in Europe were drawn up, among others by brilliant scholars such as Leibniz. Up until the time of Boniface VIII, the papacy had been recognized as having international authority, above states and sovereigns, but this had come to an end at the time of the papal exile in Avignon and had completely disappeared by early modern times, when it was clear that Christianity had become definitively divided. The new situation prompted lawyers and philosophers to make various attempts to create an international legal order, founded by the states themselves, to which national governments would be subordinate. This legal order would ensure internal peace and external security (especially against the Turks). Yet none of the projects came to fruition, and the sovereign states followed their own destinies. In the twentieth century this scene was replayed on the global scale. It is now clear that a world organization with effective power over all nations, including the super-powers, is an impossible dream; the best proof of that is the right of veto of the permanent members of the Security Council of the United Nations.

Still, in legal history when an idea has actually managed to establish a central role for itself, it tends to be pushed to its most extreme logical consequences. Some legal concepts therefore end up virtually as obsessions. Here are two examples. The first is the rise of pontifical theocracy, which is certainly the most striking model of an ideology taken to extremes. From the eleventh century onwards, this theory, which is alien to the original message of Christianity, developed and came to influence every aspect of the institutions of the church until the crisis of the fourteenth century. In turn, church practice and legislation decisively affected European legal systems, both in public and private law. A second example is provided by the aspirations of the monarchy to order and to structure society as a whole. This led to the absolutist state of early modern times. Here too an embryonic idea, that a monarch designated by God was destined to govern an entire society, was developed at all levels of social organization. In practice the idea was sometimes pursued to excess, and only later were the excesses moderated. Suffice it to mention torture in the criminal courts: it was the task of the sovereign to guarantee peace and so to repress crime. In order to ensure convictions, there was no hesitation in permitting witnesses to be examined secretly (already a restriction on the rights of the defence) and allowing confessions to be obtained under torture (which eliminates those rights entirely).

SOCIAL GROUPS AND PRIVATE LAW

87 The survival of man depends on his belonging to, and being protected by, a social group whose members support one another and make their own individual contributions to the group. Over the centuries various types of social group have played this part with consequences for the development of private law, which some examples can illustrate. At first, bonds of kinship constituted the most important social group (the family in the strict sense, the tribe in the broader sense). The individual had duties towards his *parentela*, and when in difficulty he could appeal to it himself. At a later stage feudal solidarity, which united the vassals of a single lord in relation both to him and to one another, became fundamental. The feudal bond entailed both rights and obligations, especially in private law. Finally, from about the twelfth century the city and the state became the basic forms of organization: from now on, belonging to a city or a kingdom took precedence over all other forms of solidarity and loyalty. The general development (as well as the integration of the church into society) can be illustrated by examples.

The law of succession is one reflection of this social development, since devolution of the property of a deceased person has been governed by very diverse legal regimes. Primitive tribes had a relatively simple scheme: the moveable property was burned or buried with the corpse, while the real property (the land) remained in the possession of the familial clan. There was therefore no problem of fragmentation on succession. When this archaic situation changed, the question arose what should happen to the estate. In the early Middle Ages, the importance of the family was still such that the property of the deceased had to remain in its possession, and the estate was divided between the children. Testamentary succession was virtually unknown, although some special forms had developed, such as donations *post obitum* or *pro anima* in favour of the church.[8] The church was disadvantaged by the exclusive devolution of estates to family members, and so encouraged a revival in the making of wills (which had been common in Roman law), at least in favour of church institutions. Its efforts were successful and, even before the renaissance of Roman law, it became customary to make a bequest in favour of ecclesiastical legatees. Meanwhile, the law of intestate succession had undergone another development, dictated by the nature and purpose of feudal law: the law of primogeniture had made its appearance. The exclusion of the younger son is to be explained by the desire to maintain the fief in its entirety, in order to ensure revenues sufficient to allow a knight to discharge his military obligations towards his lord. Fragmentation of a fief among several children would have made this impossible. Now an estate could be made up of a partible mass (*alodia*, to which the old law of succession still applied) and also an impartible mass (*feoda* or fiefs, to which the feudal principle of primogeniture applied). The Roman system of unitary succession was revived only with the *Code civil.*

The development of towns, which applied their own specific rules, also had an impact on the law of succession. Municipalities were anxious that the riches of their citizens should remain within the general economy of the town, and so they levied a special tax on property which left the town by inheritance, the *droit d'issue*. It applied whenever a foreigner acquired the property of a citizen by way of succession or otherwise, and the rate of the levy ranged from 10 to 20 per cent.[9] It was the part taken by the state which was to

[8] P. Jobert, *La notion de donation. Convergences: 630–750* (Paris, 1977; Publications de l'Université de Dijon).

[9] In Flanders it is found already in the thirteenth century, e.g. in an ordinance of Ghent dating from 1286.

end up weighing most heavily on estates, yet apart from practices such as those of King John, who demanded exorbitant *relevia* from the successors of his vassals, it is only recently that rights of succession have become fiscally significant. This trend has become more marked in our day (partly for ideological reasons), so much so that succession to relatives in some degrees is tantamount to confiscation. The burden of tax has practically nullified the legal and economic significance of the system of succession set up by the *Code civil*.

Freedom to dispose of personal landed property is another revealing social indicator. Originally, collective landed property scarcely made sense, since many tribes led a nomadic existence and left their cultivated lands as soon as they were exhausted. Later, forms of family and even individual possession of land developed, but they were still subject to collective restrictions. So far as the family was concerned, this manifested itself in a prohibition on alienating landed property without the consent of the clan. The right of recovery (*droit de retrait*) is one of the collective restrictions which survived into the *ancien régime*: when a piece of land had been sold to a third party (that is, someone who was not a member of the family), members of the seller's family had the opportunity to exercise their right of recovery and buy the property back, so reintegrating the family patrimony. Similarly, feudal lands were long considered inalienable, because they were thought to attach directly to the person (and the personal qualities) of the vassal. This principle was later attenuated, although alienation could still not take place without the consent of the feudal lord. Ultimately, fiefs became freely alienable.[10] It is obvious that restrictions on the sale of land constituted an obstacle to the economic growth of cities, at a time when the need for credit and capitalization of rents demanded that land should be marketable. The towns therefore encouraged the individualism of entrepreneurs, to the detriment of ancient family control of land. Thus, article 19 of the Charter of Ghent of 1191 authorizes the free sale of land. The charter was promulgated by the

[10] The English statute *Quia emptores* of 1290 expressly gave vassals the right to alienate: J. M. W. Bean, *The decline of English feudalism* (Manchester, 1968), 79–103. The freeing of land from all collective restrictions (whether family, feudal, religious or the communal ones of primitive agrarian communities) was one of the main trends in European legal development, which led to individual ownership of land and to the integration of land into the ordinary economic system.

countess of Flanders, who had legislative power permitting her to implement such a change in the law.[11]

In the Middle Ages and the *ancien régime* society was made up of orders and guilds. They had their own administration, rules and jurisdictions.[12] They also had their own legal status: the clergy and nobility not merely enjoyed the usual fiscal privileges, but also benefited from privileges in criminal law (such as an exemption from torture).[13] This social organization under the *ancien régime* had its implications for private law: often only the great landowners had the right to sit in the courts (this was already the case for the Frankish *mallus*). Similarly, there was discrimination in favour of the landed proprietors or *viri hereditarii* of the towns; their evidence and their declarations before a court had greater weight than those of their fellow citizens. Privileges were the order of the day under oligarchic regimes, but the democratization of political institutions, especially in the Italian towns, brought about a development towards the other extreme: the evidence of a nobleman was then given less weight than that of another citizen. The privileged position of the *viri hereditarii* (whose words or oath were probative and prevailed over the evidence of any other person) none the less appears once more in an entirely different context: article 1781 of the 1804 *Code civil* makes a distinction between declarations by employer and by employee: 'the master is believed on his affirmation'.[14]

THE INTELLECTUAL AND MORAL CLIMATE

The law of evidence

88 Law adapts to intellectual developments (or *mentalités*). In some periods, man has felt keenly that he was subordinate to transcendental forces or supernatural beings, and that he was part of a cosmic universe beyond his observation, knowledge and comprehension. At other times, logical and rational thought – exemplified by

[11] The text is in W. Prevenier, *De oorkonden der graven van Vlaanderen (1191-aanvang 1206)* II: *Uitgave* (Brussels, 1964; Commission royale d'histoire. Actes des princes Belges, 5), 15: 'There is such freedom in the city of Ghent that, if somebody desired to sell or mortgage property within the jurisdiction of the city, he was allowed to, whether foreigner or citizen, and nobody could contest it on the ground of any relationship by blood or marriage.'

[12] The numerous extant rules of the guilds and corporations have scarcely yet been studied.

[13] As a corollary, in criminal law the higher classes were sometimes subject to more severe penalties than the lower.

[14] See above, section 6.

empirical scientific and mathematical research – has been predominant. The transition from one *mentalité* to another – from a Platonic to an Aristotelian cosmology – has its repercussions for the law of evidence. Nor should it be forgotten that some peoples have at some stage lived under a religious governing class, which demanded that individuals and the community should respect and observe religious precepts (often enshrined in sacred texts). Such clerical dominance has in several cases been extremely important for the history of European private law.

During the twelfth and thirteenth centuries, the law of evidence underwent a fundamental transformation from a primitive and irrational system to an advanced rational system.[15] Under the old system, even in civil matters (especially in cases about landed property) the courts relied for proof on divine signals in the shape of ordeals. This might take the brutal form of the judicial duel, or the subtler form of the oath supported by oath-helpers. In the first, the party or champion who managed, with a blow of the sword or club,[16] to triumph over his adversary was thought to have had divine assistance in order to achieve victory, which implied that his cause was just. In the second case, it was presumed that possible perjurers would unfailingly meet with divine retribution, and that the fear of celestial wrath would dissuade most people from swearing a false oath.[17] Of course there was awareness in the early Middle Ages of proof by documents and witnesses, but these methods could readily be challenged or neutralized, for instance, if two opposed groups of witnesses insisted on their conflicting evidence. To escape from the impasse, it was then necessary to resort to the judicial duel and an appeal to the divinity.

The whole question, however, was entirely transformed by a profound change in European *mentalités*. A new law of evidence, essentially the one which is still in use, was worked out. It was based on critical and rational evaluation of documents, testimony and real evidence. To establish the reasons for this transition from a magical conception of the universe to a more rational conception is a historical problem which has not yet been resolved; but it is clear that the

[15] See *inter alia* the volumes *La Preuve* in the *Recueils de la société Jean Bodin* XVI (1965–).

[16] Here too class differences played their part, for in a duel a knight used his sword and the peasants their clubs.

[17] Even nowadays the law of civil procedure provides for oaths, whether supplementary or determinative of the action.

transition had implications for the law of evidence. The archaic system, introduced under Germanic influence, had to be abandoned, although it was difficult to decide with what to replace it. In Europe experiments were made with various systems, some derived from the *Corpus iuris*, others (such as the jury) inspired by existing, rudimentary methods which were then developed into a true system of evidence.

One aspect of the modernization of the law of evidence was the increased use of writing. After a period in which writing was virtually unknown, from the twelfth century onwards written proof became widespread, even in agreements between ordinary people. Particularly remarkable is the use of 'authentic' documents – that is, documents 'authenticated', declared worthy of faith, by people or institutions who had public authority to do so. There was a good deal of variety in the form of documents, and in the authorities responsible for their composition or authentication, and this depended in particular on the importance of learned law in the region. In the south, a profession of notaries developed, following on from the Bolognese School of Law. They were invested with public authority by the pope or emperor, prepared by elementary studies in law, and could then establish themselves in the towns and compose and produce authentic documents.

Notaries progressively spread into the northern regions, but in the Netherlands there was no standard notarial practice until the sixteenth century. In the north a quite different means of authenticating documents was evolved, the *œuvres de lois*: the contracting parties went before a court and presented their agreement to it; it was then entered in judicial records, and an extract could be delivered to the parties, although this was not an essential formality. Voluntary jurisdiction was exercised by the ordinary or feudal courts, or by the tribunals of aldermen, together with their other judicial activities. During the later Middle Ages this system became extremely important, and even in early modern times it survived against the competition of notaries. The church courts, especially the officialities[18] also exercised this non-contentious jurisdiction.

Originally, written (and *a fortiori* authenticated) evidence was optional and did not take precedence over proof by witnesses. But the point was highly controversial. A lawyer as distinguished as Pope

[18] See above, esp. section 52.

Innocent III could still declare himself firmly in favour of proof by witnesses: 'the word of a living man prevails over the skin of a dead ass' (i.e. a parchment). Customary law had sayings such as 'witnesses prevail over letters' or 'viva voce witnesses overcome letters'. But it was inevitable that authentic documentary proof should become the standard. The legislation of the Italian towns had moved in this direction even in the fourteenth century (Naples in 1306, Bologna in 1454 and Milan in 1498). In France the main steps in the development were the *Ordonnance* of Moulins of 1566,[19] which provided that, for a transaction in excess of 100 pounds, only written proof would be admissible, and also article 1341 of the *Code civil* of 1804.[20] In Belgium the principle is to be found in the *Edictum Perpetuum* of 1611. In England it was accepted in the eighteenth century that a document could not be challenged purely on the basis of oral evidence.[21] And in some contracts, particularly those concerning land, the law was not satisfied with mere written evidence but required an authentic notarial document.[22]

Lending

89 Changing conceptions of morality, and religious authorities and doctrines, also had important consequences for private law. It is not surprising that they often collided with the policy of the secular authorities. Two illustrations will suffice: lending and marriage.

The economic expansion of the West during the later Middle Ages led to a resurgence in lending. Methods of credit had already been developed and legally recognized in Roman antiquity, but had

[19] See above, section 48.

[20] 'Any matter exceeding the sum or value of 150 francs must be documented before notaries or under private signature, even in the case of voluntary deposits, and proof by witnesses is not admissible as to the content of the documents, or as to what was said before, at the time or since they were written, even if that relates to a sum or value of less than 150 francs. This is without prejudice to what is prescribed in statutes relating to commerce.'

[21] Cf. J. Gilissen, 'Individualisme et sécurité juridique: la prépondérance de la loi et l'acte écrit au XVIe siècle dans l'ancien droit belge', *Individualisme et société à la renaissance* (Brussels, 1967), 35–57; G. Verneillen and G. van de Perre, 'De historiek van de beperking van het bewijs van verbintenissen door getuigen', *Rechtskundig weekblad* 32 (1968–9), col. 817–50.

[22] The requirement of writing was also extended to areas other than evidence. Nowadays it is impossible to imagine a statute which is not printed and published; earlier, matters were otherwise, and it was only the word of the king which had any legal weight. On the learned law, see G. Dolezalek, 'Scriptura non est de substantia legis. A propos d'une décision de la Rote romaine de l'an 1378 environ', *Diritto comune e diritti locali nella storia dell'Europa* (Milan, 1980), 51–70.

disappeared during the first centuries of the Middle Ages. It is extremely difficult to launch a private commercial or industrial enterprise unless at least part of the necessary funds can be borrowed, and, since the temporary use of capital is advantageous, it is normal that it, like materials and labour, should be rewarded. In other words, loans are repaid with interest. Here, however, the needs of economic development collided with religious precepts, for ever since Christian antiquity the church had prohibited lending at interest (*usura*). The prohibition had not only been maintained by the fathers of the church, but had also been enshrined in church law. The ecumenical council of Nicaea of AD 325 prohibited the clergy from agreeing to loans at interest; lay people were initially merely advised by the church against this practice, but the prohibition was subsequently extended to them. A capitulary of Charlemagne of AD 789 unequivocally set out the prohibition: 'it is absolutely forbidden to everyone to lend anything against interest'. Any form of interest, that is any case in which the lender received more than he had lent, was treated as usury and so as a sin. The general condemnation therefore did not apply only to exorbitant rates of interest ('usury' proper), which had been obtained by exploiting a position of strength against the debtor.

This moral attitude corresponded to the mentality of the feudal world, for which any gain, even if it arose from perfectly legitimate commercial operations, represented sin and conduct contrary to social mores. Although in the West this conception is nowadays hard to comprehend, it is still to be found in Islamic countries where religious objections to interest (i.e. usury) still apply. During the last centuries of the Middle Ages, European man had to live in a dilemma: lending at interest had become common in practice, but the church refused to withdraw its prohibition.[23] Secular legislation sometimes reinforced ecclesiastical principles, as for instance an ordinance of 1199 pronounced by Baldwin IX, count of Hainaut and Flanders.[24] As a result medieval commerce had to resort to a series of subterfuges and fictions which allowed it to develop a

[23] Texts could be prayed in aid not merely from the Bible ('lend without hoping for anything in return') but also from Greek philosophy ('money does not create money').

[24] W. Prevenier, 'Een economische maatregel van de Vlaamse graf in 1199: het verbod der leningen tegen interest', *Tijdschrift voor geschiedenis* 78 (1965), 389–401. The text of the ordinance is published in W. Prevenier, *De oorkonden der graven van Vlaanderen (1191 – aanvang 1206)* II (Brussels, 1964), no. 124, 276–8 (Comm. royale d'histoire. Actes des princes belges, 5). On Baudouin IX: *Nat. biografisch woordenboek* I (Brussels, 1964), col. 225–38.

flourishing and indispensable system of credit, while at least formally respecting religious restrictions: sale on condition of repurchase, mortgage (*mortuum vadium*, where the creditor enjoyed the fruits of the property given in security), bills of exchange, interest on arrears (which was allowed by the canonists in certain circumstances). Little by little, moral theology agreed to recognize interest as the price of credit, and to authorize it so far as equitable. This reasoning could be reconciled with the theological theory of the 'just price', according to which each economic good had a *iustum pretium* which ought – especially in credit agreements – to be adhered to.

In spite of this, objections of principle to interest as usury survived in Catholic countries to the end of the *ancien régime*. The highest judges and numerous distinguished authors maintained that interest clauses in contracts were completely void.[25] The French Revolution, which was little disposed to respect religious taboos and was in favour of free commerce, very early proclaimed that lending at interest was legitimate, at a rate fixed by statute.[26] A statute of 1796, authorizing citizens to conclude contracts to their own liking, had anyway been interpreted to mean that the parties themselves could fix their own rate of interest. This position was adopted by the *Code civil* (articles 1905 and 1907), although shortly afterwards the freedom of parties to set rates of interest was again restricted. Later still the freedom of contracting parties was reaffirmed,[27] but unjustified and exorbitant interest (usury) now constituted a crime punished by the criminal law. In protestant countries the doctrines of the reformers had opened the way to permitting interest. Calvin, for example, maintained that interest was admissible: according to him, it was not prohibited by the Bible, where the only prohibition was against lending at disproportionate interest, which was the sin of usury.[28] Many lawyers of the School of Natural Law and authors of the Enlightenment (Grotius, Montesquieu and Voltaire among others) were in favour of freedom of contract, including lending at interest.[29]

[25] D'Argentré, Jean Bodin, Domat, Pothier and the case law of the Parlement de Paris.

[26] Decree of the Constituante of 3–12 December 1789.

[27] In Belgium in 1865, under Rogier and Frère-Orban.

[28] His thesis was, exceptionally, followed by a non-Calvinist author: C. du Moulin's *De usuris*.

[29] Cf. J. Favre, *Le prêt à intérêt dans l'ancienne France* (Paris, 1900); V. Brants, *La lutte contre l'usure dans le droit moderne* (Louvain, 1906); J. Lameere, 'Un chapitre de l'histoire du prêt à intérêt dans le droit belge', *Bull. Acad. roy. sciences de Belgique*, classe des lettres (1920), 77–104; G. Bigwood, *Le régime juridique et économique du commerce de l'argent dans la Belgique du moyen âge* (2 vols., Brussels, 1921–2); G. Le Bras, 'Usure', *Dictionnaire de théologie catholique* xv, 2 (Paris,

The law of marriage

90 Both secular and church authorities legislated intensively on the subject of the family, which was the basic social unit. Particularly in the Middle Ages, family law was without doubt a matter largely of church competence, but its implications for society in general and the family patrimony in particular were such that secular authorities could not entirely abstain from regulation. The divergent approaches to marriage[30] taken by the secular and church authorities in fact make up one of the most interesting chapters in the history of law in Europe. The divergence also shows how a matter of private law could be a prize at stake between authorities whose systems of values and conceptions of society differed. Certainly no other institution was so much at the mercy of opposed trends and ideologies. This account does no more than trace the broad lines of development, and neglects the primitive forms still known in the early Middle Ages, such as marriage by abduction or sale.

It is absolutely fundamental to distinguish between marriage as a secular institution (a contract which affects society at large, and the particular families and their fortunes) and marriage as a sacrament (a means of grace which has a religious meaning, and symbolizes the mystic bond between Christ and his church). These conceptions of marriage relate to secular and church jurisdiction respectively, and as they evolved played a significant part in the history of the West. In the Middle Ages, the sacramental concept of the church and its courts prevailed, whereas in early modern times, and above all in the contemporary period, the secular element has become increasingly important.

According to the teaching of the church, marriage concerned only the spouses personally. Only their free will and decision counted. All interference by their family or parents was excluded, and any question of a patrimonial or dynastic nature was irrelevant. The matrimonial bond was declared indissoluble, on the faith of Scripture. Divorce, which had been admitted in Roman law, was from now on excluded. Within this basic framework, the law of marriage

1950), 2,336–72; B. N. Nelson, *The idea of usury* (Princeton, 1949); J. T. Noonan, *The scholastic analysis of usury* (Cambridge, Mass., 1957); B. Clavero, 'The jurisprudence on usury as a social paradigm in the history of Europe' in E. V. Heyen (ed.), *Historische Soziologie der Rechtswissenschaft* (Frankfurt, 1986), 23–36 (Ius commune, 26).

30 There are numerous studies on marriage. A recent, lucid and magisterial study is J. Gaudemet, *Le mariage en Occident. Les mœurs et le droit* (Paris, 1987; Cerf-Histoire).

none the less evolved. The purely consensual character of marriage recognized in the Middle Ages (that is, that marriage was formed by the free consent of the intending spouses without formalities or the intervention of a priest) was abandoned by the Council of Trent (by the decree *Tametsi* of 1563). It imposed formalities of marriage (witnesses, publicity, celebration by a priest) mainly with the aim of preventing clandestine marriages.[31] The church also developed a theory that mere consent without consummation (*copula carnalis*) constituted an imperfect marriage (*matrimonium initiatum*), which could be dissolved, by contrast with marriage where consent had been followed by sexual relations (*matrimonium ratum*). *Divortium* (after the Council of Trent: *separatio*) *quoad torum et mensam* was also introduced, that is, the physical separation also provided for in the *Code civil*. This allowed cohabitation to end without dissolution (and so prevented remarriage). Finally, the church recognized the nullity of marriage, which an ecclesiastical judge could declare on the ground of a defect in consent or other *impedimentum dirimens* (subsisting prior marriage, kinship, and so on).

Even in the most Catholic of times and places, there was a contrasting secular conception of marriage, which emphasized its social, family and property consequences, as well as its feudal and dynastic ones. This view was hostile to marriages concluded (often secretly) without the consent of relatives, because they directly threatened schemes of alliance between families and fortunes. In periods of staunch Catholicity this view, which was peculiar to the higher feudal and urban circles, could not prevail against the church, but it could express itself by civil and criminal sanctions against spouses who had married without parental consent. In the Middle Ages these sanctions consisted mainly in disinheriting the spouses or condemning the husband for abduction. In France in modern times the secular courts extended their competence to matrimonial cases, and the secular authorities also imposed rigorous regulations, traces of which are still to be found in the *Code civil*. A French *Ordonnance* of 1566 provided for the disherison of children under twenty-five who had married without parental consent. The *Ordonnance* of Blois of 1579 punished abduction, and case law treated

[31] These formalities were also generally taken up in protestant Europe, including the Republic of the United Provinces, although with some modifications. In France, the king did not wish them to be published as they were, but they were none the less introduced in 1579 by the *Ordonnance* of Blois.

a marriage concluded without parental consent as abduction. (The comedies of Molière clearly illustrate how parental, especially paternal, influence still determined children's marriages, even when they had reached majority.) Pothier considered that a marriage concluded without parental consent between spouses under twenty-five was void, and that if the spouses were under thirty the lack of parental consent would involve disherison. In the Netherlands, even in the Middle Ages municipal ordinances set out civil and criminal sanctions against those guilty of seduction, that is marriage without parental consent. In 1540 Charles V ordained that a man under twenty-five or a woman under twenty who married without parental consent lost all the advantages of the surviving spouse. By contrast, in canon law the consent of parents was not a condition at all. The *Code civil* of 1804 demanded paternal consent for men under twenty-five and women under twenty-one. Once beyond this age, children were still subject to the procedure of the *acte respectueux* ('respectful act'), which obliged them to seek their parents' advice; in case of refusal, the marriage could be concluded after a certain number of repetitions of the *acte respectueux*; see articles 152 and 153 of the *Code civil*.

The secular conception did not prevail until the age of Enlightenment, which was hostile to the exaggerated role played by the church and attacked church views on various matters. At the end of the eighteenth century, some countries introduced the option of purely civil marriage without any religious content. In the Austrian Netherlands, Joseph II abolished the jurisdiction of the church courts in matrimonial cases by edict of 28 September 1784: from now on marriage was considered a civil contract, and not in any way subject to the canons of the church.[32] The French Revolution enshrined this principle in its constitution of 1791, using the same terms as Joseph II had done in 1784: 'The law considers marriage as a civil contract only.' In the system of the *Code civil*, marriage was a solemn civil act, and only an officer of the civil state was competent

[32] Art. 1: 'Since marriage is considered as a civil contract, and the civil rights and bonds resulting from it derive their existence, force and determination entirely and uniquely from civil authority, jurisdiction over and decision of the various matters relating to it, and all that depends on it, ought to be the exclusive province of the civil courts. We therefore prohibit any ecclesiastical judge, on pain of absolute nullity, from assuming jurisdiction in any manner . . .' It is clear that religious marriage remained the norm among the population at large; here it is purely a question of jurisdiction in the event of disputes. The current position, which prohibits religious marriage taking place before civil marriage, dates from the nineteenth century (art. 16 of the Belgian Constitution).

to unite the spouses in the name of the law. Yet the vast majority of the people remained attached to religious marriage: only civil marriage had legal consequences, however, and religious marriage had now always to be concluded after civil marriage, if at all. At the same time the church prohibition on divorce was abrogated. Here the Revolution was very radical: by the statute of 20 September 1792 it authorized divorce (which was to be pronounced by a court) either by mutual consent or on a number of other recognized grounds. When this legislation came into force, the number of divorces rose considerably; in some years the ratio between divorces and marriages was as much as one to three.[33] When revolutionary zeal had abated, the legislator took a few steps backward. But in spite of some restrictions, divorce was maintained, by mutual consent or for the reasons set out in articles 229 to 232 of the *Code civil* (adultery, serious cruelty or injury, conviction of an infaming crime).[34]

FINAL CONSIDERATIONS

91 Historical research has succeeded in exploding the myths about law. It has destroyed old, time-honoured conceptions of law: that law is a body of rules decreed by an omniscient God and inscribed in the heart of man; or the product of wise decisions by venerable (but perhaps mythological)[35] ancestors; or a system deduced from the nature of society by men guided by reason. Historical criticism shows that the evolution of law has mostly not been a question of quality (*Qualitätsfrage*),[36] but instead the result of a struggle for power between particular interests, an *Interessenjurisprudenz*.[37] To advance

[33] A. H. Huussen, 'Le droit du mariage au cours de la Révolution française', *Revue d'histoire du droit* 47 (1979), 9–52, 99–127.

[34] Arts. 229–30 are among the clearest instances of discrimination, since they provide that a husband can demand divorce on the ground of his wife's adultery, while his wife can only do so if she has found her husband with his concubine in the matrimonial home. This discrimination was abolished in Belgium by art. 45 of the statute of 28 October 1974. In France, so far as divorce on grounds of adultery is concerned, the discrimination was removed by the statute of 27 July 1884 and the ordinance of 12 April 1945.

[35] Many medieval law books, much later than the great legislator Charlemagne, were still attributed to him, e.g. the supposed 'loi Charlemagne' of Liège.

[36] The term is used by P. Koschaker, *Europa und das römische Recht* (Munich, 1947), 138, of the adoption of foreign legal systems.

[37] The term of Rudolf von Jhering and his school (see above, section 76). Cf. also the notion of Bentham, according to which all statutes have or ought to have the aim of augmenting the total happiness of the community, which means that law is (or ought to be) dictated by what best serves the community: Gerbenzon and Algra, *Voortgangh*, 260.

beyond the traditional, rather naive conceptions is undeniably to deepen and enrich our understanding of the true factors involved in legal evolution. Law is a changing social structure, which is superimposed on society; it is affected by fundamental changes within society, and it is largely the instrument of, as well as the product of, those in power.

Yet lawyers ask themselves if this is an end of the matter, or whether some importance should not still be attached to permanent fundamental principles, which do not just depend on political circumstance or the actions of interested groups; in other words, whether there is a fixed star in the legal firmament. Even, for example, if the laws of Nuremberg had – formally – the force of law, they were undeniably the source of injustice. This reflexion leads to the desire for a body of stable rules, above and beyond changing statutes, and able to serve as a touchstone for assessing the validity of statutes – such, perhaps, as the constitutions and declarations of the rights of man. Lawyers also ask themselves not just about the role of law but about their own rôle in society. Here too historical research has played a demystifying role. It has shown that lawyers have often stood beside those who were powerful and well able to obtain the services of lawyers to plead their cases, compose their statutes or legitimate their claims. The point bears further examination. But at present the overwhelming impression is that the fee-earning lawyer has been a more frequent phenomenon than the revolutionary lawyer who stood up to those in power and defended the cause of the weak and the oppressed.[38] In law, then, the answers to two questions are among the most pressing demands of our time: what are the fundamental laws with which statutes ought to conform? How can we ensure that judges and advocates are independent and always ready to defend the law? Legal history allows these questions to be faced with the aid of human experience accumulated over several centuries.

[38] But we must beware of generalization. There were many judges who resisted considerable political pressure, by foreign occupiers among others, and many advocates who felt constrained to take the part of the oppressed, such as the young advocate Ernest Staes, the hero of the popular novel of that name by the Flemish author Anton Bergmann (*d.* 1874): his first victory was his successful intervention in favour of a worker who was about to fall foul of art. 1781 of the *Code civil* (see above, section 6).

General bibliography

UNIVERSAL AND EUROPEAN LAW

92 Allen, C. K., *Law in the making*, 7th edn, Oxford, 1964

Behrends, O. and Link, C. (eds.), *Zum römischen und neuzeitlichen Gesetzesbegriff. Symposion 26–27 April 1985*, Göttingen, 1987; Abh. Akademie der Wissenschaften Göttingen, Phil.-hist. Klasse, 3 F., 157

Bergh, G. C. J. J. van den, *Eigendom. Grepen uit de geschiedenis van een omstreden begrip*, Deventer, 1979; Rechtshistorische cahiers, 1

Geleerd recht. Een geschiedenis van de Europese rechtswetenschap in vogelvlucht, 2nd edn, Deventer, 1985

Berman, H. J., *Law and revolution. The formation of the western legal tradition* Cambridge, Mass., 1983

Brink, H. van den, *Rechtsgeschiedenis bij wijze van inleiding*, Deventer, 1976

Caenegem, R. C. van, *Judges, legislators and professors. Chapters in European legal history*, Cambridge, 1987

Coing, H. (ed.), *Handbuch der Quellen und Literatur der neueren europäischen Privatrechtsgeschichte*, Munich, I: *Mittelalter (1100–1500). Die gelehrten Rechte und die Gesetzgebung* (1973); II: *Neuere Zeit (1500–1800). Das Zeitalter des gemeinen Rechts*, 1: *Wissenschaft* (1977); 2: *Gesetzgebung und Rechtsprechung* (1976); III: *Das 19. Jahrhundert*, 1: *Gesetzgebung zum allgemeinen Privatrecht* (1982); 2: *Gesetzgebung zum allgemeinen Privatrecht und zum Verfahrensrecht* (1982); 3: *Gesetzgebung zu den privatrechtlichen Sondergebieten* (1986); 4: *Die nordischen Länder* (1987); 5: *Südosteuropa* (1988).

The continental legal history series, Boston and London, 1912–18; 11 vols. Association of American law schools

David, R., *Les grands systèmes de droit contemporains*, Paris, 1969; Précis Dalloz

Dekkers, R., *Le droit privé des peuples. Caractères, destinées, dominantes*, Brussels, 1953

Ebel, F. and Thielmann, G., *Rechtsgeschichte. Ein Lehrbuch*, I: *Antike und Mittelalter*, Heidelberg, 1989; Jurathek, Studium

Feenstra, R. and Smidt, J. T. de, *Geschiedenis van het vermogensrecht. Tekstenboek*, Deventer, 1973

Feenstra, R. and Ahsmann, M., *Contract. Aspecten van de begrippen contract en contractvrijheid in historisch perspectief*, Deventer, 1980; Rechtshistorische cahiers, 2

Gagner, S., *Studien zur Ideengeschichte der Gesetzgebung*, Stockholm, 1960: Acta universitatis Upsaliensis, Studia juridica Upsaliensia, 1

Gilissen, J., *Introduction historique au droit. Esquisse d'une histoire universelle du droit. Les sources du droit depuis le XIII*[e] *siècle. Eléments d'une histoire du droit privé*, Brussels, 1979

Historische inleiding tot recht. Overzicht van de wereldgeschiedenis van het recht. De bronnen van het recht in de Belgische gewesten sedert de 13de eeuw. Geschiedenis van het privaatrecht, Antwerp, 1981; new edn of the part *Historische inleiding tot het recht* 1: *Ontstaan en evolutie van de belangrijkste rechtsstelsels*, rev. A. Gorlé, Antwerp, 1986

Heyen, E. V. (ed.), *Historische Soziologie der Rechtswissenschaft*, Frankfurt, 1986; Ius commune Sonderhefte, 26

Imbert, J., *Histoire du droit privé*, Paris, 1979; Coll. Que sais-je?

Lawson, F. H., *A common lawyer looks at the civil law*, Ann Arbor, 1955: Thomas M. Cooley lectures, 5th series

Lokin, J. H. A. and Zwalve, W. J., *Hoofdstukken uit de Europese Codificatiegeschiedenis*, Groningen, 1986

Inleiding tot de rechtsgeschiedenis, Groningen, 1985

Mellinkoff, D., *The language of the law*, Boston and Toronto, 1963

Merryman, J. H., *The civil law tradition. An introduction to the legal systems of western Europe and Latin America*, Stanford, Calif., 1969

Mohnhaupt, H. (ed.), *Zur Geschichte des Familien- und Erbrechts. Untersuchungen und Perspektiven*, Frankfurt, 1987; Ius commune Sonderhefte, 32

Pound, R., *Interpretations of legal history*, Cambridge, Mass., 1946

Prest, W. (ed.), *Lawyers in early modern Europe and America*, London, 1981

Recueils de la société Jean Bodin, Brussels and Paris, 1936–

Robinson, O. F., Fergus, T. D. and Gordon, W. M., *An introduction to European legal history*, Abingdon, 1985

Seagle, W., *The quest of law*, New York, 1941

Smith, M., *A general view of European legal history*, New York, 1927

Wagner, W. 'Annäherungen an eine europäische Rechtsgeschichte, Aspekte der europäischen Rechtsgeschichte', *Festgabe für Helmut Coing*, Frankfurt, 1982; Ius commune Sonderhefte, 17, 387–420

Watson, A., *The evolution of law*, Baltimore, 1985

'The evolution of law', *Law and History Review* 5 (1987), 537–70

The making of the civil law, Cambridge, Mass., 1981

Wieacker, F., *Privatrechtsgeschichte der Neuzeit unter besonderer Berücksichtigung der deutschen Entwicklung*, 2nd edn, Göttingen, 1967

Zweigert, K. and Kötz, H., *An introduction to comparative law*, 2nd edn, trans. T. Weir, Oxford, 1989; 2 vols.

CANON LAW

93 Bras, G. le (ed.), *Histoire des institutions et du droit de l'église en occident*, Paris, 1955–
Institutions ecclésiastiques de la Chrétienté médiévale, Paris, 1959–64, 2 vols.; *Histoire de l'église*, ed. A. Fliche and V. Martin, XII, I, 2
Feine, H. E., *Kirchliche Rechtsgeschichte. Die katholische Kirche*, 5th edn, Cologne and Graz, 1972
Hove, A. van, *Prolegomena*, 2nd edn, Malines and Rome, 1945; Commentarium Lovaniense in codicem iuris canonici, I, I
Plöchl, W., *Geschichte des Kirchenrechts*, Vienna: I, 2nd edn 1960; II, 2nd edn, 1962; III, 1959; IV, 1966

ROMAN LAW

94 Cortese, E., *La norma giuridica. Spunti teorici nel diritto comune classico*, Milan, 1962–4; 2 vols.
Feenstra, R., *Fata iuris romani. Etudes d'histoire du droit*, Leiden, 1974
Hermesdorf, B. H. D., *Schets der uitwendige geschiedenis van het Romeins recht*, Utrecht and Nijmegen, 7th edn, 1972
Koschaker, P., *Europa und das römische Recht*, Munich and Berlin, 1947
Meijers, E. M., *Etudes d'histoire du droit*, ed. R. Feenstra and H. F. W. D. Fischer, Leiden, 1956–73; 4 vols.
Spruit, J. E. (ed.), *Coniectanea Neerlandica iuris romani. Inleidende opstellen over Romeins recht*, Zwolle, 1974
Vinogradoff, P., *Roman law in medieval Europe*, Oxford, 1929; 2nd edn by F. de Zulueta

FRANCE

95 Aubenas, R., *Cours d'histoire du droit privé. Anciens pays de droit écrit* I, Aix-en-Provence, 1956
Brissaud, J., *Manuel d'histoire du droit privé*, Paris, 1908
Chenon, E., *Histoire générale du droit français public et privé*, Paris, I, 1926; II, I, 1929, ed. F. Olivier-Martin
Craveri, P., *Ricerche sulla formazione del diritto consuetudinario in Francia (XIII–XVI)*, Milan, 1969
Declareuil, J., *Histoire générale du droit français*, Paris, 1925
Dumas, A., *Histoire des obligations dans l'ancien droit français*, Aix-en Provence, 1972
Ellul, J., *Histoire des institutions*, Paris, 1961–9; 5 vols.
Esmein, A., *Cours élémentaire d'histoire du droit français*, 15th edn by R. Génestal, Paris, 1925
Giffard, A. E., *Droit romain et ancien droit français. Les obligations*, Paris, 2nd edn, 1967; Précis Dalloz

Hilaire, J., *Introduction historique au droit commercial*, Paris, 1986; Coll. 'Droit fondamental', ed. S. Rials
Lebigre, A., *La justice du roi. La vie judiciaire dans l'ancienne France*, Paris, 1988
Lepointe, G., *La famille dans l'ancien droit*, Lille, 1937
Droit romain et ancien droit français, Paris: *Les biens*, 1958; *Régimes matrimoniaux, libéralités, successions*, 1958; *Les obligations en ancien droit français*, 1958
Olivier-Martin, F., *Histoire du droit français des origines à la Révolution*, Paris, 1948
Ourliac, P. and Malafosse, J. de, *Histoire du droit privé*, Paris, I: *Les obligations*, 2nd edn, 1969; II: *Les biens*, 2nd edn, 1971; III: *Le droit familial*, 1968, Thémis. Manuels juridiques
Ourliac, P. and Gazzaniga, J.-L., *Histoire du droit privé français et l'an mil au Code civil*, Paris, 1985; Coll. 'Evolution de l'humanité', fondée par H. Berr
Patault, A.-M., *Introduction historique au droit des biens*, Paris, 1989; Coll. 'Droit fondamental'
Raynal, J., *Histoire des institutions judiciaires*, Paris, 1964; Coll. Armand Colin, 381
Regnault, H., *Manuel d'histoire du droit français*, Paris, 2nd edn, 1942
Rousselet, M., *Histoire de la magistrature française des origines à nos jours*, Paris, 1957; 2 vols.
Timbal, P. C., *Droit romain et ancien droit français. Régimes matrimoniaux, successions, liberalités*, Paris, 2nd edn, 1975; Précis Dalloz
Tisset, P. and Ourliac, P., *Manuel d'histoire du droit*, Paris, 1949
Villers, R. and Giffard, A. E., *Droit romain et ancien droit français. Les obligations*, Paris, 1958; Précis Dalloz
Viollet, P., *Histoire du droit civil français*, Paris, 3rd edn, 1905

GERMANY AND AUSTRIA

96 Amira, K. von, *Grundriss des germanischen Rechts*, 4th edn by Eckhardt, K. A., I: *Rechtsdenkmäler*; II: *Rechtsaltertümer*, Berlin, 1960–7; Grundriss der germanischen Philologie, 5, 1, 2
Baltl, H., *Osterreichische Rechtsgeschichte. Von den Anfängen bis zur Gegenwart*, Graz, 3rd edn, 1977
Brunner, H., *Deutsche Rechtsgeschichte*, I, Leipzig, 2nd edn, 1906; II, ed. C. von Schwerin, 2nd edn, Munich and Berlin, 1928
Coing, H., *Epochen der Rechtsgeschichte in Deutschland*, Munich, 2nd edn, 1972
Europäisches Privatrecht, I: *Alteres gemeines Recht (1500 bis 1800)*; II: *19. Jahrhundert. Uberblick über die Entwicklung des Privatrechts in den ehemals gemeinrechtlichen Ländern*, Munich, 1985–9
Conrad, H., *Deutsche Rechtsgeschichte*, I: *Frühzeit und Mittelalter*, 2nd edn, Karlsruhe, 1962; II: *Neuzeit bis 1806*, 1966

Flossmann, U., *Osterreichische Privatrechtsgeschichte*, Vienna and New York, 1983
Kaufmann, E., *Deutsches Recht. Die Grundlagen*, Berlin, Bielefeld, Munich, 1986
Kern, E., *Geschichte des Gerichtsverfassungsrechts*, Munich and Berlin, 1954
Köbler, G., *Bilder aus der deutschen Rechtsgeschichte von den Anfängen bis zur Gegenwart*, Munich, 1988
Rechtsgeschichte. Ein systematischer Grundriss der geschichtlichen Grundlagen des deutschen Rechts, Munich, 2nd edn, 1978; Vahlen Studienreihe, Jura
Kroeschell, K., *Deutsche Rechtsgschichte*, I: *bis 1250*; II: *1250–1650*; III: *seit 1650*, Hamburg and Opladen, 1972–89
Laufs, A., *Rechtsentwicklungen in Deutschland*, Berlin, 3rd edn, 1984
Mitteis, H., *Deutsche Rechtsgeschichte. Ein Studienbuch*, 14th edn by H. Lieberich, Berlin, 1976
Planitz, H., *Deutsche Rechtsgeschichte*, 3rd edn by K. A. Eckhardt, Cologne and Graz, 1971
Schlosser, H., *Grundzüge der neueren Privatrechtsgeschichte. Ein Studienbuch*, Heidelberg, 5th edn, 1985; Uni-Taschenbücher, 882
Schroeder, R., *Lehrbuch der deutschen Rechtsgeschichte*, 7th edn by E. von Kunszberg, Berlin and Leipzig, 1932
Schwerin, C. von, *Grundzüge der deutschen Rechtsgeschichte*, 4th edn by H. Thieme, Berlin and Munich, 1950
Stintzing, R. and Landsberg, E., *Geschichte der deutschen Rechtswissenschaft*, I; II; III, I, 2, Munich, Leipzig, Berlin, 1880–1910
Thieme, H., *Ideengeschichte und Rechtsgeschichte. Gesammelte Schriften*, Cologne and Vienna, 1986; 2 vols.; Forschungen zur neueren Privatrechtsgeschichte, 25/I, II
Wesenberg, G., *Neuere deutsche Privatrechtsgeschichte im Rahmen der europäischen Rechtsentwicklung*, 3rd edn by G. Wesener, Lahr, 1976

BELGIUM AND THE NETHERLANDS

97 Blécourt, A. S. de and Fischer, H. F. W. D., *Kort begrip van het oudvaderlands burgerlijk recht*, Groningen, 7th edn, 1967; reprint of 1959 edn with additions by J. A. Ankum
Brink, H. van den, *The charm of legal history*, Amsterdam, 1974; Studia amstelodamensia, III
Rechtsgeschiedenis bij wijze van inleiding, Deventer, 1976
Britz, J., *Code de l'ancien droit belgique, ou histoire de la jurisprudence et de la législation, suivie de l'exposé du droit civil des provinces belgiques*, Brussels, 1847; 2 vols., Mémoires Académie royale des sciences, 20
Cerutti, F. F. X., *Hoofdstukken uit de Nederlandse rechtsgeschiedenis*, Nijmegen, 1972
Defacqz, E., *Ancien droit belgique ou précis analytique des lois et coutumes observées en Belgique avant le Code civil*, Brussels, 1846–73; 2 vols

Dekkers, R., *Bibliotheca belgica juridica. Een bibliografisch overzicht der rechtsgeleerdheid in de Nederlanden van de vroegste tijden af tot 1800*, Brussels, 1951; Verhandelingen Koninklijke Vlaamse Academie Wetenschappen, Klasse der letteren, XIII, 14
Feenstra, R., *Romeinsrechtelijke grondslagen van het Nederlands privaatrecht. Inleidende hoofdstukken*, Leiden, 4th edn, 1984
Gerbenzon, P. and Algra, N. E., *Voortgangh des rechtes*, Alphen aan de Rijn, 5th edn, 1979
Godding, P., *Le droit privé dans les Pays-Bas meridionaux du 12e au 18e siècle*, Brussels, 1987; Académie royale de Belgique, Classe de lettres
Goede, A. de, *Nederlandse rechtsgeschiedenis*, Leiden and Amsterdam, 1949–53; 2 vols.
Heijden, E. J. J. van der, *Aantekeningen bij de geschiedenis van het oude vaderlandse recht*, 7th edn by B. H. D. Hermesdorf, Nijmegen and Utrecht, 1965
Heijnsbergen, P. van, *Geschiedenis der rechtswetenschap in Nederland. Beknopt overzicht der geschiedenis onzer rechtswetenschap tot 1900*, Amsterdam, 1925
Hermesdorf, B. H. D., *Rechtsspiegel. Een rechtshistorische terugblik in de Lage Landen van het herfsttij*, Nijmegen, 1980, ed. P. J. Verdam
Kunst, A. J. M., *Historische ontwikkeling van het recht*, Zwolle, I, 2nd edn, 1969; II, 1968
Korte voorgeschiedenis van het Nederlands Burgerlijk Wetboek, Zwolle, 1967; Uitgaven van het Molengraaf Instituut voor privaatrecht te Utrecht, I
Maes, L. T., *Recht heeft vele significatie. Rechtshistorische opstellen*, Brussels, 1979
Monté ver Loren, J. P. de, *Hoofdlijnen van de ontwikkeling der rechterlijke organisatie in de noordelijke Nederlanden tot de Bataafse omwenteling*, 5th edn by J. E. Spruit, Deventer, 1972
Pitlo, A., *Niet alleen artikel één. Een vleug notariële cultuurgeschiedenis*, Amsterdam, 1982; Ars notariatus, XXVI
Samenwinninge. Tien opstellen over rechtsgeschiedenis geschreven ter gelegenheid van het tienjarig bestaan van het interuniversitair Instituut Nederlands Centrum voor rechtshistorische documentatie, Zwolle, 1977
Smidt, J. T. de *et al.*, *Compendium van de geschiedenis van het Nederlands privaatrecht*, Deventer, 3rd edn, 1977, in collaboration with R. Feenstra
Strubbe, E. I., *De luister van ons oude recht. Verzamelde rechtshistorische studies*, Brussels, 1973; Rijksuniversiteit Gent. Publikaties van de Fakulteit der rechtsgeleerdheid, 5
Zeylemaker, J., *Geschiedenis van de wetenschap van het burgerlijk processrecht (Praktijkrecht) in Nederland van de aanvang tot 1813*, Amsterdam, 1952; Geschiedenis der Nederlandse rechtswetenschap, IV, I

ITALY

98 Bellomo, M., *Società ed istituzioni in Italia tra medioevo ed età moderna*, Catania, 2nd edn, 1977

Besta, E., *Avviamento allo studio della storia del diritto italiano*, Milan, 2nd edn, 1946

Leicht, P. S., *Storia del diritto italiano. Le fonti*, Milan, 3rd edn, 1947

Pertile, A., *Storia del diritto italiano della caduta dell'impero romano alla codificazione*, 2nd edn by P. del Giudice, Turin, 1896–1903; 7 vols.

SPAIN

99 Broca, J. M. de, *Historia del derecho de Cataluña*, I, Barcelona, 1919; repr. 1985 as *Textos jurídics catalans. Escriptors* I/I

Galto Fernandez, E., Alejandre Garcia, J. A. and Garcia Marin, J. M., *El derecho histórico de los pueblos de España*, Madrid, 3rd edn, 1982

Garcia-Gallo, A., *Manual de historia del derecho español*, Madrid, 3rd edn, 1967; 2 vols

Gibert, R., *Historia general del derecho español*, Granada, 1968

Lalinde Abadia, J., *Iniciación histórica al derecho español*, Barcelona, 3rd edn, 1983

Perez-Prendes, J. M., *Curso de historia del derecho español*, Madrid, 1973

Tomas y Valiente, F., *Manual de historia del derecho español*, Madrid, 3rd edn, 1981

Vance, J. T., *The background of Hispanic-American law. Legal sources and juridical literature on Spain*, Washington, D.C., 1937

ENGLAND

100 Baker, J. H., *An introduction to English legal history*, London, 3rd edn, 1990

Holdsworth, W. S., *History of English law*, London, 1903–72; 17 vols., many re-edited, vols. XIV and XV by A. L. Goodhart and H. G. Hanbury, vol. XVII general index

Plucknett, T. F. T., *A concise history of the common law*, London, 5th edn 1956

BIBLIOGRAPHIES, DICTIONARIES AND PERIODICALS

101 *Bibliografie Nederlandse rechtsgeschiedenis*, Amsterdam, 1971– ; Nederlands centrum voor rechtshistorische documentatie

Deutsches Rechtswörterbuch. Wörterbuch der älteren deutschen Rechtssprache, ed. R. Schröder and E. von Künszberg, Weimar, 1914–

Gilissen, J. (ed.), *Introduction bibliographique à l'histoire du droit et à l'ethnologie juridique*, Brussels, 1964–88

Handwörterbuch zur deutschen Rechtsgeschichte, ed. A. Erler and E. Kaufmann, Berlin, 1964–

Hattum, M. van and Rooseboom, H., *Glossarium van oude Nederlandse rechtstermen*, Amsterdam, 1977

Lepointe, G. and Vandenbossche, A., *Eléments de bibliographie sur l'histoire des institutions et des faits sociaux (987–1875)*, Paris, 1958

Planitz, H. and Buyken, T., *Bibliographie zur deutschen Rechtsgeschichte*, Frankfurt, 1952; 2 vols.

Ragueau, F. and Laurière, E. de, *Glossaire du droit français*, 2nd edn by L. Favre, Niort, 1882

Stallaert, K., *Glossarium van verouderde rechtstermen*, Leiden, 1886–93; 2 vols.; vol. III by F. Debrabandere, Handzame, 1977

The American Journal of Legal History, Philadelphia, 1957–

Annali di storia del diritto, Milan, 1957–

Anuario de historia del derecho español, Madrid, 1924–

Bulletin de la commission royale des anciennes lois et ordonnances de Belgique. Handelingen van de koninklijke commissie voor de uitgave der oude wetten en verordeningen van België, Brussels, 1848–

Bulletin of medieval canon law, Berkeley, 1971–

Glossae. Revista de historia del derecho europeo, Murcia, 1988–

Ius commune. Veröffentlichungen des Max-Planck-Instituts für europäische Rechtsgeschichte, Frankfurt, 1967–

Journal of Legal History, London, 1980–

Law and History Review, Ithaca, 1983– ; Cornell Law School and American Society for Legal History

Rechtshistorisches Journal, Frankfurt, 1982–

Revue d'histoire des facultés de droit et de la science juridique, Paris, 1982–

Revue historique de droit français et étranger, Paris, 1855–

Rivista di storia del diritto italiano, Rome, 1928–

Tijdschrift voor Rechtsgeschiedenis. Revue d'Histoire du Droit. The Legal History Review, Dordrecht and Antwerp, 1918–

Verslagen en mededelingen van de vereniging tot uitgaaf der bronnen van het oudvaderlandse recht, Utrecht, 1880–

Zeitschrift für neuere Rechtsgeschichte, Vienna, 1979–

Zeitschrift der Savigny-Stiftung für Rechtsgeschichte: Germanistische Abteilung, 1880– ; *Romanistische Abteilung*, 1880– ; *Kanonistische Abteilung*, 1911– ; continuing the *Zeitschrift für Rechtsgeschichte*, 1861–78 and *Zeitschrift für geschichtliche Rechtswissenschaft*, 1815–50

Index